New York City
STREET SMARTS

# SAUL MILLER

New York City STREET SMARTS

HOLT, RINEHART AND WINSTON · *New York*

Library of Congress Cataloging in Publication Data

Miller, Saul.
　　New York City street smarts.
　　1. New York (N.Y.)—Description—1981–　　—Guide-
books. 2. New York (N.Y.)—Social conditions. I. Title.
F128.18.M535 1983　　917.47'10443　　82-15566
ISBN Hardcover: 0-03-060378-1
ISBN Paperback: 0-03-060379-X

First Edition

Design by Jacqueline Schuman
Maps by David Lindroth
Illustration page 94 by Laura Hartman.

Printed in the United States of America
10 9 8 7 6 5 4 3 2 1

ISBN 0-03-060378-1 HARDCOVER
ISBN 0-03-060379-X PAPERBACK

*For Alice*

New York is a place where you can get the best of everything, even the best of the worst.

—*H. L. Mencken*

# Contents

**PART TWO**

## Neighborhoods and Boroughs

# Maps and Illustrations

# Author's Note and Acknowledgments

Nothing in New York is easy, and that includes writing a book about New York. If the truth be known, the *raison d'être* for writing *Street Smarts*—to share my favorite restaurant with readers as I had with visitors and friends over the years—was destroyed when, just a few months into my research for the book, that restaurant burned to the ground, and its owners announced they would retire rather than rebuild. (In case you're curious, it was an Italian restaurant called Stella's, located in the Coney Island section of Brooklyn. Stella's was a remarkable restaurant that served excellent Italian food at prices so low you had to laugh; where strips of flypaper that hung from the light fixtures and large bottles of orange soda that graced the tables somehow managed to enhance the ambience rather than detract from it; and where a loyal following—principally New York City cops, working-class Coney Islanders, and would-be radical lawyers from Manhattan trying to impress their dates with their working-class ties—returned time and again despite the fights that would invariably break out in the kitchen and sometimes on the floor of the dining area itself.) Despite having lost my favorite eating place and the major reason for writing this book, I forged ahead, nonetheless.

I also continued with the book even after a group of young street toughs ran me out of the neighborhood where I had rented an office to write and where I had worked productively for nearly a year. Apparently, these young men had had their fill of "that guy above the pizza parlor" who worked odd hours, was always pacing and looking out at them, and had the bad sense—the utter gall—to tell a cop to make them turn down their blaring radios. I was told, in no uncertain terms, that I'd be a lot safer somewhere else. I moved out the next morning. Luckily, a friend and neighbor came to my aid, and within a day of moving out of my comfortable office above a pizza parlor I was happily ensconced in a comfortable office above a funeral home. And it was there that I was able to complete *Street Smarts*.

Between these two major setbacks, as if things were not difficult enough, fate and circumstance plucked me from New York City and plunked me down in Binghamton, New York, where I was forced to toil for more than a year. Needless to say, it becomes substantially more difficult to write a book about New York City—especially one that attempts to capture the feel of its neighborhoods and whose research depends upon being out on its streets—when one is two hundred miles from the city. The task is sort of analogous to trying to write about ocean life while living in Nebraska. Both the book and I survived Upstate New York.

If writing this book wasn't an altogether easy job, it was at least made somewhat less difficult because of the help, encouragement, and good cheer offered by a number of friends and acquaintances. I'm particularly thankful to the following people who shared their favorite places and favorite New York City anecdotes with me: Jordan Wright, Bill Martin, Trudy Martin, Jeff Ambers, E. A. Hull, Laurie Friedlander, Elspeth Macdonald, Nick Macdonald, Ted Nordman, Judy Lee, Billy Herbert, Joe Boyle, Margo Rappoport, Galen Kirkland, Dave Rougé, Virginia Normandia, Ann Cunningham, and the late Oscar Lewitz. New Yorkers all.

Thanks also to Don Blake and Jane Blake of Endwell, New York, for giving me some insight into what Upstaters think of New York City; to Will Osborn of Boston, because I owe you one; to Les Moran of Liverpool, England, for asking all the right questions; and to Michael Paris and his supporting cast of Dutch visitors (Anton Freling, Emmeken Peeters, Oliva Peeters, Kristien Kerstens, and Nicolette Smabers) for giving me the confidence that what I had to say about the city was interesting, at least, to some people, albeit foreigners.

My thanks to Harriet Hoffman, Elnora Bode, and others at the Pottery Loft, located down the hall from my office, who let me come visit during what must have seemed to them to be an inordinately large number of writing breaks; to Bill O'Brien and Joe Falcone for being atypical New York City landlords; to Milton Miller for conceptualizing the illustration of how to fold *The New York Times* on a crowded subway; to Molly Friedrich of the Aaron Priest Literary Agency for selling the book; to Natalie Chapman of Holt, Rinehart and Winston for buying it; and to both Natalie and Jo Goldberg, also of Holt, for their excellent editing job.

Though most of the research for *Street Smarts* was done on the streets of the city rather than in its libraries, I would like to acknowledge those books about the city I did read and whose influence on me I'm sure crept into the pages of this book. They include: *New York: A Guide to the Metropolis* by Gerard Wolfe, *Bricks & Brownstone* by Charles Lockwood, *New York/New York: An Architectural Overview* by John Halpern, and *The City Observed: New York—A Guide to the Architecture of Manhattan* by Paul Goldberger, for what they say about the city's architecture; *The Streets Were Paved with Gold* by Ken Auletta, for what it says about the 1975 fiscal crisis; *Managing Mailer* by Joe Flaherty, for its insight into New York City politics; *New York: The Centennial Years 1676–1976* edited by Milton Klein, *The New Yorkers: A Profile of an American Metropolis* by Andrew Hacker, and *The Abuse of Power* by Jack Newfield and Paul Du Brul, for what they say about various aspects of New York City. I also want to acknowledge *Neighborhood: The Journal for City Preservation*, published by the New York Urban Coalition, for its many fine articles about the city's neighborhoods, and *Plan for New York City: A Proposal* by the New York City Planning Commission, for what it says about every facet of New York City life and, in particular, its neighborhoods. (This last work, incidentally, is a wondrous six-volume study published in 1969—and discarded shortly thereafter—which is a must read for those who consider themselves serious students of the city. My advice is go to the library, dust off the volumes, and begin reading.)

Finally, I want to thank Alice Miller, to whom this book is dedicated, and for whom that dedication is but a small repayment for all of the work and advice she gave.

# Introduction

It is assumed that you will have little difficulty finding the Empire State Building, the World Trade Towers, the U.N., Central Park, and the Statue of Liberty. It is further assumed you'll know what to do once you get there.

Although *Street Smarts* doesn't totally ignore these and others of the better-known attractions—for it accepts the fact that you will want to see some of them—it does believe that you can't come to understand and appreciate New York solely by visiting tourist spots or by eating at overpriced Midtown restaurants. To really know the city, you must realize what it would be like to live, work, and play here.

Therefore, *Street Smarts*—as though it were a native New Yorker showing you around—is more interested in pointing out sights off the tourist-beaten path. As your surrogate New Yorker, it is particularly intent upon anticipating things you may see or wonder about along the way. In other words, *Street Smarts* will try to fill in the gaps between tourist sights to provide some of the fabric and texture of city life.

You may, for example, be curious about alternate-side-of-the-street parking, the absolute bane of New Yorkers who own cars. How does it work, and how might complying with its rules alter a New Yorker's life-style? Are you aware of how much a month it costs to garage a car in New York, and that it can cost as much as people in other cities pay for rent? How hard is it to find an apartment here, and just how expensive are apartments anyway? Is it true that you must be fabulously wealthy to live in Manhattan? What do Manhattanites think of Staten Islanders and vice versa? Do New Yorkers ever elect Republicans?

Or perhaps you'll want to be told just how safe the streets and subways really are. Where do kids go to school in New York? Are there even any kids who live here? In some parts of the city it may seem there are none. What kind of place is New York for raising a family? Is the city actually on the brink of bankruptcy? What's a bialy? Maybe you just want to know the meaning of IRT, SRO, MoMA, SoHo, DUMBO, TKTS, WTC, or Page Six. (The "New York City Glossary" at the end of the book defines many of these abbreviations and acronyms which New Yorkers take for granted but which you may find utterly befuddling. It also lists and explains phenomena unique to New York City: the Pooper-scooper law, the John Hour, shopsteading, home-delivered seltzer in syphon bottles, gridlock, face places, Guardian Angels, and brownouts, to name but a few.)

*Street Smarts* will answer these and a lot more of the questions you will undoubtedly have as you travel about the city. It will respond to your queries as it guides you through *all* parts of the city and explains *all* aspects of New York City life. For unlike the scores of other New York City guidebooks, which either focus on Midtown or describe the city solely through its museums, restaurants, or architecture, *Street Smarts* tells all about Midtown Manhattan but downtown Brooklyn too; museums but also politics; architecture *and* people. The New York that is a $2.00 cup of coffee and the New York that is a 35¢ cup of coffee as well; a $5.00 movie and a 79¢ movie, boutiques and pushcarts; Greenwich Village and Carroll Gardens; Fifth Avenue and Flatbush Avenue; skyscrapers and houseboats; racial tensions but incredible tolerance too; a demanding city, but also a very giving one.

The New York City of *Street Smarts*, then, is not necessarily "another" New York, an underground New York, or the "real" New York. Rather, it is the New Yorker's New York.

### Organization of the Book

New York is not an easy town to take in. No one would ever say it engenders immediate understanding. Rather, the city tends to confound, dazzle, overwhelm, and, yes, even offend. Hence, in Part One: "The Facts of City Life," *Street Smarts* tries to provide the background you'll need to come to grips with a lot of what you'll observe here. The information in this section is not historical in the sense of early history. Instead, it deals with what you could consider recent history.

There are, for instance, discussions about the ethnic and racial mix of the city; politics in New York; housing, schools, transportation, restaurants, crime, entertainment, the media; the cost of living, the cost of doing business, the price for safety.

What happened here fifty or a hundred years ago may be fascinating, but it won't necessarily shed much light on contemporary New York City affairs. To understand a city like New York, which changes so often and so quickly, you'll need to know what's occurred here in the last five or ten years—or even last year. And that's what *Street Smarts* will tell you.

Since New York is essentially a city of neighborhoods—a collection of separate and distinct ones—it seems to make the most sense to guide you around the city neighborhood by neighborhood, which is the purpose of Part Two, "Neighborhoods and Boroughs."

You'll be taken through *every* Manhattan neighborhood, and this includes those above 96th Street—mid-Manhattan's Maginot Line, so to speak—should you decide to venture that far north. And you should.

Although *Street Smarts* will guide you into all five boroughs, it won't take you to every neighborhood in the outer boroughs as it does in Manhattan. It would like to, for it believes any New York City neighborhood is as interesting and as integral a part of the life of the city as any other. But, like the New Yorkers of whom it speaks, *Street Smarts* is pragmatic if nothing else. It accepts the reality that most newcomers to the city will spend their initial months here exploring Manhattan rather than the outer boroughs and that most visitors are going to spend most of their time, especially if it's limited, in Manhattan as well. If you should journey out of Manhattan, it will typically be for a particular attraction or event, and not simply to gad about some random outer-borough neighborhood. (Unless, of course, the neighborhood is Brooklyn Heights, a bona fide tourist attraction in itself.)

Thus, though *Street Smarts* won't discuss every neighborhood in the Bronx, it will describe those around, say, Yankee Stadium (The Concourse), the Bronx Zoo (Pelham Parkway), and the Botanical Gardens (Belmont), for there is an excellent chance you'll visit those tourist spots. Similarly, *Street Smarts* will take you around the neighborhoods near the Brooklyn Museum (Crown Heights), the Brooklyn Botanic Gardens (Park Slope), the Children's Museum

(Bedford-Stuyvesant), and Coney Island (residential Coney Island and Brighton Beach), since those attractions are likely to lure you to those particular Brooklyn communities.

Although it's unlikely that you'll spend much of your stay in New York touring Staten Island (unless you've just moved there), you probably will take a ride on the Staten Island Ferry, so you might as well walk around at least one Staten Island neighborhood—St. George, where the ferry docks. And though you might not want to trek to the outermost parts of Queens, you might consider a five-minute subway ride from Midtown Manhattan to Astoria, a truly intriguing Greek residential and commercial center.

Since New York is an eminently walkable city (remember, twenty blocks doth one mile make), *Street Smarts* leads you around on the assumption you'll be touring on foot (thus entries in each "Of Interest" section are in rough geographical order as you walk, generally from south to north). If you plan instead to bus or taxi through neighborhoods—well, you'll miss many of the out-of-the-way places that are divulged. If you came through Brooklyn on a tour bus, for instance, you would never be able to delight in Warren Place, perhaps the loveliest mews in all New York City; or Montgomery Place, one of the most architecturally diverse residential blocks in the city; or the new artists' quarter underneath the Manhattan Bridge, which will reveal what Manhattan's SoHo probably looked like ten years ago, before it was discovered by realtors and the original artist-settlers were forced out.

Like any true New Yorker, *Street Smarts* is constantly recommending restaurant "discoveries." These are mostly neighborhood places—often not the kind you would just happen upon yourself nor the sort that you would discover by reading restaurant reviews in the *Times*. These are typically restaurants that one would hear about only through word of mouth, dining spots that New Yorkers rave about and recommend to each other: a wonderful Greek or Thai restaurant in the theater district that is among the handful of restaurants in that part of town not overpriced; a great little Italian place in the Greenpoint section of Brooklyn where they make their own fresh pasta; or any number of Indian restaurants in the East Village where excellent food is offered at dirt-cheap prices.

Finally, *Street Smarts* does not pretend to give an exhaustive account of each neighborhood it describes. Visitors and newcomers to New York tend to be inundated with things to see and do; sometimes it becomes difficult to make any choice at all. Overstimulation that leads you to want to just hole up in your hotel room is a common New York City malady, and *Street Smarts* won't make it worse by barraging you with 100 shops you must visit, 150 restaurants you must try, or 80 buildings you absolutely must see in each neighborhood. Instead, you'll get a digestible amount of information and a manageable number of places to visit—enough to give you a sense of a neighborhood, to whet your appetite, to make you want to discover more *on your own*. After all, the prospect of discovery just around the corner is what makes exploring the city's neighborhoods such great fun. *Street Smarts*, then, won't do all the work for you. Just enough.

# PART ONE

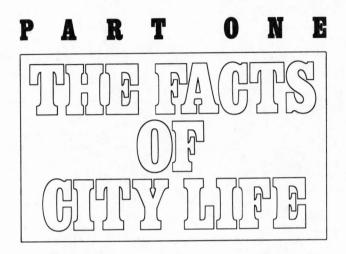

THE FACTS
OF
CITY LIFE

# 1 Places

## Boroughs

There's a lot more to New York City than just Manhattan. In fact, Manhattan is but one of the city's five boroughs, and not even the largest at that. (Brooklyn, Queens, the Bronx, and Staten Island—*not* Long Island—are the others.)

To visitors, in particular, Manhattan evokes hundreds of images. But mention any of the "outer boroughs," as they're called, and hardly a thing comes to mind. The outer boroughs are ciphers. One might recall that Brooklyn is where people are said to talk funny, or that the Bronx has a zoo, or that Staten Island is where a ferry goes to, but beyond that, one probably knows little else about these other boroughs.

It's not surprising. After all, Manhattan is where most of the tourist attractions are; it is the center of finance, commerce, communications, shopping, and entertainment. In a word, Manhattan is glamour—page-one news. The outer boroughs are more mundane—lucky to make page twenty. When someone makes a movie about Manhattan, it's called *Manhattan*. A film about Brooklyn has to be titled *Saturday Night Fever* to attract an audience.

But if Manhattan is the star of the drama that is New York, the outer boroughs are the all-important supporting cast. Manhattan may provide the jobs, but Staten Islanders fill them. Manhattan stages the plays, but residents of the Bronx buy the tickets. Manhattan publishes the newspapers, but Brooklyn prints and distributes them. Airlines have corporate headquarters in Manhattan, but the airports themselves are in Queens. If Manhattan is New York's head, then the outer boroughs are its body. You should, therefore, know some things about *all* of New York's boroughs.

Manhattan is a borough of mostly the very rich and the very poor. The middle class and the poor claim the outer boroughs as their home. Manhattan is the preserve of singles and young marrieds. The outer boroughs belong more to families. Most New Yorkers feel that Manhattan's tight housing market—apartments hard to find, small, and expensive—along with its not very good nor very safe public schools make it ill-suited for raising a family. The conventional wisdom is that Manhattan may be fine for work and play, but not for family living (unless you're loaded).

Manhattan, furthermore, is the borough of the transplant. When the Kansan moves to New York City, it is to Manhattan that he or she comes. The other boroughs are more exclusively the domain of native New Yorkers. In that sense, many of us feel the outer boroughs are more authentically New York.

No matter where New Yorkers live, we're more likely than not to work in Manhattan. Almost 65 percent of all jobs in the city are located there. By contrast, only 1.5 percent are on Staten Island.

Though New Yorkers are considered cosmopolitan in most respects, we can be quite provincial about the borough in which we happen to live. Manhattanites, for example, proclaim they could never live in any other borough (until, of course, they move to Brooklyn, discover its glories, and become inveterate Brooklyn chauvinists). You won't have to look very far to find Manhattanites who have never made the twenty-minute trip to Staten Island. Or if they admit to having been in Queens or the Bronx, it usually turns out to mean they drove through on their way into New York.

Outer-borough residents, for their part, can't as easily ignore or avoid Manhattan. For one thing, they probably work there. But as incredible as it may seem, there are many outer-borough residents who "go into the city"—though Manhattan may be but three subway stops away—as seldom as possible. To Brooklynites ensconced in Canarsie, Marine Park, or Brighton Beach, Manhattan seems overpriced, overcrowded, and overrated. To elderly couples living quietly in Queens or the Bronx, Manhattan can seem awfully intimidating.

Manhattanites hold the notion that it is in Manhattan only that one leads a truly urban life. After all, it is a borough of apartment dwellers, as one would expect in the city. In the outer boroughs, however, you find private homes. In parts of Brooklyn—Sheepshead Bay or Mill Basin, for instance—there are not only homeowners but boat owners as well. And there are shopping malls in the outer boroughs too. Manhattanites consider Queens to be a suburb, and Staten Island . . . well, it's almost rural. And if Manhattanites feel the life-style in the other boroughs is less than urban, they feel the same way about their values and politics. Manhattanites, who rarely vote for Republicans, cannot forget that Staten Islanders elect them regularly.

## Neighborhoods

You should think of each borough as an amalgam of diverse and distinct neighborhoods. What may be true of Midtown doesn't apply to upper Manhattan. The East Side and the West Side can be two different worlds. SoHo (South of Houston Street) is the essence of chic. The Lower East Side just east of SoHo is anything but chic. South Jamaica in Queens is poor, but that doesn't reflect the rest of Jamaica, which is essentially middle-class. Riverdale in the Bronx bears about as much similarity to the rest of the Bronx as Las Vegas does to the rest of Nevada. It is precisely because New York neighborhoods are so various that Part Two is organized as a neighborhood-by-neighborhood guide. It's also why you should see many neighborhoods before you start drawing conclusions about the city.

Neighborhoods are the city's saving grace. They provide us with not so much a sense of community as a sense of place. Ask us where we live and we're more likely to say Gramercy Park or Washington Heights or Harlem than to say we live in Manhattan. We will almost always say we live in Flushing, Forest Hills, Kew Gardens, or Rockaway rather than say we live in Queens.

Particularly in Manhattan, life-style—or the idea of a certain life-style—is very much tied to neighborhood. Therefore, choosing where we live is based on a lot more than just pragmatic considerations. Just as one does not buy a Cadillac for its good gas mileage, one does not live in the West Village for its good, cheap housing, nor on Central Park South for its proximity to the local public schools.

We are all very aware—perhaps to a fault—of neighborhood identities and scenes. We know about the "Swinging Singles Upper East

Side," the "Jewish Intellectual Upper West Side," the "Gay West Village," "Artsy SoHo," "Loft-Dwellers' TriBeCa (*Tri*angle *Be*low *Ca*nal Street)," "Brownstoners' Brooklyn," and so on. Nor does it take newcomers very long to become alert to these things. Thus, it was no surprise that when the Richard Nixons moved to the city in 1979, they chose a town house in the East Sixties. (Nor was it a surprise when they sold that same town house two years later for a cool $2 million profit and moved to New Jersey. But be that as it may.) Where else would the Nixons have possibly moved to? Certainly not to the Upper West Side. There is some elegant housing there (the Dakota on Central Park West at 72nd Street is perhaps the city's most exclusive apartment building), but who could imagine Dick and Pat living within a couple of blocks of a seedy Single Room Occupancy hotel? Or could you see the Nixons being stopped for change by a West Side bag lady or being encountered by a West Side liberal intellectual? The Nixons could never have moved to Greenwich Village, lest they discover a gay couple living next door. Or how about Dick and Pat converting an old industrial loft in SoHo? How inconceivable is the image of the Nixons living among Jewish families along Pelham Parkway (the Bronx), in Flatbush (Brooklyn), or in Rego Park (Queens)?

One distinctive thing about New York's neighborhoods, especially in Manhattan, is that they can change dramatically from one block to the next. Recently, someone remarked that she felt as though she had moved into an entirely new neighborhood by moving just five blocks—from West 99th Street up to 104th. Along with her five-block move, however, she acquired a new subway stop, new bus stop, new Chinese takeout restaurant, and new local movie theater. By comparison, moving from one borough to another would seem tantamount to moving cross-country.

Of course, the diversity of New York's neighborhoods makes it a particularly difficult city to govern. To be responsive to each neighborhood requires the wisdom of Solomon and then some. There was, not long ago, an attempt to decentralize the governance of the city—to give more powers to the neighborhoods. In fact, when Norman Mailer ran for mayor of New York in 1969 (he was serious about it, too), he campaigned on the issue of making New York City a separate state—the fifty-first—and establishing each neighborhood as an independently governed city. But Mailer lost and has since gone back to writing books. His plan never came to pass, and by the end of the 1970s, most of the experiments with decentralization were deemed either too ineffective, too inefficient, or too expensive. Politicians have since reclaimed much of the power once delegated to community boards, and about the only vestige of decentralization is that veritable New York institution—the block association. Some ten thousand of them dot the city, and though they don't wield much power, you will discover that their block parties provide some of the very best street entertainment in the city.

With the demise of decentralization, neighborhoods again scream about not getting what they need or want. Neighborhoods outside of Manhattan's central districts gripe the most. They complain of what they call the "Manhattan bias"—as when, in the snowy winter of 1969, Queens got its streets plowed about a week after Manhattan (an affront Queens residents still remind us of, about every third week, though almost fifteen years have elapsed).

Part of the bias, outer-borough residents will tell you, comes from the fact that most of the city's decision-makers are Manhattanites, and whatever they decide, they do through Manhattan blinders. Other boroughs also feel that decisions are made to benefit Manhattan primarily. Manhattanites seem to subscribe to the theory that what is good for Manhattan neighborhoods will filter down and benefit neighborhoods elsewhere—if Times Square is spruced up, New Yorkers all over the city will be better off. However, there seems to be no analogous feeling that if, say, the Bushwick section of Brooklyn is improved, everyone in the city would similarly benefit. The result is that new construction projects get planned for Times Square and not for Bushwick.

Still, diversity of neighborhoods—however hard to govern and to satisfy they may be—makes New York livable. It is only because there is a diversity of neighborhoods that there can be a sense of neighborhood, and it is that which makes the city other than the anonymous place so many visitors and nonresidents accuse it of being. And it is precisely for this reason that so many of us are alarmed by the creeping gentrification that we observe throughout the city. This is the phenomenon by which lower- and middle-income neighborhoods as well as industrial or nonresidential neighborhoods are "upgraded" so that the city's once diverse neighborhoods become uniformly residential and uniformly upper-income.

The trend to gentrification is discussed in chapter 6, "Housing," but for now suffice it to say that the homogenizing effect of gentrifi-

cation threatens to level and thereby destroy the city's neighborhoods. If the West Side is upgraded so that it becomes identical to
the East Side, in effect one neighborhood will then be lost to the
city. If TriBeCa becomes indistinguishable from SoHo, then what
had been two neighborhoods become just one.

It is in this way that neighborhoods will fall victim to gentrification's disappearing act. And if that should ever happen, the city will
have succeeded in attracting upper-income people back into New
York, but in regaining a tax base it will have lost its soul.

# 2 People

## Population

Population size, like almost everything else in New York, is a subject that stirs up controversy. Population figures for the city vary by as much as a million from one estimate to the next. Some argue that the population of New York is just over 7 million. Others insist it is actually well over 8. Most would probably agree it is somewhere in between.

THE OFFICIAL STATISTICS

According to the Census Bureau, the city's population in 1980 was just under 7.1 million. Although this makes New York America's largest city by far—Chicago, the second, is less than half as large—it ranks New York as only ninth or tenth in the world. Shanghai, Mexico City, Tokyo, Peking, Calcutta, Moscow, Bombay, and Manila—in that order—are all larger than New York. Perhaps by now, so too are São Paulo, Seoul, and even London.

Those who have always considered Manhattan as synonymous with New York City will be surprised to know that Manhattan is only the third most populous of the city's five boroughs, and, in fact, that 80 percent of New Yorkers live outside of Manhattan.*

The 1970s took their toll. The 1970 census gave New York's popu-

*New York City's 7.1 million residents are distributed as follows: 2.2 million in Brooklyn; 1.9 million in Queens; 1.4 million in Manhattan; 1.2 million in the Bronx; and 0.4 million on Staten Island.

lation as 7.9 million, so the 7.1 million figure for 1980 represented a decline of 10 percent. And the population dropped in all boroughs except Staten Island. The Bronx was hurt the most, losing 20 percent of its population in the decade. Queens lost the fewest (only about 5 percent). Staten Island—quiet, unspectacular Staten Island—actually grew by almost 20 percent. (This must be proof that Staten Island is really a New Jersey suburb only pretending to be a borough of New York City.)

To a lot of New Yorkers, this decline in the city's population reflected a decline in the city itself. Why else would so many people leave? While New York City lost 800,000 people, the population of the United States as a whole was growing, so things in New York must have been particularly bad; or so the thinking went.

In truth, New York's population decline was probably less symptomatic of what was happening here in particular than what was happening in large, old, cold, northern industrial cities in general. Chicago, Cleveland, Pittsburgh, and St. Louis, for example, actually had greater population losses. New York, along with these other cities, simply could not keep pace with the likes of Houston, Dallas, San Antonio, Phoenix, San Diego, and San Jose—among the cities whose populations grew the most—with their warm weather and their new industries. Die-hard New Yorkers naturally find this explanation hard to accept. It's difficult enough for us to understand how anyone could live anywhere else but New York City, but for New York to lose out to, say, San Antonio—no matter how many consecutive days of sunshine it can boast—is truly befuddling.

Perhaps the more important change in the city's population is not the decline itself, but rather the shift in its composition. The 1970s—especially from 1970 to 1975—were a time during which the city witnessed middle-class New Yorkers leaving in droves. (The out-migration seemingly slowed by the end of the 1970s, what with "urban renaissance" and all.) Most who left were white. Those who remained, or those who newly arrived, were more likely to be both poor and nonwhite. So a city that in 1970 had been only about 30 percent nonwhite had become just under 50 percent nonwhite by 1980. Today blacks and Hispanics comprise half the population of both Manhattan and Brooklyn. In the Bronx, the population is more than 60 percent black and Hispanic. Though Queens still has a white majority, it's a substantially smaller majority than it was ten years ago. Among the five boroughs, only Staten Island remains over-whelmingly white.*

THE UNOFFICIAL STATISTICS

Many insist that not only has the city's population *not* decreased since 1970, but it has actually increased and is closer to 8 million than to the 7 million officially claimed. They argue that the official figures are grossly understated, since they omit thousands upon thousands of hard-to-find poor and non-English-speaking New York-ers as well as reluctant-to-be-found illegal aliens. Estimates of the number of uncounted illegal aliens alone range from 350,000 to 1.5 million.

Of course, both those who support the official 7 million figure and those who claim an unofficial 8 million are not without political motives. Many who support the Census Bureau count—who argue it was not an undercount and that the population of the city has in-deed declined precipitously—buttress their argument by pointing to the steep decline in the use of city services—hospital-bed use, school enrollment, subway and bus ridership, and so on. They then go on to argue for deep cuts in the city budget. Their reasoning is simple. A drastic reduction in population justifies a drastic reduction in the lev-el of city services provided.

On the other hand, New Yorkers who contest the official statistics tend to argue for an increase in city services. They point out that among the thousands uncounted by the census, most are poor and thus represent not a lessening of a demand on city services but an increase.

Whom should you believe—the population inflators or deflators? If one is to judge by the difficulty of getting a seat on a subway or bus, a show ticket, or a table in a restaurant, one tends to believe those who maintain that official statistics are greatly understated.

In the meantime, whether we boast about New York's size or com-

*In 1970 New York City was 67 percent white, 21 percent black, 10 percent Hispanic (primarily Puerto Rican), and 2 percent "other" (mostly Asians, primarily from Hong Kong and Taiwan). In 1980 the city had become 52 percent white, 24 percent black (including many West Indians), 20 percent Hispanic (including many Cubans, Do-minicans, Colombians, and Ecuadorians), and 4 percent "other" (primarily Asians still, but now including many Koreans, Japanese, Vietnamese, Indians, and mainland Chinese).

plain about it, we all have to be somewhat awed by a city so large we can only know its size give or take a million.

(The difficulty of counting the city's population was never so apparent as it was during the 1980 census. Mayor Ed Koch actually went so far as to propose a bounty system whereby city employees would be paid $10 for each previously uncounted resident they got to fill out a census form, though the Census Bureau ultimately nixed the plan for paying a bounty before it was tried. And in 1980, the city also wound up taking the Census Bureau to federal court to try to get it to adjust the population figures upward to account for the arguably large number of uncounted residents.)

If the 1980 census revealed how difficult it is to count New York's population, it proved how problematical it is to collect accurate housing statistics for the city as well. The census was planned with the rest of America in mind, not New York City. For instance, the census form had no category to account for the hundreds of residential lofts in the city that were converted from industrial space. Thus, both a 1,500-square-foot loft in SoHo and a 150-square-foot studio apartment in Queens went into the same category of "one-room apartment"! Or, since the form had a category for condominiums but not for co-ops, thousands of co-op apartments went unaccounted for. Nor did the form break down rents above $500, which is about where rents for Manhattan one-room studio apartments begin. Thus, all rental apartments that rented for more than $500—most of Manhattan below 96th Street—simply got lumped together in the catch-all category of "over $500."

## Racial and Ethnic Groups

Where else but in New York would one find kosher pizza being served to a Puerto Rican customer in a Jewish delicatessen located in a black neighborhood? (It's anyone's guess as to what language is being spoken.)

You could observe this scene in several neighborhoods around the city. Not only does it epitomize the great diversity of the city's racial and ethnic population (someone has said that the city's bilingual education program must offer classes in no fewer than thirty-seven languages), but the fact that New Yorkers would not think twice about it just proves how commonplace and how much a part of the city's natural fabric such diversity is.

Ten or fifteen years ago the ethnic components of the scene just described might have been different, for the racial and ethnic mix of the city is constantly changing. Therefore, if what you know about the city is based on books or movies about "Old New York" or if you rely on a New York City guidebook that is more than a few years old, you could be in for some surprises.

You may, for instance, visit German Yorkville on the Upper East Side only to find high-rise luxury apartment buildings where an ethnic community once throve. A German restaurant or two remain— the kind that offer oom-pah-pah music for their largely tourist clientele—but that's about it. You'll find Little Italy looking more like Little China; the population of neighboring Chinatown has fast been spilling across Canal Street into what was once an almost totally Italian community. You'll discover that the Jewish Lower East Side is now substantially more Hispanic than Jewish, and other once predominantly Jewish neighborhoods—the Grand Concourse section of the Bronx or Williamsburg and Crown Heights in Brooklyn—are now more black than Jewish. You'll learn that capturing the Catholic vote of the city doesn't mean getting only Irish and Italian support, but today means getting the Puerto Rican vote. You'll discover that Indian movies are becoming the city's new foreign film staple. You'll also notice that New York's greengrocers are no longer Greeks and Italians; now they are Koreans.

You should know that of all the changes, none has been so clear nor so dramatic as the decline in the size and visibility of traditional ethnic groups of European origin while the numbers of blacks and Hispanics have grown enormously. New York has become less Jewish, Italian, Irish, Polish, Czech, German, and Greek, and it has become more and more black and Hispanic. Now they are the two largest minority groups by far.

That's not to say that Jews, Poles, Irish, Italians, and so on don't still number in the hundreds of thousands or that they don't continue to have an obvious influence on the lifeblood and spirit of the city. More than a million Jews continue to reside here—more than in any other city in the world, including Tel Aviv—and Goldbergs still outnumber Smiths in the city's telephone directories. Jews still impart a certain Jewish sensibility and style upon the city, loom as the largest and most formidable voting bloc in city elections, and ensure that Yiddish remains a part of the city's daily lexicon. Nearly a million Italians still live throughout New York, and without the Italian communities of Little Italy, East Harlem, Carroll Gardens, Bay Ridge, Bensonhurst, Belmont, and elsewhere, the city would be a very different place—a less interesting city. Some seventy thousand Greeks remain concentrated in Astoria in Queens, making Astoria the largest Greek "city" outside of Greece. And so on.

Yet no matter how large these European ethnic groups remain or however much their influence is still felt, the point is that both their size and their presence were until recently considerably greater. One million Jews are a sizable number to be sure, but in the 1950s there were 2 million—1 million in Brooklyn alone, then and now the most Jewish of the city's five boroughs. As recently as the late 1950s, Italians were the largest foreign-language-speaking group in New York. Today they are not nearly the largest. *Il Progresso*, the city's Italian daily, may still have a circulation of 70,000 but *El Diario*, the Spanish-language paper, is read by more than 100,000 people each day. (You might be interested to know that the Yiddish-language daily, *The Jewish Daily Forward*, has recently become a weekly, *The Jewish Forward*, since its readership declined to about 20,000 from its former peak of a quarter of a million.) If today the city had to choose a second language, it would have to be Spanish.

Changes within the black and Hispanic population have entailed more than just growth in numbers. Their composition has changed as well, particularly within the past ten years or so. You'll find both the black and Hispanic communities here to be different from those in any other city you might know.

The black population now includes a great number of West Indians. In fact, most blacks who came to New York during the 1970s emigrated not from other parts of this country but from Haiti, Jamaica, Trinidad and Tobago, and elsewhere in the West Indies. The city's "black radio station," WLIB, estimates that perhaps as much as one-third of New York's black population is now West Indian. (Since so many of the city's uncounted illegal aliens come from the West Indies, especially Haiti, no one can really be sure of their precise numbers.)

As for Hispanics, don't assume they're all from Puerto Rico. Even a lot of us New Yorkers forget, or simply ignore, the fact that most Hispanics who moved to the city in the past decade came from other places of the Caribbean—primarily Cuba and the Dominican Republic—or from mainland South America—primarily Colombia and Ecuador. Now a large percentage of the Puerto Rican population is New York–born—second- and third-generation even—while Cubans, Dominicans, Colombians, Ecuadorians, Bolivians, Venezuelans, and so on are more likely to be foreign-born and to have come to New York only recently.

(It may help to know that Cubans tend to speak both the slowest and clearest Spanish; Dominicans speak much more rapidly; and Puerto Ricans speak the most rapid Spanish of all—seemingly at breakneck speed. And since Puerto Ricans have been here the longest, their Spanish has become the most assimilated and, indeed, may sound like no other Spanish you have ever heard. Many Puerto Ricans converse in what has come to be called "Spanglish," their own inimitable blend of Spanish and English.)

WHERE THEY ARE
To fully appreciate the city's extraordinary ethnic diversity will require that you extricate yourself from mid-Manhatttan (which unfortunately tends—for visitors, at any rate—to be what a magnet is to tacks). There are, of course, French and Japanese restaurants in the Fifties, Jewish delis near the theater district, Italian ices in Central Park. There are parades on St. Patrick's Day, Columbus Day, and even Pulaski Day. But all of these things amount to a kind of ersatz ethnicity.

The more authentic ethnic life of the city is to be found in the *residential* ethnic communities outside of central Manhattan. By now the ethnic enclaves of central Manhattan (mostly of European origin) have almost all disappeared. The upwardly mobile second, third, and fourth generations moved out of these ethnic communities when they were still among Manhattan's poorest neighborhoods. Those who remained were ultimately pushed out when the neighborhoods revived, property values skyrocketed, and new buildings went up. This is what happened in Yorkville to the German, Czech, and Hungarian communities. This is what happened in Chelsea to the Irish, Greek, Cuban, and Spanish communities. And this is what is happening today in the Italian neighborhoods of the West Village upon which neighboring SoHo makes daily encroachments—where with each new boutique or restaurant and with every old building converted into expensive cooperative loft apartments, the size and character of the Italian community is further diminished.

Now the large ethnic concentrations in Manhattan are relegated to upper and lower Manhattan or to the extreme east and west sides of the island. This is where you'll observe Manhattan's most varied ethnic neighborhoods—in Chinatown and Little Italy; in Puerto Rican neighborhoods on the Lower East Side or in Spanish (East) Harlem; in the black communities of Central Harlem; in the Ukrainian section of the East Village; in the Cuban and Greek parts of Washington Heights; in the Irish sections of Inwood. And if you manage to leave Manhattan altogether and to visit the outer boroughs, you'll discover even greater diversity. As you can see from the Ethnic Map at the end of the chapter, Manhattan is not nearly the most diverse of the boroughs. Now Queens ranks first in that regard, and Brooklyn and the Bronx follow close behind. Staten Island is the least varied of the five boroughs.

Queens is also home to the more middle-class ethnics. The Greeks and Italians in Astoria tend to be more middle-income than their counterparts in Manhattan. Chinese who live in Flushing (about half the Chinese population of New York lives outside of Chinatown, mostly in Queens) are apt to be better off than those in Chinatown. Indians, Koreans, and Japanese—all concentrated in sections of Queens—tend to be well-educated, professional, and quite well off. And Queens, more than any of the other boroughs, is home to middle-income blacks and Hispanics. There are certainly some poor communities in Queens, such as black neighborhoods in South Jamaica, but none quite compare to the enormous, impoverished black ghettos and Hispanic barrios of Manhattan (Harlem), Brooklyn (Brownsville or East New York), and the Bronx (Hunts Point or the South Bronx).

Most of us would probably tell you that we consider the city's multiracial and multiethnic character to be one of its greatest attractions. This doesn't mean we romanticize it. God knows, it's not without its problems. No one is going to deny that racial tensions are very much a part of the city's landscape. We won't deny that we move about the city with our racial antennae raised high and often working overtime.

No one will paint a picture of New York as a place where all kinds of people live and work harmoniously, side by side. It's just not true, and the evidence against that notion is too glaring anyway: all-black neighborhoods in Central Harlem; the nearly all-white Upper East Side; totally Hispanic neighborhoods in the South Bronx; segregated public schools everywhere; youth gangs in Chinatown; blacks and Hasidic Jews fighting in Borough Park; 12 percent unemployment for blacks and 11 percent for Hispanics (when it was 7 percent for whites); nearly 40 percent unemployment among black and Hispanic youths; Puerto Ricans alone comprising nearly one-third of the city's welfare rolls; etc., etc.

Whether racial and ethnic disharmony is actually any worse here than in other cities is hard to say. But most would agree that tensions certainly *seem* more palpable here than elsewhere. And how could they not? In a city where East 95th Street can be part of the fashionable Upper East Side and East 96th can already be Harlem; where Central Park West in the Eighties can be white and upper-class and Amsterdam Avenue in the Eighties just two blocks west can be black, Hispanic, and poor; or where a single subway car can include as many races and nationalities as the United Nations General Assembly, tensions aren't easily ignored. And that is what ultimately distinguishes New York from other cities—not more racial and ethnic tensions, but rather less ability to avoid or ignore them and more opportunities for tensions to play themselves out publicly.

Yet despite this—despite what we call one of the social costs of living here—we still value the great racial and ethnic mix. Without it this would be a bland city. Without it we might as well all live in Oslo. This doesn't mean that in our personal lives there is necessarily much coming together between various racial and ethnic groups. In fact, for most of us there is very little. For a lot of New Yorkers, experiencing the racial and ethnic richness of the city may encompass nothing more than shopping at Balducci's in the Village, eating in Chinatown, or perhaps listening to a Jamaican steel-drum band in Central Park. None of these things engenders much understanding between people and cultures. None necessarily makes us less ethnocentric deep down. But they sure do make us *feel* that we are less ethnocentric. We feel better about ourselves since, at least, "our city" embraces, tolerates, and tries to understand so many kinds of people. If *it does*, then we feel *we do*. And unlike non–New Yorkers, we can all at least say that we haven't forsaken the city for some ethnically neutral, racially monochromatic suburb.

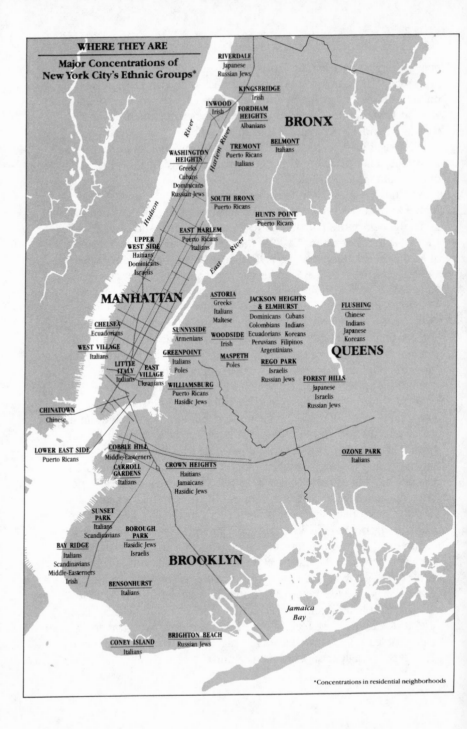

**WHERE THEY ARE**

**Major Concentrations of New York City's Ethnic Groups***

**BRONX**

RIVERDALE
Japanese
Russian Jews

KINGSBRIDGE
Irish

INWOOD
Irish

FORDHAM HEIGHTS
Albanians

WASHINGTON HEIGHTS
Greeks
Cubans
Dominicans
Russian Jews

TREMONT
Puerto Ricans
Italians

BELMONT
Italians

SOUTH BRONX
Puerto Ricans

HUNTS POINT
Puerto Ricans

EAST HARLEM
Puerto Ricans
Italians

UPPER WEST SIDE
Haitians
Dominicans
Israelis

**MANHATTAN**

CHELSEA
Ecuadorians

WEST VILLAGE
Italians

LITTLE ITALY
Italians

EAST VILLAGE
Ukranians

CHINATOWN
Chinese

LOWER EAST SIDE
Puerto Ricans

ASTORIA
Greeks
Italians
Maltese

SUNNYSIDE
Armenians

WOODSIDE
Irish

GREENPOINT
Italians
Poles

MASPETH
Poles

WILLIAMSBURG
Puerto Ricans
Hasidic Jews

JACKSON HEIGHTS & ELMHURST
Dominicans   Cubans
Colombians   Indians
Ecuadorians  Koreans
Peruvians    Filipinos
Argentinians

FLUSHING
Chinese
Indians
Japanese
Koreans

**QUEENS**

REGO PARK
Israelis
Russian Jews

FOREST HILLS
Japanese
Israelis
Russian Jews

COBBLE HILL
Middle-Easterners

CARROLL GARDENS
Italians

CROWN HEIGHTS
Haitians
Jamaicans
Hasidic Jews

OZONE PARK
Italians

SUNSET PARK
Italians
Scandinavians

BAY RIDGE
Italians
Scandinavians
Middle-Easterners
Irish

BOROUGH PARK
Hasidic Jews
Israelis

**BROOKLYN**

BENSONHURST
Italians

*Jamaica Bay*

CONEY ISLAND
Italians

BRIGHTON BEACH
Russian Jews

*Hudson River*

*Harlem River*

*East River*

*Concentrations in residential neighborhoods

# ③ Politics

Most people think of New York as a one-party town, a Democratic town. It is, more accurately, a liberal town. With the demise of the political club—machine politics—the city's large and independent liberal voting blocs—Jews, blacks, Hispanics, unions—now ensure victory for the political liberal. Just being a Democrat is no longer sufficient.

In fact, given a choice between a Democrat and a more liberal Republican opponent, we might very well elect the Republican. John Lindsay was elected mayor in 1965 when he ran as a Republican but was the most liberal candidate in the race; and he was reelected in 1969, when he ran as the candidate of the Liberal Party, since he had lost his own party's primary to a more conservative Republican foe. U.S. Senator Jacob Javits, perhaps then the most liberal Republican in the Senate, always garnered strong support from the city's Democratic voters.

Of course, it's not often that a liberal will run as a Republican. Republican candidates here are typically conservative (often getting the backing of the city's Conservative Party), and ordinarily they find the political waters chilly, if not downright icy. There are only a few conservative voting districts in the city. They crop up as scattered enclaves, in neighborhoods whose population is largely white, Catholic, and over forty—the major traits of New Yorkers who vote for conservative Republicans. Mostly these neighborhoods are in Brooklyn (Bay Ridge, for instance); Queens (Ridgewood, Douglaston, and South Ozone Park); and most of Staten Island. Manhattan has historically been the city's most liberal borough; the "Silk Stocking District" along the Upper East Side is its one clearly Republican stronghold, and even so, that district supports moderate-to-liberal Republicans.

These isolated conservative districts have little impact on citywide or statewide elections. The city remains on the whole a liberal-Democratic bastion. (Democrats, by the way, outnumber Republicans by almost 5 to 1—about 2 million registered Democrats and about 440,000 Republicans.) And that's why general elections here seem to hold so little interest for many of us compared to the Democratic primaries. It is in the Democratic primary that the real dogfights are waged, that there is legitimate suspense as to who will win, and that the eventual winner in the general election will be chosen. More often than not, the general election is anticlimactic, at best. At worst, it's soporific.

You may find certain features of the city's political landscape surprising, even ironical. For example, despite our image as being politically savvy, when it comes to electoral politics, you'll discover that New Yorkers tend to be terribly apathetic. In the past few mayoral elections, only about 30 percent of those who could have voted actually did. Though we seem to respond a bit better in national elections, New Yorkers are still a long way from being model citizens. In recent presidential elections the percentage of voter turnout in the city was only about half of what it was in neighboring suburbs in Nassau and Westchester counties.

Some say low voter turnout is due to the fact that the city has such a large poor black and Hispanic population—groups that historically have been reticent at the polls, particularly when there are no black or Hispanic candidates to vote for (and in New York there rarely are). Others ascribe voter indifference to the fact that the city's problems, in both number and magnitude, appear to many as being beyond the ability of politicians to solve. In other words, why bother?

Although you would think that running a city as large and as complex as New York would require that politicians have broad bases of support, they now almost never do. Three-way races (two Democrats—one as the Liberal Party candidate—run against a Republican) typically leave the winner with less than 50 percent of the vote.

If it is difficult for a candidate to win a majority in a general election, to do so in a Democratic primary has become nearly impossible. No fewer than seven candidates ran in the 1977 Democratic mayoral primary—a primary more crowded than a subway at rush hour and one that might have made some wonder whether the simplicity and efficiency of the political machine might not be preferable. The six major contenders—all liberals—split the vote as follows: 20 percent, 19 percent, 18 percent, 17 percent, 14 percent, and 11 percent (the seventh candidate polled 1 percent). The results, to say the least, represented something less than a mandate from the people. (The 1981 mayoral election was exceptional in that Mayor Koch, then running for a second term, ran as both the Democratic *and* Republican candidate. The 1981 mayoral election was unexceptional in that despite Koch's claim that his election with 75 percent of the vote represented a mandate from the people, the election had the lowest voter turnout in twenty years. Less than half of those registered to vote actually did.)

Whereas blacks and Hispanics win offices in other cities—often where they represent a much smaller percentage of the population than they do in New York (as in Los Angeles), neither a black nor a Hispanic has ever won a *citywide* office here. Perhaps this is not so surprising when you consider that it wasn't until 1973 that New York elected its first Jewish mayor. And this is in a city that has the largest Jewish population of any city in the world. It wasn't until 1977 that a woman was first elected to a citywide office, and that was to the position of City Council President.

Frankly, this record is kind of embarrassing to liberal New Yorkers. We badmouth Los Angeles unmercifully, yet Los Angeles has elected a black mayor. We pooh-pooh San Francisco as just a pretty place, yet it's put its feminism where its mouth is and elected a woman mayor. Atlanta even had a Jewish mayor before we did!

That blacks, Hispanics, and other minority groups have not been successful in winning city offices may result not so much from our lack of racial and ethnic consciousness as from the excess of it. Not only do minorities identify strongly with their group, but they also usually see other groups as antagonists. Elections here are the arena where polarized and often hostile groups square off. One group does not usually get the support of others, and it is precisely that cross-group support that a minority candidate needs to win.

When three Jews, a black, a Puerto Rican, and an Italian ran in the 1977 Democratic mayoral primary, one read more about Jews, blacks, Hispanics, and Catholics than about issues. Predictably, the vote split almost precisely along ethnic and racial lines. In the predominantly Jewish voting district that includes Brighton Beach and Sheepshead Bay in Brooklyn, for instance, the top vote-getter among the Jewish candidates beat the black candidate by a 25-to-1 margin. Conversely, in Brooklyn's nearly all-black Bedford-Stuyvesant section, the black candidate beat the top vote-getting Jewish candidate by 10 to 1. The Puerto Rican was overwhelmingly the winner in largely Hispanic districts such as the South Bronx, and the Italian won big over all others in heavily Catholic neighborhoods such as Bay Ridge in Brooklyn. Only in the few voting districts with a racial and ethnic mix—as on Manhattan's Upper West Side—was the vote spread out somewhat evenly among the several candidates.

If in certain of its political features New York differs from other cities, there is one way it does not, one way it is identical to any other American city: We too elect only lawyers.

Despite the city's vast array of talented people in all kinds of professions, in the past seventy years all but one of our mayors have been attorneys; the one exception was Abe Beame, an accountant! In most every other aspect of city life New York offers unimaginable diversity, if nothing else. In all fields but politics New York is a veritable smorgasbord; in politics it's strictly McDonald's.

# 4 Money Matters

## Public Sector

For New Yorkers the year 1975 stands out as a watershed (nearly our Waterloo). It was the year of our great fiscal crisis, the year we came within a hair's-breadth of going bankrupt. The financial capital of the world—a city brimming with men and women expert in the handling of big money deals—had to admit publicly it had not managed its financial affairs very well. It was like an investment banker confessing he could not balance the family checkbook. The irony was not lost on anyone.

And we discovered then the real feelings the rest of the country harbors toward us. Although the federal government ultimately came through with loans to help bail us out of our financial difficulties, it wasn't until we were made to jump through a few hoops and then assume the posture of the supplicant. We won't forget the government's initial nose-thumbing to our plea for aid. The sentiments of the federal government were captured in a *New York Daily News* headline: FORD TO CITY: DROP DEAD.

We will always remember how Senator Proxmire, chairman of the Senate Finance Committee, came snooping around the city to see how we were managing our affairs. We won't forget how humiliating it was to have Proxmire riding around on New York City garbage trucks to observe municipal productivity—as if he'd know it if he saw it.

We'll never forget, nor forgive, our fellow Americans from Iowa, Arkansas, Idaho, Oregon, and elsewhere who urged the government not to lend us any money—certainly not *their* tax money. Apparently they felt that if we had been irresponsible and profligate, then we deserved to go bankrupt. It was all right for the government to bail out farmers, aircraft industries, car makers, dictatorships, and any number of other worthy causes; but New York was another matter. People were saying they really didn't care if New York went bankrupt; it was just a dirty, old, smelly, crime-ridden, immoral city anyway. And it was smug and arrogant to boot. The rest of America passed judgment and concluded that if there has to be a choice between the survival of New York City and, say, an automobile manufacturer, well then, give them a Chrysler any day.

CAUSES OF THE FISCAL CRISIS

In the spring of 1975 the city found itself unable to borrow money it needed to pay an upcoming city payroll and other obligations. Credit markets to which the city had gone time and again suddenly closed their doors. Only by virtue of some eleventh-hour loans from the city's municipal unions' pension funds and from the federal government was New York able to meet its immediate obligations and stave off bankruptcy.

Although the immediate crisis, bankruptcy, was both precipitated and averted in 1975, the crisis had in fact been several years in the making; and the blame falls mostly upon the city's politicians.

Several administrations, dating back to at least the mid-1960s, had been fiscally irresponsible. They had, year after year, spent more money than New York had, and to bridge the budget deficits they faced, they simply borrowed the money they needed. Unfortunately they never told anyone about it. For years we were under the impression that the budget was balanced. No one knew that it was only because money had been borrowed to do so.

When credit markets closed up for the city, it was because New York had by then simply borrowed too much too many times. The deficit for 1975 alone was nearly $2 billion (the city spent $13 billion; revenues were about $11 billion). It had actually reached the point where the city was borrowing money just to pay back the money it had previously borrowed. In the spring of 1975 when moneylenders finally said no more loans, New York City owed debts—accumulated over the years by borrowing to make up budget deficits—totaling $12.5 billion. Now would you lend that man money?

(Though this kind of deficit borrowing had gone on through several administrations, it was somewhat ironical that the bubble should burst during the administration of the Honorable Abe Beame. He was elected mayor not for his leadership abilities, nor his charisma, nor his vision, but solely for his financial acumen. He was an accountant, a former Director of the Budget, and a former City Comptroller. To use the Yiddish parlance, he was a money *maven*. So it was to him that in 1974 we entrusted our $13-billion-plus annual budget—a city budget that was larger than the budgets of most states, including New York State, and one that exceeded the annual budgets of some entire countries.)

Not only had politicians spent money the city didn't have, they had failed to collect revenues they might have. It's been suggested that if the city had collected all the monies it was owed—uncollected sales, real estate, and income taxes, as well as uncollected parking, traffic, and other fines—it probably could have come close to making up its yearly deficits without having to borrow money. If the city had been able to collect taxes from the 150,000 tax-exempt properties located throughout the five boroughs, it certainly would have made up the deficits. The World Trade Center alone, since it is owned by a government agency (the Port Authority of New York and New Jersey), escaped about $65 million in taxes each year. And, if the city had been able to eliminate the several hundred million dollars lost each year in Medicare and Medicaid frauds, it might have been financially flush rather than nearly bankrupt.

Though politicians were the main culprits in bringing on the fiscal crisis, they were not the only ones. Other members of the rogues' gallery include the municipal unions, banks, the state and federal government, and middle-class taxpayers who had abandoned the city.

Unions: For extracting wages and benefits the city couldn't afford; not more than the union members deserved nor more than the cost of living in New York City warranted, but simply more than the city could pay for. Banks: For being remiss in allowing the city to accumulate $12 billion in debts and then abruptly turning off the tap when the city was desperate for funds. The state and federal governments: For not assuming a larger share of the cost to the city for providing a high level of city services, and for sticking New York City with a welfare tab of nearly $1 billion in 1975—the city's 25 percent share of a total $3.7 billion in welfare and Medicaid costs.* Middle-class taxpayers: For deserting the city throughout the 1950s, 1960s, and 1970s for the suburbs and beyond and thereby leaving New York with a dwindling tax base at a time when more and more poor people—who pay less taxes and make greater demands on city services—entered.

RAMIFICATIONS OF THE FISCAL CRISIS

If the 1975 fiscal crisis was several years in the making, it has been and continues to be several years in the unmaking. And we still suffer from its effects, daily and graphically. On the assumption that the crisis was primarily the result of overspending—as opposed to, say, undercollecting revenues owed—the 1975 crisis has since been the justification for drastic budget cuts and other unprecedented austerity measures. The crisis has been the excuse for the subsequent massive job layoffs, reduction in city services, and elimination of other benefits and amenities.

In 1975 the City of New York employed close to 300,000 workers. By 1980 that number had been reduced to about 200,000 and by 1982 to fewer than 200,000. The budget of virtually every city agency has been slashed. Since 1975 the city has laid off—or has failed to replace those who quit or retired—several thousand policemen, firemen, teachers, and sanitation workers, to name but a few of the city's most essential employees. Between 1975 and 1982, the work force of the Police Department shrank about 20 percent; the Fire Department, 10 percent; and the Sanitation Department, 20 percent. To those who never thought the city did a very good job of delivering services with 300,000 employees, it's a mystery how it can even presume to do an adequate job with one-third fewer workers.

Since 1975, schools and hospitals throughout the city—mostly in poor neighborhoods, by the way—have been closed; police patrol cars, which once contained two officers, now often have just one; welfare rolls have been cut, though there has been no reduction in the number of poor people nor in the need for assistance. In 1975 the subway and bus fare was 35¢. Since the crisis it has been raised

---

*In most other states, the localities' share of welfare costs is much less than the 25 percent share in New York. In some states, the localities make no contribution to welfare costs at all. Rather, the state picks up the entire tab.

to 50¢, then 60¢, then 75¢, and the talk lately has been that it will have to be raised again to $1.00 or more. Special Sunday and holiday half-fares and other discounts on public transportation have been scrapped. The City University, which had been built upon a commitment to provide a free education—and continued that tradition for a hundred years—now charges tuition. And the belt continues to be tightened.

Of course, politicians proudly proclaim that the financial ship has been put back in shape. They promised a balanced budget by 1982, and they did better than that by producing one in 1981. Actually in 1981 there was a surplus of a couple of hundred million dollars. (This was after anticipating a deficit. So although coming up with an unexpected $200 million surplus might seem preferable to an unexpected $200 million deficit, it still doesn't instill confidence about the ability of the city's money people to *balance* a budget.) For its austerity measures, the city was rewarded, also in 1981, when the major securities-rating services endorsed the city's notes and bonds as creditworthy—for the first time since the fiscal crisis.

The worry, however, is that in the process of producing balanced budgets, some of the essential elements of city life, such as a reasonable subway fare, adequate police and fire protection, enough hospitals, and so on, might be irrevocably lost. We worry that the cure might prove far worse than the disease.

## Private Sector

Headlines decry the city's economic woes, but to many, such as visitors who come here only to see a show, dine out, or shop, the evidence seems to belie what the newspapers are saying. Broadway tickets cost $30 and $40 or more, but theaters are packed; restaurants are outrageously expensive, yet it's difficult to get a reservation; Bloomingdale's, Saks, Bergdorf's, and Bendel's are as crowded as ever; expensive furs outnumber the down parkas on Fifth Avenue; nannies tending children seem omnipresent.

Yet you can be sure that if you travel outside of Midtown Manhattan, and outside the posh East Side in particular, you will discover that business does not always go on as usual. In spite of the apparent wealth in the fancy parts of town, travel to other neighborhoods and to other boroughs and you will discover that when hit in the pocket-book the vast majority of New Yorkers, like anyone else, hurt too.*

In fact, the city's economy tottered through most of the 1970s, and a great many New Yorkers suffered because of it. In 1969 the city provided 3.8 million jobs—the most ever—but by the end of the 1970s, that number had shrunk to just 3 million. Between 1969 and 1977 (things supposedly began to get better in 1977), unemployment in New York City tripled.

Rather than being unaffected by economic downturns, New York usually suffers more than other places. When unemployment nationally stood at 7 percent in 1977, it was 10 percent here. By 1979 when the national unemployment rate had dropped to under 6 percent, here it still hovered near 9 percent. During 1981 unemployment rose nationally to 7 percent again, and in the city it again surpassed 10 percent. (Both New York City and the nation as a whole experienced more than 10 percent unemployment during the "depression" of 1982.)

The more optimistic among us now say that the city's economy is on the upswing, and has been since late 1977. There are several signs: an increase in the number of jobs; a decrease in unemployment, at least prior to the Reaganomics-induced national recession of the early 1980s; more middle-class families moving back into the city; and fewer businesses now leaving.

The truth is that there is an awful lot of contrary evidence that makes such optimism somewhat suspect. The total number of jobs here may have increased since 1977, but that gain has been limited primarily to Manhattan, Queens, and Staten Island. The number of jobs has increased only slightly in Brooklyn, and in the Bronx the number has actually declined. If citywide unemployment has dropped from time to time, it's because whites have found jobs. Unemployment among the city's Hispanics has remained about the same since 1977, and for blacks it has worsened. If the city's tax base has been growing because middle-class taxpayers are moving back to the city and businesses are deciding to remain here, this has been

---

*According to the 1980 census, although Manhattan ranks number 14 out of 3,132 counties in the United States in per capita income, the Bronx, for example, ranks number 2,270. The borough-by-borough breakdown for New York City is as follows: Manhattan is number 14 nationally with a per capita income of $10,889. Queens is number 309 with $4,046, Staten Island number 316 with $3,745, Brooklyn number 1,805 with $3,072, and the Bronx number 2,270, with a per capita income of $2,943.

limited almost exclusively to Manhattan—and more specifically, to Manhattan below 96th Street. Elsewhere around the city, things are not nearly so rosy.

What makes it impossible to be sanguine about the city's economic future is a certain fundamental problem that will not easily or simply go away. That is, New York has become a predominantly white-collar town but still retains a substantial blue-collar population. (To say the city is a white-collar town is, by the way, also a way of saying that it's not a union town. Despite the apparently endless union negotiations that go on and the strikes that nearly cripple the city seemingly every few months, this union activity is mostly limited to the large, powerful, and very vocal municipal workers' unions. Outside of municipal workers, most of the city's work force remains nonunionized.)

Whereas in 1950 factory work accounted for about one-third the total number of jobs in the city, by the mid-1970s factories provided only about one-sixth. We lost our manufacturing businesses to the Sun Belt, to the South, and to suburbs everywhere. And the more New York declined as a center of manufacturing, the more it grew as a financial and services center. Skilled jobs increased, while unskilled jobs declined.

The problem is that the city's unskilled population did not decrease as well. Rather, the size of the poor, undereducated, and unskilled population burgeoned. The continuing influx of illegal aliens adds to the already swelling numbers of unskilled workers. So the problem is one of skilled jobs and unskilled workers—the dichotomy that might be called the ring around New York City's white collar. (It was recently predicted that in the immediate future, 7 out of every 10 job openings would be white-collar.) Until that dichotomy disappears, the prognosis for our economic health can never be good.

## Cost of Living

No one lives here to save money. It's just too damn expensive.

You'll very likely hear both rich and poor New Yorkers bemoaning the high cost of living here. Just recently a Manhattan couple, both lawyers in their thirties and the parents of one young child, unabashedly declared in a *New York Times* article that despite a combined annual income of over $100,000, they considered themselves to be middle-income at best. At the same time, more than 800,000 city residents on welfare rail against the cost of living, because while in New York it has probably increased by about 75 percent since 1974, the size of the welfare grant has increased by only 15 percent. And that increase didn't come until 1981, when the basic grant for a family of four was raised from $258 to $296 a month, not including food stamps and the separate monthly grant for rent.

Whereas the federal government said the average American urban family of four needed $23,000 after taxes to live in "moderate comfort" in 1981, the New York City family of four, by contrast, needed $25,000. Only three other American cities were more expensive—Anchorage, Honolulu, and Boston, in that order.

To be more accurate the government should have come up with at least two cost-of-living figures for the city—one for Manhattan below 96th Street and another for everywhere else. Not that New Yorkers outside of Manhattan live cheaply; New Yorkers in all boroughs are still the most heavily taxed people in the United States. In every borough we still tend to pay nearly 30 percent of our incomes for housing, while the rest of America pays closer to 25 percent. And all of us must pay outrageously high gas and electric bills extorted by Consolidated Edison, our friendly overpriced utility company.

Living in Manhattan, though, remains even more expensive in almost every respect than living in the outer boroughs. That's why so many choose not to live in Manhattan. The cost of housing there, for example—whether on the Upper East Side, Upper West Side, in the Village, in Chelsea, Murray Hill, or almost anywhere else—can't be compared to the much cheaper housing costs of, say, Staten Island or the Bronx.

Manhattanites lead a different sort of life from that of outer-borough residents—not necessarily more comfortable, but different nonetheless. For middle-class Manhattanites, sending a child to private school is regarded not just as a comfort, but as a necessity (private schools can cost $5,000 or more per year per child). In Brooklyn, Queens, and Staten Island, however, there are still some public schools that are apparently considered both adequate and safe. For many, getting out of Manhattan in the heat of the summer is imperative (a summer share in a house on Fire Island or in the Hamptons can cost several thousand dollars), while on Staten Island, people have pools in their backyards. Manhattan families send kids to sleep-away camps. In Queens, day camps are good enough. Manhattanites garage their cars (easily costing $100 per month). Elsewhere car owners have their own garage or driveway; or there is always the street, where legal parking spots are more available than in Manhattan. Manhattanites need therapists. Staten Islanders seem not to.

It's obvious that it costs much more to live in Manhattan than in any other borough. If the government came up with two cost-of-living figures, the one for Manhattan would surely make it the most expensive place to live in the country. It may be more expensive to live in Anchorage than in Maspeth, Queens, but it is doubtful that Anchorage can be more costly than, say, Central Park South.

# 5 Buildings

## The New

There's a construction boom going on in the city. It comes after a period that lasted through most of the 1970s, during which new construction came almost to a standstill; about the only thing that got built in New York was the Citicorp Building at 53rd Street and Third Avenue. By the end of the 1970s, however, construction fences, makeshift walkways, and other pedestrian obstacles that signal building activity began to sprout again. The only problem with this boom is that it is limited to Midtown Manhattan.

By 1982 Manhattan accounted for about half the value of all taxable real estate in New York City—over $20 billion of the total $45 billion. (The latter figure does not include the approximately 150,000 parcels of tax-exempt properties—government, religious, educational, and charitable—located throughout the city. They're worth another $26 billion—and they cost the city about $2 billion each year in lost real-estate-tax revenues.) Yet even though half the value of the property of all five boroughs is already located in just one of them, resources and new construction continue to get pumped primarily into Manhattan to the exclusion of the other four boroughs.

Hence, Manhattan is getting a new convention center—despite the fact that there is already one at Columbus Circle, that Midtown can hardly bear the increased traffic the new center will bring, and that no such facility exists in any of the other boroughs. As if Manhattan were the only borough with a waterfront, only its waterfront is being

upgraded (at Battery Park City, for instance, and the stretch along the East River between 16th and 24th Streets called River Walk).*
New office buildings are being constructed almost exclusively in Manhattan.

Manhattan, likewise, is practically the sole beneficiary of all the new hotels now under construction or being planned. Every other city in the world seems to have at least a few hotels outside the center of the city. You can stay in hotels a bit outside of London or Paris or Washington, D.C. But no one would dare put up a hotel in New York outside of Manhattan. (Indeed, when the Vista International Hotel at the World Trade Center opened in 1981, it became the first major hotel to be built outside of Midtown in a hundred years. The hotel planned at the old police headquarters just outside of Little Italy in lower Manhattan will become the second. Otherwise all new hotels have been built between 42nd and 72nd Streets.) Yet it would take all of fifteen minutes to get from downtown Brooklyn, for example, into the business and tourist centers of Manhattan.

In fact, sights have been so set on the dead center of Manhattan that even the so-called Midtown construction boom has essentially been limited to a twenty-block area of Midtown, bounded roughly by 42nd Street, 59th Street, Third Avenue, and Sixth Avenue (known to visitors as the Avenue of the Americas). On the East Side this area, already perhaps the most densely developed plot of real estate in the world, has become even more built-up and further congested. Here, where empty space is more valuable than buildings themselves, developers pay $15 million for the old Bonwit Teller department store at 56th and Fifth just so they can tear it down and put up another building on the site. (When the old St. Peter's Lutheran Church got in the way of the Citicorp Building, developers razed it and then built a new St. Peter's.) Other developers pay $17 million for the *air rights* above the Museum of Modern Art at 53rd Street just off Fifth so that an apartment tower can be added atop the museum. And some corporation offers to buy St. Bartholomew's Church at 51st and Park for $100 million so that an office skyscraper can be constructed.

While perfectly good buildings in Midtown are being knocked

* Although there have been proposals to develop part of the Brooklyn waterfront between the Brooklyn and Manhattan bridges, whether that comes to pass remains to be seen.

down to make way for new ones, and new towers are being added to every building not already a skyscraper, just five miles to the north in the South Bronx, vast expanses of open space remain untouched, begging to be developed. (Indeed, the South Bronx is of so little interest to developers here that after a proposed housing project at Charlotte Street in the South Bronx fell through, officials representing the Bronx actually sought $5 billion in aid from the Soviet Union! Apparently it has not been forthcoming.)

It doesn't make much sense. But then, New York has never been known as one of your better planned cities. No part of the city was ever planned for on a large scale. Rather the city developed in bits and pieces. On a scale of one to ten—Paris being a ten and Los Angeles a one—New York might rate a three for planning. The lack of an overall design may not have been such a terrible thing when the city was first being built. It's even been said that it has been a blessing in disguise, the legacy of these planning lapses being the incredible architectural diversity the city now boasts as well as a sense about the city that it evolved naturally. More planning, many say, would have left New York with a more homogeneous architecture and with as much a feeling of spontaneity as, say, Washington, D.C. So what if we now have to live in a city of sixty-story skyscrapers built upon a street grid originally laid out to accommodate three-story town houses?

A continued lack of city planning bodes ill, however. It creates a void into which, not surprisingly, real-estate developers jump. And these developers bring about as much social responsibility and awareness to development decisions as they would bring to a game of Monopoly. If it were otherwise, the outer boroughs wouldn't complain about being sacrificed to the god Manhattan.

The rationale offered is that what is good for Manhattan is good for the rest of the city—the trickle-down theory of prosperity and well-being. But a lot of New Yorkers don't buy this argument. How could we? Manhattan property values skyrocket while those in Brooklyn and the Bronx decline; in the Bronx the decline is drastic. So where is this trickling down to? It seems more likely to be a case of what is good for Manhattan is good for developers and realtors. It remains to be seen whether what is claimed to be good for Manhattan is in reality for its benefit. Just look at what's happening.

In the theater district, at Broadway between 45th and 46th Streets, the fifty-four-story Marquis Hotel is newly built. Fine, a new hotel to swank up the seedy district. The only catch is that to make room for the new hotel, three of the city's most famous and venerable theaters—the Helen Hayes, the Morosco, and the Bijou—had to be torn down, along with the old Piccadilly Hotel, which also found itself inconveniently in the way of progress. Bad enough that we lost these beloved old buildings; but worse, you can be sure that what will replace them will not be an improvement. The one theater to be constructed within the Marquis will in no way match the beauty or achieve the intimacy of the three theaters it will replace. Nor will the new Marquis charge the modest rates the old Piccadilly offered.

Under the guise of "improving Manhattan's waterfront," a mammoth marketplace complex—shops and restaurants (as many as a hundred new eating places are projected) along with an office building and hotel—is planned for the South Street Seaport area of lower Manhattan. The developers—the same people who built similar complexes in Boston and Baltimore—boast that the "package of retail and tourist attractions" will bring 12 million tourists a year—30,000 a day—to this part of the city. Baltimore may need more tourists; Manhattan does not. And this section of Manhattan in particular certainly does not. The South Street Seaport district happens to be one of the oldest and quietest neighborhoods in all the city. With many of its original nineteenth-century buildings still intact, the neighborhood retains a certain "Old New York" ambience about it. Imagine what an influx of 30,000 people a day upon this tiny neighborhood will do to that ambience.

All over, Manhattan is becoming increasingly commercialized. To real-estate interests, it's never a question of whether more housing is needed or whether the remaining residential qualities of a neighborhood should be preserved. Rather, it's simply dollars and cents. Commercial space is far more profitable than residential space, so almost all new buildings are now devoted to commercial use.

One peculiar aspect to this commercialization trend is what is called "retailization." It is one of the newest and perhaps most virulent phenomena to hit the city in a long time. What it means is that more and more space is now being built specifically for retail establishments. What's been occurring along Third Avenue in the Forties and Fifties is an especially graphic example. There retail space rents for $50 and more a square foot per year, compared to $30 or $40 for office space or the even lower rentals commanded by apartments. So to no one's surprise, retail businesses have inundated the area. Even

when a new office or apartment building is built, the bottom floors
are devoted to retailing; and more likely than not, the retail stores are
those that belong to huge retailing chains—Radio Shack, The Ath-
lete's Foot, Waldenbooks, Baskin-Robbins, The Gap—for who else
can pay $200,000 a year for rent? And these stores remain open in
the evenings *and* on weekends. This brand of retailization brings the
kind of activity from which there is no respite: no cycle of noise and
quiet, but instead noisiness and busyness at all times.

We might not have been so enthusiastic—actually gullible—about
the idea of mixed uses within buildings, a supposedly enlightened
concept, had we known our downstairs neighbor was going to be a
Herman's sporting-goods store, open weekdays from nine to nine,
Saturdays and Sundays until six. In the suburbs you have to travel to
reach a mall. Now in Manhattan you can live on top of one.

All this for the good of Manhattan? We doubt it.

## The Old

If you find that you are spending all your time looking up at Midtown skyscrapers, then you are missing a very special part of the city-
scape. You are depriving yourself of the joy of observing bits of Old
New York—the city's oldest and most historic buildings. Unlike the
modern skyscraper, these buildings can be seen and appreciated at
street level.

To observe these historic buildings, you not only have to lower
your gaze, but you must also leave Midtown and visit the oldest parts
of the city, where the wrecker's ball has not swung as freely as in
Midtown—the financial district, the South Street Seaport, Greenwich
Village (the farther west you go, the better), Chelsea, the side streets
of the Upper East and Upper West Sides, and Harlem.

You'd be smart to venture out of Manhattan altogether and take in
some of the outer boroughs as well—neighborhoods in South
Brooklyn especially. In Brooklyn Heights alone, for instance, you
will discover some seven hundred houses built prior to the Civil
War. Adjacent neighborhoods in Cobble Hill, Boerum Hill, Carroll
Gardens, and Park Slope abound in residential dwellings of the nineteenth century.

To come here and not see what remains of Old New York is to get only a partial picture of city life. You can't really answer the question "How could anyone possibly live in New York City?" unless you spend time looking at some of the oldest buildings (Federal Hall, City Hall, Fraunces Tavern, the Schermerhorn Row Houses, and India House, all in lower Manhattan; Jefferson Market Library in the West Village and Colonnade Row in the East Village; General Theological Seminary in Chelsea; the Ansonia Hotel and the Dakota Apartments on the Upper West Side; the Lycée Française on the Upper East Side), blocks (Stuyvesant Square around East 16th Street and Second Avenue; Gramercy Park on East 20th and 21st at the lower end of Lexington Avenue; Sniffen Court off 36th Street just west of Third Avenue in the Murray Hill section; Veranda Place in Cobble Hill, Brooklyn; and President Street between Smith and Hoyt in the Carroll Gardens section of Brooklyn), and entire neighborhoods (Greenwich Village, SoHo, Turtle Bay on the East Side in the low Forties, Striver's Row in Harlem on West 138th and 139th Streets between Adam Clayton Powell, Jr., Boulevard, formerly Seventh Avenue and Frederick Douglass Boulevard, formerly Eighth Avenue).

Old neighborhoods and old buildings are for many of us the alternative to living in high-rise apartment complexes in densely populated parts of the city. Instead we can live in a floor-through apartment in a nineteenth-century brownstone on a quiet tree-lined block in Park Slope, Brooklyn; or in a whitestone on West 105th Street just off Riverside Drive in Manhattan.

Unfortunately, many people don't seem to be that interested in seeing the city's older, and therefore smaller, buildings. They don't make up the New York that the visitor, to be sure, has heard so much about. The visitor comes here looking for the mighty triad—the Empire State Building, the World Trade Center, and Rockefeller Center. But whether you're interested or not, you have to understand that old neighborhoods and buildings are tremendously important to those who live here. In a city built for the most part on a grand scale, older, smaller buildings provide a human dimension. In a city famous for creating fads and for flaunting its avant-gardism, the old provides a much-needed tie to the past. And in a city that becomes cooler with each new steel-and-glass tower, buildings of mortar, brick, and wood generate a reassuring warmth.

The importance of preserving the old was not always so obvious to us. For years historic buildings were perfunctorily razed just because they happened to be in the way of some developer's plans. Down they came, and no one raised much of a fuss. In fact, it wasn't until 1965 that the city finally got around to establishing a Landmarks Preservation Commission to designate, and thereby protect and preserve, historic buildings and districts. (The map at the end of this chapter pinpoints most of the city's historic districts.) Imagine what London or Paris would look like today if those cities had waited until twenty years ago to create some mechanism to prevent the wholesale destruction of their oldest structures.

Nowadays the threatened destruction, or even alteration, of an old and historic building is sure to summon forth some protest. Protecting old buildings became *the* issue of the late 1970s and has carried over into the 1980s. The imminent destruction of an old building is more likely to arouse demonstrations than a transit-fare hike or the closing of a municipal hospital.

Battles on behalf of some historic building seem to be waged daily. Sometimes the fight is to save a single building, like the clash on the Upper West Side to save the Rice Mansion on 89th Street and Riverside Drive; or more recently the fights to save St. Bartholomew's Church on Park Avenue at 51st Street or the Morosco Theatre in the theater district.

Other times the efforts are to save entire neighborhoods. One of the loudest confrontations in recent years was over the proposal to create the Upper East Side Historic District. The plan was to give landmark status to an area that encompasses most of the East Sixties and Seventies between Fifth and Lexington Avenues. And though historic-district status was ultimately won, it wasn't before a long and drawn-out battle.

To be sure, part of what accounts for protests on behalf of historic preservation is that old is now chic. We knew it was when we observed hordes of young professionals on the Upper West Side, in Park Slope, in Fort Greene, in Clinton Hill, and even in Flatbush buying up old houses for renovation. And if we didn't know it then, it certainly became apparent when in the 1970s Jackie O.—not known for her involvement in protest politics—spearheaded a movement to save Grand Central Terminal from the monstrous office tower that was planned for construction atop its lovely, elegant crown. Thanks to Jackie and friends—plus a little help from the U.S. Supreme Court—Grand Central can still be observed in its original grand form.

A PRE-1900 ARCHITECTURAL OVERVIEW*

You should know that Manhattan was developed from the bottom up. You'll discover the oldest parts of the borough to be the lower portions—the financial district, the Lower East Side, the Village. Similarly, as the population of Manhattan spilled over into the other boroughs (Manhattan was the first of the five boroughs to be developed), people first settled in those sections of the outer boroughs nearest to Manhattan, and they are now the oldest neighborhoods in each of the boroughs—Brooklyn Heights, Cobble Hill, and Boerum Hill in Brooklyn; the Mott Haven section of the Bronx; Hunter's Point in Queens; St. George, Stapleton, and New Brighton on Staten Island.

Start at the tip of Manhattan and walk up and you'll pass through a chronology of early American urban architecture. Major clusters of Federal-style architecture (built from about the time of the Revolutionary War to the 1830s) remain in the South Street Seaport neighborhood just east of the financial district; in the Charlton-King-Vandam neighborhood just below the Village; and, of course, throughout Greenwich Village itself, particularly in the western sections. There are no Federal buildings in Manhattan above 14th Street. Outside of Manhattan, Brooklyn Heights also includes a huge number of Federal houses built in the late eighteenth and early nineteenth centuries. (One of the distinguishing characteristics of the Federal style—and therefore your best clue to identifying that style—is its red-brick façade laid in the Flemish bond pattern. That is, bricks in each course are laid alternately long side out, end out, side out, end out. . . .)

During the 1830s and 1840s, the Greek Revival style flourished. (It's similar in appearance to the Federal style, but it lacks the Flemish bond. Rather, the red bricks are laid out with the long side out throughout. Also, the generally smooth, unbroken façade of both the Federal and Greek Revival building is more likely to be broken on the later-built Greek Revival dwelling—often by the column-supported portico built around the front door.) Houses in this style can be found all over Greenwich Village—check out Washington Square North, in particular—and to a lesser extent in Chelsea (evidence that the settlement of Manhattan had advanced above 14th Street) and just above the East Village, for example Stuyvesant Square. Outside of Manhattan, Brooklyn Heights and Cobble Hill, just over the Brooklyn Bridge, teem with Greek Revival dwellings.

Starting in the 1840s, the now-famous New York brownstone began to sprout. Though today the term "brownstone" is used to describe any manner, style, and color of New York City town house or row house, originally it was meant to characterize only those dwellings whose façade was indeed covered with brownstone slabs 4 to 6 inches thick. (These slabs, consisting of a kind of sandstone, covered a brick construction.)

Brownstones were first built in the Gothic Revival style during the 1840s and 1850s. Many remain standing throughout Greenwich Village and Chelsea. In Brooklyn they can be observed in Brooklyn Heights, Cobble Hill, and Carroll Gardens. (Aside from their brownstone façade, the Gothic Revival building differs from Federal and Greek Revival buildings in that the hoods above the doors and lintels above the windows are more prominent and much more ornamented.) Even more elaborately ornamented brownstones built in the Italianate style between the 1840s and 1870s are clustered in those same neighborhoods as well.

Middle and Upper Manhattan were developed in the latter part of the nineteenth century. Row houses built in the late 1800s used a variety of styles, often resulting in eclectic and truly ornate-looking residences. Town houses all over the Upper East and West Sides and throughout Harlem represent the many different styles used during the time, including a variety of materials for façades—brownstone, whitestone (limestone), red brick, yellow brick, and so forth. In Brooklyn, the Park Slope and Bedford-Stuyvesant sections are the best and most obvious neighborhoods to visit to observe the kinds of dwellings constructed in the late nineteenth century. Montgomery Place in Park Slope has perhaps the loveliest and most varied collection of late-nineteenth-century town houses in all of New York City.

The emergence of the apartment building toward the end of the nineteenth century ushered in the era of "modern" architecture. So much, then, for Old New York.

## Beyond Old and New

For those of you who couldn't care less about old or new, or about this or that architectural style, but instead are concerned only with height, you should at least know which are the city's tallest buildings.

The five tallest buildings in New York, with the year they were constructed and their heights are: 1) The World Trade Towers, 1970, at 1,350 feet (100 feet shorter than the Sears Tower in Chicago); 2) the Empire State Building, 1931, at 1,250 feet; 3) the Chrysler Building, 1930, at 1,046 feet; 4) the Citicorp Building, 1977, at 1,015 feet (this includes, of course, the 115-foot columns upon which it is constructed); and 5) 70 Pine Street in the financial district, 1932, at 950 feet.

It may interest you to know that when the 280-foot-high Trinity Church steeple was completed in 1846 at the head of Wall Street, it was the tallest building in all of New York. When the Flatiron Building at Fifth Avenue and 23rd Street was built in 1902, it then reigned for a decade as the city's tallest "skyscraper." It was—and still is—all of 286 feet high. Then in 1913 the Woolworth Building at 233 Broadway in the Civic Center area was completed, and at 850 feet it was the city's first true skyscraper. It remained the tallest building in the city until the 1930s, the heyday of skyscraper construction in New York.

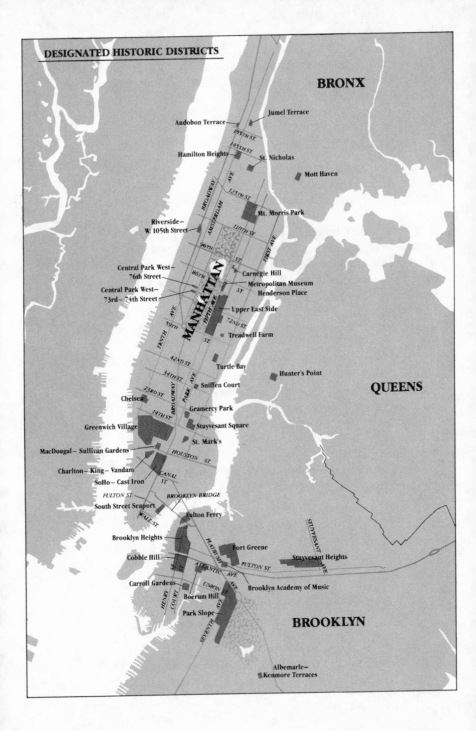

DESIGNATED HISTORIC DISTRICTS

BRONX

Jumel Terrace
Audobon Terrace
145TH ST
Hamilton Heights
St. Nicholas
Mott Haven
BROADWAY
AVE
125TH ST
Mt. Morris Park
AMSTERDAM
110TH ST
Riverside—
W. 105th Street
96TH
ST
Central Park West—
76th Street
86TH
Carnegie Hill
Metropolitan Museum
Central Park West—
73rd — 74th Street
Henderson Place
ST
FIFTH AVE.
Upper East Side
TENTH
59TH
72ND ST
AVE
FIFTH
Treadwell Farm
MANHATTAN
ST
42ND ST
Turtle Bay
Hunter's Point
34TH ST
QUEENS
BROADWAY
PARK
AVE
Sniffen Court
23RD ST
Chelsea
Gramercy Park
14TH ST
Greenwich Village
Stuyvesant Square
MacDougal — Sullivan Gardens
St. Mark's
HOUSTON
ST
Charlton — King — Vandam
CANAL
ST
SoHo — Cast Iron
FULTON ST
BROOKLYN BRIDGE
South Street Seaport
WALL ST
Fulton Ferry
STUYVESANT
Brooklyn Heights
FLATBUSH
Fort Greene
AVE
Cobble Hill
FULTON ST
Stuyvesant Heights
ATLANTIC
AVE
Carroll Gardens
UNION
Brooklyn Academy of Music
HENRY
COURT
Boerum Hill
ST
Park Slope
SEVENTH
AVE
BROOKLYN
Albemarle—
Kenmore Terraces

# ⑥ Housing

Move to any other city and it's a good bet that you'd find a job first and then worry about looking for a place to live. But things don't work that way here.

If you should decide to make the move to New York and plan to live in Manhattan, you would be smart if you did your apartment hunting before your job hunting, for the sad and simple truth is that in Manhattan, as opposed to the other boroughs, housing is a lot harder to come by than jobs. Although it may take you weeks before you get work, it could take months before you find housing. And instead of the four-room apartment in an elevator building on an excellent block for something around $550 a month you'd dreamed of, you'll probably settle for a fifth-floor walk-up studio apartment on a marginal block for $600 a month. Or else you'll take an apartment in Queens.

Nowadays a spacious, affordable apartment in a "good" Manhattan neighborhood (which to most apartment seekers means south of 96th Street) is about as common as milk in glass bottles. Any New Yorker lucky enough to have such a place is not about to give it up—not even when he or she dies. In Manhattan apartments get passed down to offspring. And not just twelve-room penthouses, but small—perhaps one-bedroom—apartments as well. Whereas in other parts of the country divorce battles are usually waged over the issue of who will get custody of the children, in New York the ugliest and most protracted custody battles are more likely to be fought over the apartment.

When Ed Koch was first elected mayor of New York, he refused to abandon his three-room, rent-controlled (which means rent increases are limited to a fixed amount) apartment in Greenwich Village. Luckily he was allowed to live in Gracie Mansion—the official residence of the mayor of New York and the city's answer to the White House, so to speak—*and* keep his apartment. But had he been forced to choose one or the other—to choose between the twenty-room mansion and the three-room apartment—you can be sure he would have opted for the apartment. He knew he couldn't be mayor forever, and if he ever wanted to live in the Village again— where the number of shops that sell homemade ice cream surpasses the number of apartment vacancies—he knew that he'd better have an apartment waiting for him at the end of his term.

In a sense New Yorkers have only themselves to blame for the housing crunch. We've created it. It's not as if there aren't enough apartments available in the city. There happen to be some two million rental apartments throughout the five boroughs. And whether you agree on a population figure for New York of seven or eight or even nine million, you would think that the supply could satisfy the demand.

The problem is that the supply of housing is in one place—outside of Manhattan—and the demand is in another—in Manhattan. The forces of supply and demand go askew, for despite the scant availability of housing in Manhattan, untold numbers of New Yorkers, nonetheless, would never consider living anywhere else in the city. In New York you are *where* you live, as opposed to what you eat or what you do or anything else that might give definition to persons in other places. In New York one chooses a neighborhood because of a life-style associated with it. And whereas the life-styles associated with Manhattan emerge from the pages of *New York* magazine or the "Home" and "Living" sections of the *Times*, the life-styles identified with the outer boroughs belong strictly to *Family Circle*. If you seek the fast lane of urban life, you must live in Manhattan. The Bronx, Queens, Brooklyn, and Staten Island are for those content to stay far over to the right. Or so the thinking goes.

The degree to which one's identity is tied to place of residence rather than the residence itself is why for so many of us it is far preferable to live in a tiny cubicle of an apartment with a hotplate across from Lincoln Center than to have an eight-room house in Brooklyn, albeit only a twenty-minute subway ride away. The conventional wisdom of urban chic requires that one live in the city, not just near it. And *the city* is Manhattan.

Therefore, though apartment vacancies might run as high as 15 or 20 percent in the northern Bronx, newcomers to the city will still pound the pavements of the fashionable Upper East Side where apartment vacancies hover near the zero mark. And in any event, newcomers don't usually know that the city even extends above 96th Street or below the Village (nor do many middle-class Manhattanites). And though apartments in Flatbush, Brooklyn, may rent for $100 per room, most young professionals would rather pay $300 per room for an apartment in the sophisticated neighborhood of, say, the East Seventies and Eighties, where there is a night life. In Flatbush the day ends at 6:00 P.M.

The family moving back into the city after a stint in a Westchester suburb will pay $800,000 for a brownstone in the West Eighties off Columbus Avenue—near Central Park, the Museum of Natural History, cafés, cafés, and cafés—before paying a quarter as much money for twice as much house in, for instance, Jamaica Estates, Queens. If one is going to live there, one might as well stay in Westchester.

While the newly divorced bachelor would cut off his leg to get a loft in trendy SoHo or TriBeCa, he would only laugh at the thought of a loft on Staten Island. And for a gay couple, a windowless garret anywhere in the Village is preferable to the entire bottom floor of a large house in, for example, Bay Ridge, Brooklyn, a family-oriented neighborhood and a community that is not too accepting when it comes to matters of life-style and sexual preference.

If we find housing tight because we choose to focus on but ten of the three hundred square miles that are encompassed within the city, then we deserve what we get. You might say we have made our bed and now must sleep in it. The only problem is finding an apartment for the bed.

If you doubt that this is a problem, consider these facts of Manhattan life:

•The apartment vacancy rate on both the East and West Sides of Manhattan below 96th Street (above which many believe is Harlem, though in truth, Harlem on the West Side at least does not begin until 125th Street) is about 1 percent. Five-percent vacancy is considered healthy.

•South of 96th Street in Manhattan a one-room studio apartment

rents for anywhere from $400 to almost $1,000 per month depending on where it's located. The range for a one-bedroom apartment is
roughly $700 to $2,000. Two-bedroom rents *begin* at about $800;
three-bedroom at about $1,700. (This as of 1982.)

•Though sound budgeting principles dictate that one spend not
more than 25 percent of one's gross income for rent, more than half
of all New Yorkers who rent spend 30 percent or more of their income on rent.

•When a three-bedroom apartment recently became available on
the Upper East Side, despite the advertised rent of nearly $2,000 a
month, two hundred people competed for the apartment.

•Manhattan rents increase on the average of 15 to 20 percent a
year. Incomes don't increase at anywhere near that rate.

•Not too many years ago singles who shared apartments typically
shared four-, five-, and six-room apartments. Now two people will
share a one-room studio and actually feel fortunate to have found
one.

•At least half the apartments in Manhattan are occupied by just one
person. According to the 1980 census, the average number of persons in a Manhattan household was 1.96, the lowest figure in the
country except for Kalawao, Hawaii, and it's a leper colony. Every
other place in the United States had at least 2 persons per household.
The national average is 2.8 persons per household. (Looking around
at a family gathering recently, a New Yorker observed that the 20
family members at the dinner table represented 16 separate housing
units. And hence the housing crunch.)

•New Yorkers consider it neither unusual nor immoral to pay off a
building superintendent or some other building personnel for information about apartments now, or soon to be, available as well as for
the right to preferential treatment. Such bribes are often the *sine qua
non* for finding an apartment. Anyone who finds a particularly desirable apartment without making such a payoff is the exception.

•Almost all apartments are now rented through a broker. Just five
or so years ago this was not the case. Today brokers pervade the
housing rental market, and they typically charge a fee paid by the
renter equal to 10 percent of one year's rent at the very least. Brokers' fees of 15 percent are not unusual, in which case you would
have to pay almost $1,000 for the privilege of renting a $500-a-month
studio apartment.

•All over Manhattan, couples who have nominally divorced or separated continue to live in the same apartment. It is not always possible for one person to move out upon splitting up. That requires a place to move to. In Manhattan that could take some time. The large apartments on the Upper West Side, along West End Avenue for example, are ideal for this arrangement of estranged couples continuing to live together. These apartments allow for the respective parties to live at separate ends. A duplex apartment would probably be even better; an entire brownstone just perfect.

•And if the rental market wasn't bad enough already, since the late 1970s rental units have been disappearing right and left by being converted to cooperatives. In 1981 somewhere between 75,000 and 100,000 apartments that had previously been rented are said to have been converted to co-ops. In that same year, the average price for a Manhattan co-op was also said to have been $65,000 to $75,000 *per room*; on top of which a maintenance fee of anywhere from $500 to $2,000 a month would be required.

The Manhattan housing market will probably get a lot worse before it gets any better. The alternatives available are very limited. In other places where the demand warrants increasing the supply, you just build more housing. But not in Manhattan.

In case you haven't noticed, there's not a great deal of space left in Manhattan for much of anything. During the 1970s practically no new housing got built. Now what little new housing that does get constructed is almost always luxury housing—more often than not, expensive cooperatives or condominiums rather than rental units. So, while new co-ops are being built atop the Museum of Modern Art, where a one-room studio will sell for $200,000, middle-income housing is becoming but a faint memory. And building co-ops rather than rental units in a city where close to 75 percent of the population are renters makes about as much sense as putting up low-income housing projects in Beverly Hills. (Proof that New York is the quintessential city of apartment *renters* is the fact that a book about the rights of New York City renters could become a best-seller, as did *Super Tenant*.) New construction, in short, holds out no possibility of easing the Manhattan housing crunch for the average apartment seeker.

The alternative of moving to less desirable Manhattan neighborhoods—more euphemistically, "not yet discovered neighborhoods"—or moving out of Manhattan altogether provides only limited and temporary relief on the housing squeeze: limited because there will always be that hardcore who will never live anywhere but in Manhattan—newcomers to the city, singles, upwardly mobile childless couples, and so on. In fact, for thousands who have moved to the outer boroughs, the move was thinkable only after having lived for a time in Manhattan and only after having had a chance to live out their Manhattan fantasies.

Also, there are only so many places that anyone would consider as an alternative to Manhattan. If one is going to venture out of Manhattan then you can be sure that person will not venture too far out. Brooklyn Heights or Park Slope, practically in the lap of the Brooklyn and Manhattan bridges, respectively, is one thing. Canarsie or Flatbush is quite another matter. Woodside, Queens, from which the Manhattan skyline is reassuringly still in sight, may be acceptable. Rego Park, in the deeper parts of Queens, would not be.

In any case, moving to less fashionable Manhattan neighborhoods or moving deeper into another borough provides a relief that can only be temporary. It lasts just as long as it takes *The New York Times* or *New York* magazine to put its imprimatur upon the neighborhood by announcing that there are still cheap apartments available in the East Village, or in Long Island City, Queens, or in Boerum Hill, Brooklyn. Three weeks later the available apartments in that neighborhood are no longer cheap. Three months later no apartments are available. A year later your once inexpensive apartment has been converted to a co-op, and you either come up with $100,000 to buy it or you're checking out the ads for apartments to rent once again. Thank you "Living" section of *The New York Times*!

No, the housing situation is not likely to improve. So, if it's good, affordable housing that you're after, New York is not the town for you. We, on the other hand, accept this fate. Our housing plight is in a way our common bond. It's part of what makes us New Yorkers. The problem of finding housing also gives us something to talk about. You might even find our obsession with the subject of housing insufferable. We, on the contrary, almost never tire of it. Renting and subletting; rent control and decontrol; co-ops and condos; raw space and finished space; working lofts and living lofts; Donald Trump and Mitchell-Lama. The subject of housing has no limits.

# Gentrification (or, the "Co-op"tation of New York)

One aspect of the city's housing scene warrants specific mention, since it threatens to change the face and character of the city irrevocably despite its appearance only recently, is the phenomenon of gentrification. It is the "upgrading" of once-run-down neighborhoods, or of neighborhoods that were previously industrial or otherwise nonresidential. The dearth of housing in already desirable neighborhoods has been the motive force behind the need to gentrify these other sections of the city.

The improvement of neighborhoods is achieved principally through housing. Luxury housing is gentrification's primary vehicle, the co-op conversion its god. Since only the rich can afford co-ops (in Manhattan they start at around $100,000; in the other boroughs co-ops are somewhat less expensive), putting up a co-op or converting a rental building to a cooperative means rich folk will follow. Expensive shops and boutiques then follow rich folk into the neighborhood. Chic can't be too far behind.

You know that the gentrification scenario has played itself out when a rent-controlled building for low- and middle-income tenants has been converted to $100,000-plus co-ops (as has happened all over Chelsea, for example); when the local hardware store has been replaced by a shop that specializes in the preparation and sale of gourmet picnic lunches (as you will discover all along Columbus Avenue on the Upper West Side); and when the name of a neighborhood has changed, for instance, from Hell's Kitchen to Clinton (the name now given to the West Thirties, Forties, and Fifties west of Eighth Avenue). Gentrification is the luring of the upper classes into neighborhoods where but a short time ago they feared to tread.

The powers-that-be seem to encourage gentrification. The city offers attractive tax breaks to developers who refurbish old residential buildings or who convert nonresidential structures into housing— empty warehouses, courthouses, churches, fire stations, office buildings, cement factories, closets, shoeboxes, and anything else that doesn't move. (A cartoon in a recent issue of *The Village Voice* depicted the Statue of Liberty as the Liberty Towers Co-op Apartments—a cynic's view of just how far the conversion phenomenon might extend.) The rationale for these incentives is that the supply of housing desperately needs to be augmented and should therefore be stimulated. (It would certainly be interesting to know whether the city revenues lost by these real-estate-tax abatements were offset by the upper-middle-income-tax base the housing is presumably attracting to, or retaining in, the city.)

Yet many of us remain dubious, at best, about whether the supply of housing actually does increase through conversions and so forth. Aside from the fact that only the well-to-do can afford the housing that results from upgradings and conversions, we would like to know how the housing supply is increased if an SRO (single room occupancy) hotel for transients on the Upper West Side that is home to a hundred tenants gets converted into large, high-priced apartments which then rent to twenty people. How is the supply of housing augmented if the ten families squatting in an abandoned building on the Lower East Side are forced out by refurbishment, and those ten families are then replaced by ten single occupants? How is the demand for housing lessened if tenants in a middle-income building in Boerum Hill are displaced when the building goes co-op, and those tenants are suddenly and frantically looking for new apartments to rent? (An owner of a building can convert it to a co-op once 35 percent of the building's present tenants agree to purchase their apartments upon the conversion. This means that up to 65 percent of a building's occupants can be forced out as a result of a co-op conversion.)

Perhaps of more concern than its effect on the housing market is gentrification's influence on the texture and composition of the city. Gentrification has a homogenizing effect. Wherever it goes it leaves its pall of sameness. Neighborhoods of mixed racial and economic character become uniformly white and upper-income. Neighborhoods of artists, writers, actors, plumbers, printers, secretaries, the unemployed, and the unemployable become neighborhoods of mostly lawyers and accountants. Neighborhoods of parents and children become neighborhoods of adults only. And neighborhoods of hardware stores and beauty parlors and luncheonettes and shoe-repair shops and bakeries and barbershops become neighborhoods where one can buy little else besides coffee beans, imported mustard, and brunch.

For those of us who have always loved and valued the city's great variety—its hallmark—the leveling influences of gentrification (the 1980s version of urban renewal) pose a huge threat—the threat that the city's patchwork quilt of diverse neighborhoods will be transformed into one large, white satin sheet. The East Seventies certainly have a place among New York's many different neighborhoods, but that place is on the Upper East Side; not throughout the city, which is where gentrification threatens to extend it.

#  Schools

## The Public School System

A kid can get a terrific education growing up in New York, but that education may more likely come from the theaters, museums, movie houses, and streets than from the city's schools. All New York City kids grow up street-smart. Only some grow up school-smart.

Let's face it. No one lives in New York because of its great school system. In fact, you can safely assume that the suburbs around New York City are filled with former New Yorkers who left the city primarily because they lacked faith in its schools. It was a combination of too few adequate public schools and too few affordable private schools that sent these once inveterate city dwellers scurrying to some quiet, safe, somnolent suburban school district in New Jersey, or in Westchester County, on Long Island, or even as far away as Connecticut.

Actually, the public school system here is probably no worse than most other large urban school systems. In many respects it may even be somewhat better. New York's, incidentally, is by far the largest public school system in the United States. It is supported by a budget of more than $3 *billion* a year and has over 900,000 students, more than 50,000 teachers, and 1,000 schools; which is why we don't try to refer to them by name but instead by number—P.S. (Public School) 128 or I.S. (Intermediate School) 243, for example.

Sure, absenteeism runs pretty high in New York schools—about 20 percent, or 200,000 students on any given day—but in what large urban school system isn't absenteeism that high? Many of the city's school buildings are run-down (out of the thousand schools, a grand total of ten were painted during a recent year), but no other large old northeastern city will have its schools featured in *School Beautiful* either.

Though New York City public schools are now about 70 percent black and Hispanic, making them about the least-white institution in the city, Detroit and Newark and even Los Angeles public schools are not any less nonwhite, nor any less segregated. When it comes to violence in the schools, and racially motivated violence specifically, New York City schools are veritable centers of pacifism when contrasted to, say, South Boston. And though half the city's public school students read below their grade level, half read at or above their grade level, which is about the national average.

But what makes New York unusual among cities with large urban school systems is that within a generally mediocre system, there are a few absolute gems. Some would argue that finding them may be more difficult than discovering bargains at Bloomingdale's, but no one can deny they exist. And they are without parallel.

What other city's public school system can boast a Bronx High School of Science, from which a diploma carries more prestige than a Harvard degree; which counts among its graduates more Nobel Prize–winners than any other school in the country, or in the world for that matter; and which each year sends almost a third of its graduating class on to Ivy League schools?

Or what about the High School of Performing Arts, where each year hundreds audition for the chance to attend; which perpetually churns out graduates who go on to become celebrities (Liza Minnelli, Al Pacino, the late Freddie Prinze, Ben Vereen, and Pinchas Zukerman among them); and about which Hollywood would make a movie (*Fame*)?

Most low-income New Yorkers just succumb to the public school system and hope for the best. And indeed, city public school students are now predominantly from poor or working-class families. If you're Catholic, middle-class, and a believer in strict discipline, you send your kids to parochial school (though apparently more and more non-Catholics, blacks especially, are now attending the city's parochial schools). And if you're wealthy, you send your children as a matter of course to one of the three hundred private schools located here, for wealthy New Yorkers avoid public schools perhaps even more assiduously than they avoid public transportation. Two hundred thousand mostly white parochial school students and fifty thousand mostly white private school kids help explain the urban conundrum of how a city that is 50 percent white can have a public school system that is 30 percent white.

If you're a middle-income New Yorker, but not Catholic, well, you've got a problem. Parochial school is not a likely alternative, and unless you're willing to go into hock or have a benefactor, a private school is out of the question. Tuition at a private high school will run anywhere from $4,000 to $5,000 or more per kid per year. No problem certainly for the likes of Robert Redford, Jackie Onassis, or Calvin Klein. Nor may the tuition present much of an obstacle when mom is a lawyer and dad a television producer or some such thing. But the high tuition does effectively eliminate the option of private school for most who are middle-income.

The challenge for most middle-class New Yorkers, then, is to find the few good, even excellent, public schools amidst the junk heap, and then somehow maneuver through the system to make sure your kid gets into one of them. The task tends to be least problematical at the elementary school level, for there happen to be more good elementary schools here than there are good junior highs or high schools. Elementary schools tend to be neighborhood schools, and thus are usually as good as the neighborhood in which they're located. So if, for example, you live on the Upper East Side, in the West Village, in Riverdale, in Park Slope, or in any number of middle-class Queens neighborhoods, you'll not likely have too many qualms about the quality of the local public school. Of course, if you should live in the South Bronx, on the Lower East Side, or in Bedford-Stuyvesant or Brownsville in Brooklyn, then it's a completely different story.

Finding reasonably good junior and senior high schools presents the greatest challenge, and it is at those levels that the system truly tests a New Yorker's mettle, separates the fair-weather New Yorker from the confirmed New Yorker. More New Yorkers abandon the public schools, or abandon the city altogether, when their kids reach junior high than at any other time. Of course, for those who are politically liberal, committed to both public education and to integrated schools, the decision to yank a kid out of the public schools induces no small amount of liberal guilt. But guilt notwithstanding, after a mugging incident or two in a school hallway or bathroom, or on the way to or from school, the decision becomes quite a bit easier to make. "I can't use my children to promote a cause," or "We won't sacrifice our child to prove a point" have become the contemporary shibboleths of liberal New Yorkers. So when Michael Harrington, the writer and socialist, announces that he is moving his family out of the city—to Scarsdale no less—or when Nat Hentoff, *The Village Voice* writer and First Amendment addict, admits to sending his daughter to a fancy-shmancy private school, he elicits nods of agreement and understanding rather than accusations of hypocrisy.

Not to abandon the public schools, but to work the system to your best advantage, takes a certain amount of ingenuity, maybe even subterfuge. It may, for instance, require that you establish a false address so that you can send your child to a superior school located in a neighborhood other than your own—perhaps even in another borough. To accomplish the ruse, you might use the address of a friend or relative, and then install a phone there in your own name in order to have a phone bill as proof of your residence within the school district.

Or, circumventing the system may entail dredging up some course offered in a school outside your neighborhood which no school in your district offers. The policy of the Board of Education is to allow transfers for the purpose of taking a special course or program. So on the basis of, say, the availability of flute lessons at one school and their unavailability at another, a transfer can be arranged and will be sanctioned. (In fact, not only does the Board of Ed allow such transfers, it actually condones them. It may even encourage the transfer, for the practice is the major guise under which white, middle-class parents ensure their children don't get stuck in a predominantly black and Hispanic school. Without such a policy, the city's junior and senior highs would be able to retain even fewer middle-class students than they now do. And the Board of Education knows this better than anyone.)

When your children are about to enter high school—if you've outwitted and outlasted the system that long—you cross your fingers and pray they get into one of the highly competitive academic high schools or into one of the specialized highs. All excellent schools, the competitive academic highs (Bronx Science, Brooklyn Polytechnic, and Stuyvesant) and the specialized high schools (Performing Arts, and Music and Art) are for many New Yorkers their ace in the hole; they keep thousands of middle-income New Yorkers in the city and save thousands more from the impoverishing experience of financing a private school education.

These schools are truly godsends. More than anything else, they explain how New Yorkers survive the public schools. (Citywide, only one in two high school students manages to graduate.) It hardly matters that the Bronx High School of Science is in the northwest Bronx and you live on Staten Island, or that Stuyvesant is on East 16th Street in Manhattan and you live in Queens. Although the idea of allowing your teenager to commute to school an hour each way by subway or bus is unfathomable to anyone who doesn't live in New York, here the practice is commonplace. Some 70 percent of the students at Manhattan's Stuyvesant High, for example, come from Brooklyn and Queens. Some 95 percent of its students travel to Stuyvesant by public transportation. (Not surprisingly then, Stuyvesant has a Commuters Club, surely the only such student organization of its type anywhere. Its newsletter is called *The Straphanger*.)

Say what you will about the New York City public schools. At a time when school boards all around the country are banning books for their espousal of Darwin's theory of evolution, to its credit, the New York City Board of Education recently rejected two biology textbooks for just the opposite reason: their endorsement of creationism. And not many school boards nowadays are about to do that.

## Higher Education

You hear it said that Boston is the ultimate college town. Maybe it is, if only because Boston feels so much like a college town. In Boston, a rather small city after all, the presence of college students is felt everywhere—a constant reminder that the colleges are there. Here students don't make that much of an impression on the surface feel of the city. While Boston caters to its students, New York merely lets them be.

We'll concede that Boston probably does have a slight edge when you compare private colleges, though New York runs a close second. New York, however, is the public university city nonpareil. Counting undergraduates alone, the City University of New York (CUNY) enrolls close to 200,000 students at eighteen branches. This makes CUNY indisputably the largest city university. Years ago it was also the best.

There was a time—lasting through the 1950s and perhaps through part of the 1960s—when CUNY's student body was largely middle-class and largely Jewish. It was thought to be a place where one could receive both an excellent *and* a free education. Indeed, there's always been a certain mystique about the bright boy who studies physics at City College and then goes off to Harvard Law School to become editor-in-chief of the *Law Review*; or the literature major from Brooklyn College who then gets a Ph.D. from Princeton and winds up teaching at Yale. (A certain Daniel Patrick Moynihan, a one-time City College student himself, milked the mystique for all its worth in a successful race for the U.S. Senate.)

Today, CUNY students are much less middle-class and definitely much less Jewish. More than a third of the enrollment at the four-year senior colleges is now black and Hispanic, and more than half at the two-year community college branches. Also, CUNY has apparently lost some of its academic rigor. It's said that the courses with the largest enrollment are currently the remedial courses. CUNY no longer sends very many of its graduates on to the Ivy League.

If you ask a New Yorker why the academic quality has fallen and why the middle class has forsaken CUNY, nine out of ten middle-income New Yorkers will attribute the changes to open admissions, a policy initiated in 1970 that guarantees a place in the CUNY system to every graduate of a city high school regardless of grades. Previously one needed an 80 to 90 average to get into a senior college (some demanded higher averages than others) and at least a 75 to qualify for a community college.

As admission standards came down, the middle class began to go elsewhere. Their exodus was further encouraged when a few years ago CUNY began to charge tuition, thus ending its hundred-year tradition of offering a free education. As long as you now had to pay to attend an inferior CUNY, a lot of New Yorkers decided they would just as soon pay a little more for the chance to go away to school. Middle-class students who years ago would have gone to CUNY almost automatically are now more likely to attend one of the State University of New York (SUNY) campuses. Today SUNY is to middle-income New Yorkers what CUNY used to be.

It's easy enough to badmouth open admissions and to bemoan

the loss of prestige CUNY has suffered since. But let's be realistic. Open admissions was about as inevitable as bilingual subway announcements. Open admissions merely acknowledged the changes among the city's high school graduates—they were less white, less middle-class, and less prepared to do college-level work. Admission standards and academic standards *had* to change accordingly. And if a CUNY degree is no longer the entree to Harvard Law that it once was, it's still a potential meal ticket—which a city high school diploma is not—for 200,000 students. Now that should earn it some respect.

What's New at The New School?
One really can't talk about the city's schools without at least some mention of The New School for Social Research, more affectionately and familiarly known as The New School.

Though hardly any New Yorker can tell you much about its undergraduate school—or even knows that there is one—and only a few New Yorkers know anything about the graduate school, almost all New Yorkers can wax eloquent about The New School's adult division. Unlike the other components, the adult evening division has celebrity status in the city.

Offering more than 1,500 courses a semester, from "Single in New York—a New Strategy" to "Troubador Poetry" to "Beyond Crossword Puzzles" to "Elementary Arabic" to "Cloisonné Enameling" to "Conversations with New York Moviemakers" to "Quiche," The New School is less a school than it is an event. The New School is to adult education what Macy's is to retailing: the prototype or industry leader. The New School brings respectability to dilettantism. It also provides a place where singles can meet besides singles bars and the waiting-rooms of shrinks' offices.

This is not to say that there is no intrinsic value in the courses themselves. The potential practical worth of "Co-op Buyer's Workshop," "Urban Crime," "Animal Photography," "Breakfast and Brunch Cookery," and "Creative Divorce," for example, should speak for itself. Yet we take New School courses mostly for fun and often, frankly, with the hope of meeting someone "interesting." The New School is more a social than an academic experience. Nothing wrong with that.

As a visitor or newcomer, you'll want to know that The New School is located in the Village, with a building on Fifth Avenue at

13th Street and another just around the corner at 66 West 12th Street. Inside, you'll be able to pick up a copy of the famous *New School Bulletin*, the publication of which is among *the* publishing events of the year. A quick read through the course listings and descriptions will tell you more about the current concerns, sensibilities, and fads of New Yorkers than reading five years' worth of back issues of *New York* magazine. Perusing the catalog is also terrific fun. Where else would you come across a course in "The Intensive Journal Life Context Workshop" or one in "Peking Duck"?

# 8 Subways

Visiting New York without riding the subways would be like going to Lourdes and not testing the waters. If your intention to find out what it's like to live in New York is earnest, then you simply must ride on the city's subways—and not just once, and not just for three stops, and not just before or after the rush hour. In fact, if one had to pick the single most uniquely New York thing you could possibly do, it would be to take the IRT Seventh Avenue subway from 42nd Street at 5:00 P.M.—uptown to the Bronx or downtown into Brooklyn.

To know the subways is to know New York, for they are an integral part of both the physical and psychic character of the city. San Francisco without its cable cars would essentially still be San Francisco as we know it, but New York without its subways would not be New York. Subways are to New York what freeways are to Los Angeles, canals to Venice, or bicycles to Amsterdam. Subways largely define New York, impose a certain sensibility upon the city, and determine the pace at which we New Yorkers must go through life.

There is no one who lives here whose life is not touched by the subways. That's not to say that every New Yorker rides them every day and everywhere, for that's not the case—although some 3.5 million riders do actually ride the subways daily. But even when New Yorkers don't ride the subways, but instead take taxis or buses, drive their own cars, walk, or stay close to home, they do so mostly *in response to* the subway system. For despite the seemingly inevitable delays and breakdowns—about fifty of the six hundred trains needed to provide full service are taken out of service because of mechanical breakdowns each day—subways remain the fastest and cheapest way to get around the city. Sometimes it takes a subway strike to make us realize this. During the first day of the last strike, which was in the spring of 1980—the previous one was in 1966—only three-quarters of the workers employed by the city got to work; the number of cars entering Manhattan tripled; and the number of traffic accidents doubled. And while Queens commuters were driving all the way up to Westchester so they could then take a Conrail train into Manhattan, Brooklynites were driving out to New Jersey, where they could then catch the PATH train back into the city.

So, if New Yorkers take cabs, for example, it's not because they particularly want to pay exorbitant fares—about $2.00 per mile plus 10¢ for every 45 seconds you sit in traffic plus a tip—to mostly stand still on the city's traffic-clogged streets. Rather, they are shunning the subways.

Of course, no New Yorker finds the subways pleasant. They can assault your senses at two stages. First, the stations (if you think the present beige paint is sickly looking, you should have seen the royal blue that preceded it), then the cars and the ride itself (52 tons of garbage are removed from the subways each day). Of all the campaign promises city politicians make, including those to cut taxes and balance the budget, the promise "to ride the subways each day with the people of New York" is the hardest one to keep. Mayor Koch made that pledge and after about three days in office announced he would try to ride the subways at least once every two weeks or so. A far cry from every day.

Can you blame him? Responding to the cliché that the subways at rush hour are like cattle cars, someone actually researched the Department of Agriculture's regulations for the transportation of cattle, and in a letter to *The New York Times* concluded that cattle must be transported under better conditions than riders on New York City subways! According to federal regulations, each animal must have at least five square feet of space, and cars must be heated in the winter and ventilated in the summer. To legions of New York City strap-hangers who fight for five square inches of space and who find the subways heated in the summer and overheated or freezing in the winter, these cattle-car regulations must sound as though they could describe subway conditions in some urban utopia.*

---

*The condition of subway cars could improve in the near future, at least on the IRT line. The city recently ordered 325 new cars from Japan (all expected to be in service

Still, almost all New Yorkers ride the subways at least from time to time. Middle-income or wealthy New Yorkers may make the distinction between using the subways for work but not for play—for which purpose they'll take a cab or use their own car—or, they'll use the subways during the day but not at night. Poor New Yorkers, though, use the subways for all occasions at all times of the day. But it is the rare New Yorker indeed who will never ride the subways.

If a New Yorker avoids the subways altogether—given the expense or slowness of the alternatives—it can only mean he or she has absolutely no tolerance for discomfort or feels uptight around poor people, or has a paralyzing fear of crime (or all of the above). These attitudes are essentially antiurban, and are certainly misplaced in New York City, the most urbanized 300 square miles in the world.

The small minority of New Yorkers who harbor these feelings to the extent that they *never* ride the subways set themselves apart from the great majority of us who do ride them. In fact, the differences in attitudes and values between those who take subways and those who don't are so clear and so vast that it is hard to imagine that a New Yorker who does could ever be best friends with one who doesn't.

As a neophyte, don't expect to master the subways immediately. You are, after all, taking on the world's largest and certainly most complex subway system. With 23 different lines (by comparison, the Paris Metro has 16 lines and the London Underground only 9), more than 700 miles of track, 600 trains, and 6,000 subway cars, the New York City subway system is not one to be attacked headlong.

It can even take New Yorkers years before we come to know the subways well. It's true that some never make any real effort to grasp the intricacies of the system and are content to know only the one or two lines we use to get to work. Thousands of Upper East Siders, for instance, may never take any train but the IRT Lexington Avenue, and then never above 96th Street or below Wall Street. Many an Upper West Sider stays within those same boundaries while traveling only the IRT Seventh Avenue train. Manhattan residents who have never taken the subways into another borough might not know that in Brooklyn, Queens, and the Bronx, there are stretches where the

---

by 1985) and another 825 from Montreal (all expected to be in service by late 1987) to replace IRT cars now twenty-five to thirty-five years old.

subways, seemingly surfacing for a breath of air, travel above ground.*

Yet, even among the most ambitious and intrepid New York subway riders, you'll find that there are always some parts of the mammoth system that are unknown and unexplored. Ask a Manhattanite who fancies herself a well-seasoned subway rider if she's ever traveled on the GG, for example; or someone from Queens if he's ever been on the B train; or a Bronx resident if she's been on the J. Ask anyone if he has ever traveled the Franklin Avenue shuttle. More likely than not, he never has.

Only subway aficionados will know and will have ridden all the lines. These are New Yorkers who make a study of the subways, ride them just for fun on the weekends, pay repeated visits to the New York City Transit Exhibition near Borough Hall in Brooklyn, tour the subway yards and the operations maintenance facilities, and read books about the city's subway system.† And even they may have to consult their subway maps every now and then.

So, the advice to you is to ease into the system. First of all, don't be cowed just because a subway map looks less like a subway map than an instruction manual for the wiring of a television set, or because you erroneously believe your Eighth Avenue A train is going to stop at 72nd Street and the next thing you know you're at 125th Street, or because you hear over the loudspeaker that your D train has just turned into an F.

Then, don't be reluctant to ask anyone who looks knowing for directions and guidance. New Yorkers who are quite reticent and imprecise when it comes to giving street directions can be expansive, even overly precise, when asked for subway directions. We feel that

---

*As a way of determining just how well New Yorkers know the subways, you might use the following tests: *Not at all*: if they don't know that the Broadway local, Seventh Avenue local, no. 1 train, and the West Side IRT local are all just different names for the same train. *Pretty well*: if in addition to using the shuttle at 42nd Street to get crosstown, they use the no. 7 Flushing train at 42nd Street and the LL at 14th Street; and if they don't go into an utter panic when they go just one stop too far in the easterly direction and find themselves in Queens. *Very well*: if they know that in traveling downtown one can transfer from the IRT Lexington Avenue train to the IND F train by getting off at Bleecker Street and walking underground to the Broadway-Lafayette stop on the F line, but that one cannot do the reverse, transfer from the F to the Lex going uptown.

†The best book about the New York City subways is *Uptown, Downtown*, by Stan Fischler, published as a paperback in 1976 by Hawthorn Books.

our knowledge of the subways is our very own little body of esoterica that no one else knows, so we sometimes like to flaunt it.

Despite the inevitable confusion, the mistakes, and the time spent being lost, you should take some solace in knowing that after you've developed the least bit of facility in maneuvering around the New York subways, you will find getting around on the subways of any other city in the world—Paris, London, Madrid, Mexico City, Munich, or Washington, D.C.—mere child's play.

## How Safe Are They?

No doubt you have been led to believe that anyone who rides the New York City subways is a crime victim in search of a perpetrator. Well, the reality of the situation is not quite that grim.

This is not to minimize subway crime. With something like two hundred felonies committed each week—and who knows how many more that go unreported—subway crime is a real problem.

Still, it's important to have some kind of perspective on the matter of subway crime. There are felonies and there are felonies, and unfortunately crime statistics that get reported in the media—certainly those that get headlined—don't usually make the distinctions.

While the news media would have you think that a murder a minute is committed on the subways, in truth, there have been fewer than twenty subway murders a year for the past several years. (When you consider the millions who use the subways during the course of a year, the incidence of subway murders is actually very low.) While the crimes you most often read about are rapes, attempted rapes, assaults, and armed robberies, in fact, the overwhelming majority of subway felonies are of a nonviolent nature—larcenies of the purse-snatching, purse-opening, pickpocketing, necklace-snatching variety. (Something like 40 percent of all subway thefts are necklace-snatchings. Thus, you can theoretically reduce the chances of being robbed by almost half simply by leaving your gold necklace at home or in your hotel.)

This doesn't mean that you are expected to be appeased by the fact that you're more likely to be robbed than robbed *and* raped. Nor should you have a sense of absolute equanimity about riding the subways. They are not the safest places in town, to be sure—though they are probably somewhat safer than the streets. But riding the

subways, contrary to popular belief, is not quite tantamount to taking your life in your hands.

Remember, also, that most subway crimes take place in the stations—on the platforms and, especially, in the passageways that con-
nect platforms—rather than in the subway cars themselves. (It is for
this reason that many of us—particularly women—will at 14th Street,
for example, transfer from the IRT to the IND via the street rather
than the dark, dingy, often secluded block-long passageway that
connects the lines underground. This method of transferring will
cost you an extra fare, but those who do it consider it money well
spent.) So once you actually get on the subway, you can breathe
somewhat easier.

Also, you might be interested to know that generally the safest
subway stations are in Queens. None of the Queens stations have
made the ten-worst crime station lists in recent years. The Ely Avenue
Station in Queens, along the IND line, is considered one of the very
safest stations in the city (along with the Cortlandt Street and Rector
Street stations in Manhattan on the BMT line). The highest-crime stations are consistently those at 42nd Street. Eighth Avenue and 42nd
Street is, hands down, the worst crime station. The 42nd Street stations at Sixth Avenue, Times Square, and Grand Central all rank up
there among the ten worst in the subway system.

Finally, despite all the talk about subway crime, the fact remains
that most New Yorkers who don't ride the subways avoid them more
because they are unpleasant than because they are unsafe.


## The Great Graffiti Debate

Talk to New Yorkers about subway graffiti, and you'll discover that
most of us will fall into one of four camps: those who love it; those
who hate it; those who ignore it; and those who find the debate over
graffiti more objectionable than the graffiti itself.

The genesis of the subway graffiti phenomenon can be traced
back to the late 1960s and the omnipresent scrawl of "Taki 183"—his
name and presumably the street (183rd) he lived on. When graffiti
on the subways first appeared as a phenomenon—something more
than just the random scribblings of a few people—it was terribly chic
to argue its virtues. Subway graffiti was hailed as authentic urban
street art. Madison Avenue and SoHo art galleries had shows featur-

ing subway graffiti; books of graffiti art were published; museums organized graffiti exhibitions. There was even a time when it was fashionable for East Siders of the Sutton Place, Beekman Place, Fifth Avenue, and Park Avenue set—the sort of New Yorker who doesn't even ride the subways—to throw parties to which they would invite members of Puerto Rican street gangs and have them cover an all-white penthouse wall or two with graffiti.

Sociologists maintained that graffiti was a legitimate response to the aggressions spawned by city life. Psychologists offered the opinion that subway graffiti was cheery, and in the otherwise dreary environs of the subways, graffiti should bring smiles to the faces of subway riders. Supporters of subway graffiti in general concluded that in the context of a subway system beleaguered by crime, breakdowns, delays, and crowded and uncomfortable cars, anyone who would complain about graffiti had to have a warped sense of priorities.

To all of this, opponents of graffiti offered a resounding "Bull!" Graffitists were vandals pure and simple, and anyone who argued otherwise was pandering to a criminal element. And not only was graffiti unsightly, they said, but it also made it impossible to read what precious few subway maps riders were able to find.

Now that subway graffiti has been with us for ten or twelve years, it's likely that many of the original opponents of graffiti—if they continue to ride the subways, that is—largely ignore it, having become inured over the years. Perhaps only the MTA (Metropolitan Transportation Authority) itself has managed to maintain the vehemence of its opposition. If anything, the MTA has escalated its opposition. Today the Authority spends several million dollars a year in its fight against graffiti, and this includes payment for a special antigraffiti squad of plainclothesmen as well as for "graffiti-proof" paint for inside the cars and polyurethane for outside. (Neither the paint nor the polyurethane really works, of course. They don't make it harder to write graffiti, but rather easier to wash off once it's on. Whether the new cars ordered for the IRT line will be graffiti-proof, as advertised, remains to be seen.) And most recently, the MTA has allocated over $20 million to install double-width chain-link fences—with razor-edged metal coils on top of and between fences—around all the subway yards as part of an effort to keep graffitists out of the yards—where, in fact, most of the graffiti is done. At the Corona yards in Queens, besides the fence and coils, the MTA has used two German shepherds—Suzy and Red—to patrol the yards.

By now graffiti supporters and detractors alike must wonder how the graffiti fad has lasted more than a decade in New York, while elsewhere—Philadelphia and Boston, for instance—it survived but a few months. In some cities, such as Washington, D.C., subway graffiti hardly appeared at all.

A decade later a lot of us are wondering whether perhaps the graffiti "fad" is a fad at all.

# ⑨ Other Means of Transportation

## Buses

The city's buses play second fiddle to its subways. Bus travel just doesn't dominate the collective consciousness of New Yorkers the way subway travel does, even though a couple of million New Yorkers ride buses each day.

Even New Yorkers who take buses more often than subways, or to the exclusion of subways, still think of the city as one of subways and not buses. It's really the reverse of what you find in London, where buses prevail in the city's identity and self-image. This may explain why the experiment a few years ago to introduce London-style double-decker buses in New York aroused about as much interest here as would a sale on power lawnmowers.

Though buses in New York have a much poorer record of keeping to their schedules than subways, subway delays are what everyone screams about. While maintenance of subway cars has been bad, maintenance of buses has been abysmal. Before the recent addition of new buses, something like a thousand of the city's four thousand buses were out of commission at any given time. And yet again, subway breakdowns and subway accidents are what make news.

Masses of New Yorkers will invariably leap over or crawl under subway turnstiles to protest each transit-fare hike, yet one never hears of an organized protest on the city's buses. If the price of gold soars to $600 an ounce, subway crime suddenly goes up by 40 percent (gold necklaces are snatched), but the incidence of bus crimes remains the same. When cracks are discovered in the undercarriages of both new subways and new buses, it is the subway cracks that make most headlines and the subway manufacturer the City of New York winds up in protracted litigation with, while the bus matter is settled more quietly, out of court.

That the same incident which creates a roar with respect to the subways will create a whimper when it concerns buses can only be attributed to the failure of buses to grab our attention as subways do. There are at least two reasons for this.

First, buses don't make New York unique. What place doesn't have buses? You can visit Cleveland if it's buses you want to see. On the other hand, only a relative handful of cities in the world have subways, and none quite like New York's. (Remember, we offer the best of the worst.)

But the other and probably more important reason why buses and subways elicit completely different responses from us is that we don't depend upon buses the way we do subways. Certain Manhattanites will say they need buses to get crosstown—and, in truth, the crosstown buses probably are the most useful ones—but that "need" is of a very different order from that of residents of the Bronx, Brooklyn, or Queens who work in Manhattan and ride the subways to work each day. While there are a number of ways besides the bus to get from East 59th Street to West 59th—including the alternative of walking—the subway is the only viable way for someone to get from the northwest Bronx into Midtown Manhattan by 9:00 A.M.

If buses are used by choice, subways are used by necessity. If subway strikes tend to cripple the city, bus strikes actually tend to seem to ease the street traffic. Subways, to put it succinctly, are a matter of life and death, while buses are mostly a matter of convenience. And it is this difference that explains why the city's buses have never really captured our imaginations.

Nor are they likely to capture yours.

There actually has been one bus-related incident that has garnered as much attention and created as much noise as anything that has ever happened on the subways. The matter relates to bus shelters.

A few years ago the city had a firm construct and install bus shelters in Manhattan modeled on shelters in Paris—boxlike structures built of shatterproof glass. After the "Manhattan experiment" proved successful, the city asked for bids on a contract to install these shelters throughout the five boroughs.

With visions of these shelters at all ten thousand of the city's bus stops, the prospect of a lucrative bus-shelter contract with the City of New York touched off some pretty vigorous competition. Apparently a bit too vigorous, for at least one competing company tried to flex some muscle at City Hall, and the next thing we knew "The New York Bus Shelter Scandal" was born. The city comptroller's office, a state assemblyman, and a prominent law firm were implicated. In fact, in the 1981 race for city comptroller, the bus shelter scandal was seemingly the only issue. (The incumbent won, nevertheless.)

One of the curious aspects of the whole affair is why the city ever decided to extend the shelters beyond Manhattan in the first place. Obviously, it deemed the experiment in Manhattan a success, but to the objective observer it seemed like anything but. The shelters proved not to be "graffiti-proof" as claimed; advertisers often shunned their use as mini-billboards because the cost of advertising was too high; and a good number of the shelters were destroyed in heavy winds.

Of course, it shouldn't surprise anyone that what had worked so well on the streets of Paris did not work in New York, for historically what has been imported from abroad to the streets of New York has often not caught on. Witness, most recently, double-decker buses from England, mopeds from Italy, Peugeot taxicabs from France, bike lanes from Holland, and street sweepers from the People's Republic of China—all short-lived experiments at best.

The bus shelter debate goes on.

## Taxis

Though every movie made about New York City would lead one to believe that New Yorkers travel only by cab, that's just not so. Characters in Woody Allen films may take cabs all places all the time, but the average New Yorker does not. A recent study concluded that the typical New York taxi user is a thirty-five-year-old white woman who makes $27,000 a year and lives in Manhattan below 96th Street.

If cabbies had to rely upon New Yorkers to make a living, they'd starve. Certainly we take taxis—some of us frequently, almost all of us at least from time to time—but it is the out-of-town visitor and businessman upon whom taxi drivers depend for their livelihood. Which is why cabs stick close to Midtown tourist haunts—and why any New Yorker who is a frequent cab user would have to be a Manhattanite, for only in Manhattan are taxis common.

If the most obvious trait about mid-Manhattan is the overwhelming presence of yellow cabs, the most glaring characteristic outside of Midtown, particularly in the outer boroughs, is their absence. Count the taxis in mid-Manhattan—say, between the Village and 96th Street—add to them those cabs at the airports or in transit between the airports and Midtown, and you will account for all but about six of the city's twelve thousand yellow medallion (licensed) cabs.

If you doubt that this is so, you should sometime try finding a cab in Brooklyn or on Staten Island. Or, to approach the challenge from another angle, try getting a taxi in Manhattan that will take you to the Bronx—far away from the tourist trade and a trip which for the driver holds the specter of having to return to Manhattan without a fare.

The greatest challenge of all is to convince a cab driver to take you to what are thought to be high-crime areas—the South Bronx, Bedford-Stuyvesant, Williamsburg, East New York, and Harlem, for example. These neighborhoods are off limits as far as most taxicab drivers are concerned, and they will flatly refuse to drive passengers there—particularly at night—despite New York City laws and TLC rules to the contrary (TLC being the Taxi and Limousine Commission, not tender loving care).

Bad enough that banks "redline" poor black and Hispanic neighborhoods, that is, not provide mortgages or home-improvement loans to *anyone* who lives in these neighborhoods; or that certain retailers refuse to grant credit cards to *any* applicant whose Zip code falls within poor, high-crime areas; or that insurance companies refuse to insure *any* properties in those sectors. But who would have guessed that cabbies—the putative salt of the earth—would join the likes of bankers, credit managers, and insurance brokers by redlining these neighborhoods as well? One would have expected better of them.

But lest anyone doubt the indomitable spirit of the outer boroughs, about ten or twelve years ago, nonmedallion car services—which cannot cruise the street looking for passengers—as well as gypsy cabs—nonmedallions that illegally pick up street hails—began to fill the void created by the reluctance of medallioned yellow cabs to drive outside of Manhattan. Car services and gypsy cabs sprouted mostly in working-class and poor neighborhoods. Their presence is less than pervasive, and one has to phone for a car or go to the dispatching office—as opposed to stepping out onto any Manhattan street and getting a taxi just by lifting the index finger, or having one's doorman blow a taxi whistle. But at least the outer boroughs now have some cab service.

## DON'T BE TOO SURPRISED . . .

• If your cab driver shares his words of wisdom, as is the cabbie's wont, in a language you don't understand. More and more, taxi drivers here do not speak English. The reason may be that driving a hack is often the easiest, if not the only, job recent non-English-speaking arrivals to the city can find. (For whatever the reason, Israelis seem to make up the largest number of recent New York City arrivals who drive cabs for a living.)

• If you discover that you know your way around the city far better than your driver does. Driving a cab in New York City is no longer the honored profession it once was. It doesn't seem to attract the career-minded type anymore. Now cabbies drive cabs only as long as it takes them to find another job. Hence, many cabbies are neophytes. The process for getting a hack's license, moreover, is now largely perfunctory. It requires no particular knowledge of the city's streets and neighborhoods. To pass the written test here, one basically has to know where the Sheraton is, where the Empire State Building and Madison Square Garden are, and how to get to the airports. Glancing at a tourist map of the city would be adequate preparation. And although since 1981 cabbies have been required to keep a detailed map of the city in their cab, there is no guarantee that they've studied it or will ever refer to it.

• If it costs $25 to be driven crosstown. Although New York City cabs are expensive, they're not *that* expensive.* However, "taxi-hustling"—the practice of charging the unwary (usually out-of-towners) fantastically inflated fares—is becoming increasingly widespread. To reduce your chances of getting hustled, you might heed the following advice: Try to avoid broadcasting the fact that you're from out of

---

*Actually, according to *The New York Times*, cab fares here are only about the fifteenth highest in the United States among large cities. However, that ranking was arrived at by comparing fares on the basis of distance only. Comparative fares did not include such extras as charges for waiting in traffic. And since that is something you can count on doing a lot of in New York, it's safe to say that taxi fares here are among the very highest in the country.

town—in particular, avoid any appearances that you might be from the Middle East, for on the assumption that all Arabs are oil sheiks, cabbies have been known to charge $100 or more to drive Arab passengers from one airline terminal at Kennedy to another, a distance of maybe half a mile—and don't hail a cab anywhere in the vicinity of the East Side Airline Terminal (38th Street and First Avenue), for it is considered by taxi-hustlers to be a prime spot for picking up out-of-town prey.

Note: Should anyone try to convince you that New York cab fares are reasonable, you might want to remember that it costs more to take a taxi between Kennedy and Newark airports than it does to fly. The cab fare would be about twice the plane fare for the trip. (Though flying will save you money, it won't save you time. Including the time it takes to board and deplane, flying and driving take approximately the same amount of time—about 45 minutes.)

# Cars

New York may be one of the few places in the world where having a car is generally considered to be a liability rather than an asset, which is why most New Yorkers—certainly Manhattanites—don't own cars. It's why it is not unheard of—but actually typical—for a Manhattan family making $100,000 or more a year not to have a car. Their counterpart anywhere else would probably own a mini-fleet. It's also why generations of teenagers have grown up here never learning how to drive. (If in your travels you should ever meet someone twenty-five or older who does not know how to drive, you can almost bet that he or she is a New Yorker.)

In Manhattan particularly, the convenience of public transportation along with the great inconvenience of driving and parking combine to dispel any inclination to own a car. The farther from central Manhattan you go, however, the greater the likelihood of car ownership. In the outer boroughs, especially the neighborhoods of predominantly single-family dwellings in Queens, Brooklyn, and Staten Island, car ownership becomes commonplace. (Rumor has it that on Staten Island there are even a number of two-car families. According to another rumor, station wagons have occasionally been seen there.)

But it's quite clear that in Manhattan car owners are a small minority of the borough's residents. Of those who do own cars, the number who use them with any frequency are a relative handful—aberrants really, for Manhattanites with cars usually own them to get out of town, not around town.

Yet like anything else in New York, even when only a small minority of people do something, there are thousands upon thousands who make up that minority. So the minority of Manhattan car owners still accounts for a hefty number of autos—certainly enough to make finding a parking spot in even the more residential neighborhoods of Manhattan one of the greater challenges of modern-day urban life. (A New Yorker recently reported of his attempt to park in the vicinity of Broadway and 67th Street. Forty-five minutes later he settled on a spot on 87th Street—and not a totally legal parking space at that.)

But the massive numbers of autos and the colossal traffic jams can't be blamed on Manhattanites with cars. Rather, most of Manhattan's traffic problems arise from the influx of hundreds of thousands of cars *into* Manhattan each day—commuters from the outer boroughs and from the suburbs—not to mention trucks, buses, and cabs. Each weekday about 650,000 cars and trucks enter Manhattan between the hours of 6:00 and 10:00 A.M. alone. Even on the weekend, you can count more cars from New Jersey than from New York.

As if driving in Manhattan was not already difficult enough, city traffic planners recently announced that in the future they would deal with the city's traffic problems by making driving here an even greater hassle than it now is. Honestly. The theory, from the fight-fire-with-fire school of thought, is premised on the belief that at some higher level of pain, people will ultimately stop driving cars into Manhattan and switch to public transportation.

The plan includes: increasing the number of streets banned to private cars and open only to buses, taxis, trucks, and cabs; increasing the number of streets on which weekday parking is totally prohibited; increasing fines for parking violations (already raised from $25 to $35 a shot); expanding the use of towtrucks to deal with illegally parked cars; and in general, stepping up enforcement of the city's hundreds of parking and driving rules. (After one recent crackdown on double-parking in Midtown, daily tickets increased from about 800 a day to nearly 2,000 a day. The result was that the flow of Midtown traffic made a quantum leap from 5.2 miles per hour to 5.8.)

There have also been attempts to limit the number of cars entering Manhattan, first, by requiring the East River bridges to start charging a toll and then by banning all single-occupant cars from crossing an East River bridge during the morning rush hours. Both these schemes have thus far been successfully blocked by court actions, proving that the Auto Club of New York is a lot stronger than city traffic planners would have thought.

In any case, there seems to be a basic flaw in the reasoning that by making it increasingly difficult to drive in Manhattan people will cease to. That is, it has *never* been easy to drive in Manhattan—not since autos were first imposed upon streets that were built for horse-drawn buggies—and yet people have *always* driven here. Obviously, the tolerance for pain on the part of those who choose to take an auto into the city is extraordinarily high. One suspects it's much higher than city planners imagine. They might just have to ban all cars from all parts of Manhattan at all times. Period.

Although the ordeal of driving in New York is obvious to anyone who has ever driven here even one time, what may not be so apparent—not even to New Yorkers if they are not car owners themselves—is the plight of those of us who own and attempt to maintain a car. The problems and expenses of New York City car owners have to be unique. For example:

**Parking.** Manhattanites who own cars and park them on the street consider themselves fortunate whenever they find a parking spot within ten blocks of their apartment. They also consider themselves lucky if they obtain the spot in less than half an hour. In the posher neighborhoods, finding a place to park on a Sunday evening—when everyone has returned with their cars from the Hamptons, Berkshires, or Fire Island—could easily take from forty-five minutes to an hour or more. Parking problems are substantially less severe in the outer boroughs.

Those who choose not to park on the street, but to put their cars in a garage or lot instead, trade convenience for expense. Manhattan garages can cost as much as $200 a month; few cost less than $90 or $100. (The New York Skyport underneath the FDR Drive between 18th and 23rd Streets offers outdoor parking for about $20 a month and indoor parking for about $50. A fantastic bargain. The only hitch is that the waiting list for the indoor garage is said to be seven years and the one for the outdoor lot fourteen years.) In other boroughs, you can find lots for as little as $40 to $60 a month, though you might think twice before you'd choose one of these places over a more secure parking garage for your $12,000 BMW.

**Alternate-side-of-the-street parking.**    For all of us who have cars, alternate-side-of-the-street parking regulations are the absolute bane of our existence. These regulations ban parking on one side of the street one day and on the other side the following day, between specific hours, such as 8:00 A.M. and 11:00 A.M., or 11:00 A.M. and 2:00 P.M.

What this means is that if you won't be around during the day to move your car during the hours alternate-side rules will be in effect, then the night before you *must* park on the "good" side of the street. Of course, this constriction—which in essence halves the number of potential parking spots—can triple or quadruple the time it would otherwise take you to secure a parking place. Which is why in New York refusing an invitation to go someplace because you're on the good side of the street for the next day is considered perfectly legitimate and acceptable. Those offering the invitation will understand, especially if they too are car owners. Many a car owner who finds a parking spot on a Friday that's good for the following Monday will dare not budge the car for the entire weekend.

If you will be home during the day, you are free to park on the "bad" side of the street the night before as long as you're prepared to go out and move your car just before alternate-side regulations go into effect. And if you have to double-park during the time the regulations are in effect, you'll have to go out again to move your car just before the regulations cease. (What essentially happens is that when alternate side goes into effect, all cars on the wrong side of the street shift over and double-park on the good side. Double-parking is actually the only workable way cars and alternate-side-of-the-street parking regulations could coexist, and hence double-parking in order to comply with alternate-side rules is largely condoned; normally you won't be ticketed. You are, however, expected to observe double-parking etiquette, which requires that you leave a note in the car window indicating where you can be reached should the owner of the car you're blocking wish to move. Otherwise, that car has no way out except the sidewalk. Needless to say, there is hardly a New

Yorker with a car who has not at one time or another driven along a sidewalk.) 

The ostensible purpose of alternate-side parking is to allow the city's street-cleaning machines to work one side of the street one day and the other the next. Yet weeks can sometimes go by before *either* side of a street gets cleaned. (Also, a lot of New Yorkers who own cars would like to know how come, if the purpose of alternate-side parking is to allow street-cleaning, the regulations don't terminate immediately after the street has been swept.) It's at those times that car owners question the legitimacy of alternate-side regulations and the jockeying, maneuvering, planning, and general havoc it occasions—having to enlist friends to move your car for you should you have to go out of town for a few days; or going so far as to hire someone to move your car each day from side to side. (It's true. There *are* people in New York who make their living moving other people's cars from one side of the street to the other.) Some Manhattanites park their cars in Astoria in Queens, which is just over the 59th Street Bridge; there, as in other Queens neighborhoods, alternate-side parking rules are in effect but one day a week. Though it requires that you schlep out to Queens and back, at least you need not do it more than once a week.

So, while most New Yorkers carp about the disruptions caused by subway strikes, sanitationmen's strikes, tugboat strikes (tugboats transport garbage to landfills), snowstorms, street flooding, and so on, car owners relish these "crises," because for the duration of each of them alternate-side parking rules are typically suspended.

While most New Yorkers remember the winter of 1978 as one of the worst, those of us with cars remember it as one of the best. Heavy snowfalls that winter led to the suspension of alternate-side regulations for fifty or sixty consecutive days. For almost two solid months we simply forgot about our cars—left them on the streets without ever once moving them. It was heavenly.

**Insurance.**   Auto-insurance rates—particularly for collison and comprehensive, fire, and theft—are higher in New York City than anywhere else in the country.

A New Yorker who recently left the city to live in Upstate New York lamented his departure but rejoiced over his adjusted insurance premium. Upstate he paid one-third of what he had been paying in the city for exactly the same amount of coverage. Which may explain why most of the cars you see in New York with, say, Vermont plates on them don't belong to Vermonters at all. They belong to New Yorkers who, by establishing an address in Vermont, are able to register their cars there. By so doing they can avoid the high insurance premiums they would otherwise have to pay in New York if they had their cars registered here. It is estimated that some forty thousand New York City car owners have their cars registered in some other state.

**Repairs.**    Not only are auto-repair shops here among the most expensive, they're also among the most dishonest.

A couple of years ago, the federal government used a rigged car to test whether auto mechanics in the metropolitan area were doing only work that was necessary and not overcharging. Auto shops throughout New York City fared poorly; those in Brooklyn were worst of all, according to federal investigators.

Not infrequently—and certainly not surprisingly—New Yorkers take their cars to New Jersey for servicing and repairs.

**Potholes.**    Driving a car in the city without damaging its suspension or busting an axle in a pothole is a major achievement. During the winter months, pothole patrols supposedly fill upward of thirty thousand potholes a week. And potholes here are unlike any you have ever seen. Some are so deep that garbage cans have to be placed in them as a way of signaling their whereabouts and thereby preventing cars from going into them. However, if this fails, you not only hit a pothole but a garbage can as well.

So how does the City of New York deal with its pothole problems? It passes a law which prohibits anyone from suing the city for damages due to potholes. How else?

That *anyone* would keep a car in New York despite the rigors of doing so can only be a testament to the pervasiveness of our country's car culture.


WHITHER WESTWAY?

For some ten years now New Yorkers have lived without a major portion of the only highway that takes cars up the western edge of Manhattan. Ever since a truck crashed through an elevated section of the West Side Highway back in 1973—and by so doing, dramatized the advanced state of the road's deterioration—a 4.2-mile stretch of the highway has been closed, from the Battery Tunnel to 42nd Street (and more recently, on up to 57th Street as well). When you think about it, this is the equivalent of Los Angeles without 4 miles of the Santa Monica Freeway or Chicago minus a 4-mile chunk of Lake Shore Drive.

Yet somehow the city has survived—reroutings on city streets, massive traffic congestion, intolerable auto-emission pollution, and all. What we may not so easily survive, however, is the interminable debate that goes on over what should replace the fallen West Side Highway.

The debate has centered on Westway, a proposed six-lane super-highway—sunken below ground, actually river, level—on top of which would be vast expanses of parks. The cost? About $2.3 billion, give or take a few hundred million. (In predicting that its actual cost would reach about $4 billion, or $1 billion per mile, Senator William Proxmire awarded Westway one of his "Golden Fleece" awards for wasting taxpayers' money.)

Proponents of Westway have always argued that it would not only provide the highway the city desperately needs, but would create parks and save the waterfront; and, perhaps most importantly, its construction would create jobs, jobs, and more jobs. (When Ronald Reagan, a Westway booster, came to New York with a check for $85 million to be used to buy land for Westway, it was to fulfill a promise to *organized labor*. And he came on Labor Day.) That the federal government would pick up 90 percent of Westway's tab is another attraction.

Opponents of Westway have maintained that building the highway would destroy parts of neighborhoods, such as Chelsea, and would have untold horrible effects on the Hudson River. (Indeed, the most recent obstacle to building Westway was a federal judge's injunction barring any further work on Westway until its effects on fish life in the Hudson was redetermined.) And they argued that a superhighway such as Westway would only encourage the use of autos in Manhattan and add more congestion and fumes to the already congested and polluted narrow city streets, the last thing in the world the city needs. As an alternative to Westway, they proposed a less ambitious and less expensive multilane "boulevard," costing maybe not much more than half a billion dollars. The difference between what they proposed and what Westway would cost could then be used to improve the city's mass-transit system—something which is far more important than building a superhighway. (Whether or not the federal government would simply turn over the difference between the cost of Westway and a less costly alternative for mass-transit improvements was never entirely clear.)

There's obviously a lot more to both sides of the Westway spat, but that's the crux of it. In 1982 the city and state finally agreed to adopt Westway as their "official policy" for the replacement of the West Side Highway, though opponents have by no means given up the fight to prevent Westway from ever happening, and, indeed, after they won the injunction barring all further work on Westway pending a new environmental report, Westway never seemed closer to being doomed. And what's so disheartening is that should Westway ever begin to be built, it will then take approximately ten years to complete it. And Westway takes care of the stretch up to 42nd Street only. Nothing—absolutely nothing—has been said or done about the part from 42nd to 57th Street.

In our nightmares we envision ten years from now a superhighway that comes to an abrupt halt at 42nd Street, where it overlooks a gaping hole that extends to 57th. A hole that will take still *another* ten years to fill.

## Bicycles

New York is a great city for walking. It is *not* a great cycling city. Yet we sometimes forget what we're about. Or, at least, that seems to be the only explanation for how the city could ever have encouraged the use of bicycles as a means of transportation as it did just recently.

In the winter of 1979, Mayor Ed Koch visited China and observed hundreds of thousands of bicyclists pedaling about that country's cities. "If this can happen in Peking, then why not in New York?" queried the mayor. Which is like asking why not gondolas in the Bronx since they seem to work so well in Venice?

Nevertheless, the mayor returned to New York determined to encourage New Yorkers to forsake other means of transportation for bikes. The first thing he did was to establish an uptown bike lane along Sixth Avenue (Avenue of the Americas) from the Village to

Central Park, and a downtown lane that went along Seventh Avenue, then Broadway and then over to Fifth Avenue. The lanes consisted of a strip painted along the side of the street.

The problem, however, was that motorized vehicles heeded these painted lanes about as frequently as pedestrians here observe laws against jaywalking. Cars and buses drove in the bike lanes, taxis straddled them, and trucks parked right smack in their middle; all of which made the lanes worthless—nonexistent, really—so far as bicyclists were concerned.

Never one to be easily daunted, Mayor Koch then had concrete barriers constructed along the outside edge of the lanes as a way of keeping cars, trucks, cabs, and buses out. The concrete barriers did indeed keep motorized vehicles out. The hitch was that they failed to keep pushcarts, hand trucks, joggers, roller skaters, delivery men, and assorted other pedestrians out as well. Furthermore, since the barriers made swerving out of the way of these obstacles difficult if not impossible for the cyclist, the lanes became traffic hazards for both the bike rider and whatever live obstacle happened to be in the lanes at the same time.

To make matters worse, the bike lanes effectively eliminated one lane of the street to traffic. In some places—where trucks stopped to make deliveries and now had to park outside the barriers—actually two lanes of the street were removed, which did nothing for the city's traffic congestion.

All of this would have been all right and could probably have been tolerated—things might even have improved with time—had enough cyclists used the lanes to warrant the inconveniences. But instead of thousands upon thousands of New Yorkers biking along these lanes each day, only a few hundred did. At one point the mayor went out to observe the bike lanes himself and counted exactly two bicyclers—one of whom was apparently riding in the wrong direction!

After three months of relative nonuse, many accidents, untold numbers of near accidents, and much increased traffic congestion, the mayor admitted that he had made a mistake, and he ordered the concrete barriers removed. The three-month experiment cost us half a million dollars—about half the money used to erect the barriers and half to have them removed.

More recently, Ed Koch visited Egypt. Newspapers showed pictures of him riding a camel. He had a very curious-looking smile on his face. We shudder to think of what the mayor may have been contemplating.

Any New Yorker should have been able to predict that bicycling in lieu of other forms of transportation would never catch on. All we had to do was remember the fate of the moped fad a couple of years before. That lasted about four days. Now, apparently more mopeds get sold each year in Cincinnati than in New York.

We should accept New York for the kind of city it is and be comfortable with the fact that it is not a place where a bicycling culture is ever likely to develop; and perhaps that's fortunate. Just as certain places are probably better off not plunging ahead too fast toward advanced industrialization (replacing bikes with subways), New York might be better served by not making a quantum leap back to simpler times (replacing subways with bikes). After all, it's not as if New Yorkers are about to follow the example of, say, the Dutch—buy single-speed truck bikes and ride them in an orderly and sensible way. New Yorkers buy $600 ten-speed bikes; put on radio headphones that blare disco and rock music; place a whistle in their mouths to announce themselves while flying through intersections; and take off speeding and careening recklessly along city streets.

That the bike lane experiment failed may be a blessing in disguise.

# 10 Crime

## How Bad Is It?

Any city that has had thirteen bank robberies in one day (four in a single hour) as New York has, or records five murders and about eighteen hundred other major reported crimes each day, as New York does, obviously has a serious crime problem on its hands. No one would dare try to tell you it didn't—not the Chamber of Commerce, not the Visitors and Convention Bureau, not even City Hall. Not the Police Department either. New York's finest—and who should know better?—won't even live here. They typically choose instead to reside in Rockland County or some other suburb and commute.

Nowhere is the fear of crime greater or the sense of one's physical safety less than in New York. The fear of crime, in fact, rather than the incidence of crime, is what really seems to distinguish New York from almost every other large American city. In a number of other cities the crime index is actually much higher than here. Boston ranks number one; or at least it did as of the end of 1981. By contrast, New York ranks twelfth among the twenty-five largest cities in the United States.

Yet, it is highly doubtful that residents of Boston or of any of the other cities that supposedly have higher crime indexes than New York—Dallas, Denver, Seattle, and Phoenix, to name a few—suffer the kind of paranoia about crime that we do. It seems unlikely that in Phoenix or in Seattle, for example, it would be considered the norm to have at least three locks on your door (the Medeco dead bolt, the

chain latch, and the police lock make up the holy trinity of protection for New York City apartment dwellers); to have metal bars on
all ground-level windows and steel gratings on all other windows
that face out onto fire escapes; to make access to an apartment building more difficult for visitors than entry to maximum-security wings
of prisons (closed-circuit TVs, intercom-buzzer systems, and door-
men/guards are all standard—magnetometers can't be too far off);
to have cab drivers separated from their passengers by bulletproof
Plexiglas barriers; to have liquor-store salespersons and stock separated from customers by bulletproof Plexiglas "cages"; to have entry to boutiques and other fancy storefront businesses depend upon
your appearance passing muster with the salesperson who controls
the buzzer to unlock the front door. These are all typical—minimal
really—New York City precautionary measures.

Where else but here do you take out your keys a block before you
reach your apartment to avoid the need to fumble for them in vesti-
bules, entryways, hallways, or other so-called vulnerable areas?
Where else do women wear down coats over expensive evening
dresses so as not to broadcast the fact they are well-heeled? Do wom-
en in Phoenix or Seattle avoid carrying pocketbooks at night, or generally avoid going out alone after dark? Can it be possible that
elsewhere parents give children "mugger's money" each time they
leave the house as a matter of course?

These responses are all part of the standard set of urban baggage
that we carry around with us here. After living in New York just a few
months, they become instinctive reactions, and you don't shed them
very easily, not even when you leave the city. That's probably part of
the reason why New Yorkers are constantly being chided for walking
too fast wherever they go, even on country "strolls."

There are a number of reasons why New York *feels* as though it must
be the crime capital of the Western world while statistically it is far
from it. First of all, regardless of the crime index (the per capita rate
of crime, or the number of crimes per 1,000 persons), given the
enormous population of New York City, the *absolute* numbers are
always mind-boggling. Five-hundred-plus murders a year may give
Dade County in Florida the highest homicide *rate* in the country, but
eighteen-hundred-plus murders in New York City each year provide
many more headlines and hence the perception, certainly, that New
York is a far more dangerous place.

Then, although New York does not rank number one in total crime—and with respect to certain types, such as larceny-theft, actually ranks quite low—the Big Apple very significantly, and unfortunately, ranks number one in the category of robbery, which translated means muggings. Or, to put it another way, *street crime.*

It's street crime, not shoplifting, that induces us to walk around strung tighter than a drum and with our crime sensors as exposed as raw nerves. Shoplifting happens to Bloomingdale's; street crime happens to people.

That New York leads all other cities in street crime makes us especially nervous, since New York is the quintessential street city. With the exception of U.N. diplomats, bank presidents, politicians, and Park Avenue matrons with blue-gray hair and white poodles—all of whom get chauffeured around in limousines—it's nearly impossible to live here without spending considerable time out on the streets. There is no such phenomenon as going from house to car to work to car to shopping center to car to home again. Here "street" gets substituted for "car," and each time you're on the street you become a potential crime target; and that's anywhere and everywhere in the city, for although there are secure buildings in New York, there are no secure neighborhoods. (The greatest increases in crime in the past several years, as a matter of fact, have been in the more affluent sections of the city.) One's $500,000 Fifth Avenue duplex offers protection only so long as one doesn't ever leave it.

Perhaps the major reason why New York feels so much more dangerous than other high-crime cities is that street crime—as opposed to, say, murder, burglary, or arson—is not something that just occurs to other people. It can happen to you. We only read about murders, whereas muggings touch our lives much more personally and graphically. It is no exaggeration to say that there are no New Yorkers who have not been mugged or almost mugged, or who do not personally know at least a dozen people who were also either actually or nearly victimized.

There is simply no other crime that makes one feel so vulnerable as street crime. That's why all of us have thought about getting mugged. We've decided for ourselves whether it's better to carry some money rather than no money. We have all decided what we would do in different situations. Resist? Hand over our money without hesitation? Run? What if the mugger is smaller than you? What if there are two of you but just one of them? We've thought about these things because if you live here long enough, the question is not whether you will be mugged. The only question is when.

Why, then, would anyone live in such a city? There is no simple answer—nothing that is likely to make much sense to a non–New Yorker anyway. Most of us probably feel that we can weather a mugging incident. We just hope that the request to hand over our wallet will not be made at gunpoint, knifepoint, or any other point. In short, we hope our mugging experience will not be a harrowing one, and as long as it is not traumatizing, we can handle it.

Then, too, our stubbornness refuses to allow street crime to push us out of the city we love. We endure everything else—tiny apartments, exorbitant rents, cockroaches galore, traffic congestion, potholes, municipal strikes of every imaginable variety, lousy schools, smog, soot, murk, and muck. We're survivors and can survive a mugging or two as well. In a strange way, having been a crime victim makes up an important piece of that survivor's badge we all wear, and that badge is part of the ineffable bond between New Yorkers. It's more than just a topic for party chatter. Rather, it's the feeling that *we* know what it's like to fear crime daily, to be victimized by crime, and then to go on with our lives nonetheless.

Finally, when it comes right down to it, most New Yorkers—true New Yorkers certainly—if pressed, would admit that whatever our level of paranoia is in the city, it's even higher outside the city. However many locks we put on our doors, we still feel more at ease in an apartment building with the sounds of other people around us than we do in a suburban house surrounded only by the sound of the wind whistling. The elements unsettle us more than people. If the choice has to be between a crowded city street and a secluded country road, we would probably opt for the street—crime and all.

## Minimizing the Risk

Every New Yorker has his or her own favorite anecdotes about out-of-town visitors who come to the city for the first time in their lives and within three hours of their arrival have their wallet stolen or car broken into. We can always imagine how these visitors then go back and tell everyone in Omaha that of course New York is every bit as bad as they say.

Ironically, the highest-crime sections of the city are precisely those where visitors are most likely to go. By far the largest number of robberies—as well as the largest number of all other reported felonies—occur in the Midtown North and Midtown South precincts, which cover 34th to 59th Streets. Looking at crime statistics as reported by the police department, whether one looks only at robberies (street crime) or at total felonies, there seems to be an almost exact inverse relationship between the safety of a borough and the likelihood of a visitor going there. Police Department figures would indicate that insofar as crime goes, the boroughs rank in the following order (from highest amount of absolute crime to lowest): Manhattan, Brooklyn, Queens, the Bronx, and Staten Island.

A year or two ago *New York* magazine did a study of the city's neighborhoods and concluded that the following are New York's safest neighborhoods (based on robberies and burglaries): In Manhattan: Stuyvesant Town and Peter Cooper housing complexes on First Avenue between 14th and 23rd Streets (the safest neighborhood in all of Manhattan); Roosevelt Island; TriBeCa; Little Italy; and parts of the Upper East Side, specifically Fifth and Park Avenues between 59th and 86th Streets, Sutton Place, and Beekman Place. In general, the Upper East Side is safer than the Upper West Side (about 10 robberies per 1,000 residents compared to 16 per 1,000). In Brooklyn: Cobble Hill and Carroll Gardens in South Brooklyn; Greenpoint, a largely Polish and Italian community; Bay Ridge; and upper-income Brooklyn Heights. In Queens: Middle Village; Kew Gardens (where about twenty years ago Kitty Genovese was murdered on the street as some forty residents silently looked on); Douglaston and Little Neck; and Neponsit and Belle Harbor. In the Bronx: the predominantly Italian neighborhood of Belmont; Morris Park in the northeast Bronx; and the upper-class enclave of Riverdale. On Staten Island: Tottenville (the safest neighborhood in all of New York City), which is closer to New Jersey than it is to New York; Todt Hill; Emerson Hill; and Dongan Hills.

Lest you be unduly distraught over crime in the wicked city, remember that statistics indicate that the safest borough is Staten Island; the safest day of the week is Tuesday; the safest time of day is between 9:00 and 10:00 A.M.; and the safest month is February. Hence, by limiting your walking about the city to Tuesday morning strolls on Staten Island during the winter, you should be able to avoid crime on the street.

# 11 Newspapers

Though you would expect the media, communications, and information center of the world to publish a multitude of daily newspapers, we actually support just three major dailies—the *Daily News*, the *New York Post*, and *The New York Times*. If Oklahoma City has three papers, New York should have at least ten. You would think.

It's not as though the city has no newspaper tradition. At one time New York supported nineteen or twenty daily papers. As late as the mid-1950s, there were still a dozen or so dailies competing here, and not until 1965 did the *Herald Tribune* meet its demise—a paper which many New Yorkers still insist was far superior to the *Times*, eminently more readable, and with a better crossword puzzle too! (In fact, the story goes that the *Trib* carried a daily puzzle long before the *Times* did, and that each day the publisher of the *Times*, Arthur Hays Sulzberger, would buy the *Tribune* just so he could do the crossword. Only upon realizing how ridiculous it was for the owner of a paper to buy a competing paper to do its puzzle did Sulzberger hire Margaret Farrar to develop a daily crossword puzzle for the *Times*.)

Now, not only do we have but a scant three newspapers—actually two tabloids (the *News* and the *Post*) and one newspaper (the *Times*)—one could argue that two of the three aren't even New York papers. The *News* happens to be owned by the *Chicago Tribune*, and the *Post* by an Australian.

What enables us to save face—indeed, actually allows us to be supercilious about our papers—is that we can lay claim to *The New York Times*. Say what you will about the *Times*—too liberal for conservatives; too liberal for radicals; too wordy for slow readers; too chi-chi for the down-to-earth—it nonetheless should be considered a national treasure. We can forgive the *Times* for using words whose meaning we have to look up—like using "hewing to" in a headline. We can even forgive it its Wednesday "Living" and Thursday "Home" sections and the elitism and inanity that abounds in them (full of articles like "How to Find Good Household Help," "How to Tell the Difference Between Male and Female Eggplants," "Where to Find the Best French Toast in the City," "How to Return Bad Wine Graciously," "Where to Buy Truffles," "How to Build a Gazebo," "How to Say No to Dinner Party Invitations," "How to Grow Orchids on a Windowsill," and so forth). The *Times* still *is* the country's premier newspaper.

There is just no disputing that claim. What other paper even comes close? What other newspaper takes the place of going out on Saturday night, as does the Sunday *Times*? (In New York City it becomes available on Saturday night at about 8:30. If it's a little late, you'll see lines form.) What other American newspaper's reviews and columns qualify as literature as often as those of the *Times*? Vincent Canby's movie reviews, John Leonard's "Metropolitan Diary" column, and Russell Baker's "Observer" column, to name but a few obvious examples, have all been published in collected form as books. What other paper could command the price of $22, as the Sunday *Times* does in Argentina?

## The Dailies Compared

Comparing the *Times* to either the *Post* or the *News* is like comparing public television to "Laverne and Shirley." In prestige, quality, and respectability, the *Times* is in a class by itself. The *Times* is meant to inform; the *Post* or the *News* to shock, titillate, and entertain. One must actually read the *Times*; scanning headlines and looking at pictures will suffice for the other two.

Readers of either the *Post* or the *News* will go through life with a completely different view of the world from that of *Times* readers, for what these two tabloids define as news usually does not coincide with the *Times*'s definition. Often what gets reported on the front page of the *Post* or the *News* doesn't make the *Times* at all, or gets two-column-inch coverage on page 33.

While the *Times* has heavy coverage of national and international news, the *Post* and the *News* both emphasize local news. (The *Post*, in particular, carries almost no international news.) Supporters of the two tabloids will tell you that if you want to know about New York, read the *News* or the *Post*, and if you're more interested in what's happening in Namibia, then of course read the *Times*. And to a certain extent that's true. The problem with the tabloids' coverage of local New York City news, however, is that the focus is mostly crime, violence, and the goings-on among personalities about town.

Even when the papers cover the same event, they do so with disparate sensibilities. In the screeching headlines of the tabloids there is a sense of urgency and hysteria—as if New Yorkers weren't hysterical enough—that attaches to every item reported. STATEN ISLAND FERRY SMASHES INTO DOCK is headlined in the *Post* in a way that would seem more appropriate to informing the reader that World War III has just been declared.

When Ted Kennedy was still contemplating challenging Jimmy Carter for the Democratic presidential nomination—but had not yet announced his decision—the *Post* printed the following headline on its front page (in about 50-point type): JIMMY CARTER: "IF KENNEDY RUNS I'LL WHIP HIS ASS." Only slightly less inelegantly the *Daily News* announced on page one (also in huge, bold type), CARTER FIRES BARB AT TEDDY, and below that in smaller type: "If Kennedy runs I'll whip his ass." The *Times*, by contrast, ran a front-page article under the headline, KENNEDY SAYS HE INFORMED CARTER OF LIKELY SUPPORT FOR NOMINATION, and it was only in the second half of the article— continued on page 26—that one found the line, "If Kennedy runs, I'm going to whip his ——."

There you have it: a perfect example of how the three dailies report the same story and impose a sensibility upon its readers. The *Post*: crassly. The *News*: boldly and familiarly ("Teddy" rather than "Kennedy"). The *Times*: in context and discreetly—always.

Until the mid-1970s when the *Post* was sold to Rupert Murdoch, an Australian newsbusinessman, it was considered quite a decent paper; far better than the *News* and certainly more liberal—editorially, more so even than the *Times*. To a large extent the readership of the *Times* and *Post* overlapped. You read the *Times* in the morning on the way to work, and on the way home you read the *Post* (it was then an afternoon paper only).

All that changed when Murdoch bought the *Post*. He turned it into a sensationalist rag. Under Murdoch, the *Post* has become more of a combination of *Police Gazette*, *True Confessions*, *People* magazine, and *Racing Form* than a newspaper. Its editorials, which had displayed an enlightened liberalism, now echo a Cro-Magnon conservatism. You can't even say *Post* editorials reflect middle-American values, which would be bad enough in this basically liberal city. Perhaps you can call them middle-Australian values—who knows? (Undoubtedly, it was partially the lesson of the *Post* that induced the owners of the *Times* of London to add certain provisions to the sales agreement when they recently sold that venerable paper to this same Rupert Murdoch. Taking no chances, provisions written directly into the terms of the sale forbid Murdoch to alter the tone, character, or editorial policy of the London *Times*. Oh, if only the previous owner of the *Post* had had such foresight.)

What's certain now is that no self-respecting *New York Times* reader would be caught dead reading the *Post*, unless, of course, one does so for the sports coverage alone. Sports buffs agree that the *Post*'s sports pages are first-rate, albeit overly smug and macho in tone—the sense that information comes from either hiding under a locker-room bench or tippling a few beers with the boys in the back of the team plane. Which may help explain why the *Times* can have a few women sportswriters on staff—and even had a woman serve as sports editor not too long ago—whereas the notion of a woman writing sports for the *Post* is really farfetched. Ditto for the *News*.

In the meantime, while the *Post* deteriorated in quality under Murdoch, the *News* was being upgraded. Articles grew in length and substance; the number of pictures was reduced (previously the *News* was known as the picture newspaper); international news coverage increased; and bright, thoughtful columnists were added. The *News*—once considered decidedly inferior to the *Post*—nowadays competes head-on with the *Post* for its readers. When the *News* recently began to publish an afternoon edition that would compete with the *Post*, the *Post* had to immediately counter by putting out a morning edition of its own that would compete with the *News*. Many will argue that the *News* is today a better paper than the *Post*; more reputable certainly.

In any event, the breakdown is clear. The readership of the *Times* is mostly white-collar; that of the *Post* and *News* more pink and blue. If *Times* readers are embodied by Manhattanites—monied, college-educated, well read, cosmopolitan—the audience for the *Post* and

*News* is more likely to be found in the outer boroughs and in middle-income and working-class suburbs surrounding the city. (Both the tabloids, therefore, see *Newsday*, the Long Island daily, as a major competitor. The *Times*, on the other hand, couldn't care less about *Newsday*.) It's why the *Times* gets carried in attaché cases, the *Post* and *News* under the arm. It's why New Yorkers buy the *Times* just for the crossword puzzle and the tabloids just for the comics. And it's why the *Times* gets discussed over cocktails at dinner parties on the Upper West Side, the *Post* and *News* over beers in neighborhood bars in Queens.

## The Village Voice

*The Village Voice*, the city's most famous weekly newspaper, is a hip, cynical, witty, acerbic, antiestablishment alternative to the dailies. The *Berkeley Barb*, *Rolling Stone* magazine, and *I. F. Stone's Weekly* rolled into one, the *Voice* is for those whose political views are to the left of liberalism; whose theater tastes lie to the south of Broadway; and whose preference in film points to Paris rather than Hollywood.

The *Voice* aims at those who prefer modern dance to the Radio City Music Hall Rockettes; who listen to music more often in clubs and cafés than in concert halls; who attend galleries as often as museums; who know more about tarot cards than bridge; who prefer dope to beer; and who consider "anthroposophical" a household word. The *Voice* speaks to New Yorkers more likely to attend a Gay Liberation march through the Village than a ticker-tape parade up Broadway in honor of astronauts or fifty-two American hostages returned from Iran.

Though present-day writers for the *Voice* may not be in the same league as Norman Mailer, Katherine Anne Porter, Kenneth Tynan, or others who contributed articles during its early years in the mid-to-late 1950s, you can still always depend upon *Voice* articles to be lively—full of pizazz. The *Voice*'s brand of journalism indulges a personal, subjective style of writing of the sort the *Times* eschews. Nor are writers for the *Voice* above using its pages for waging internecine battles. Who can forget when a contingent of *Voice* staffers dissociated themselves from a Feiffer cartoon that used the word "nigger"; and the following weeks of seemingly interminable articles in which staff members argued whether or not the cartoon was racist?

Actually, there is a strong suspicion that the strength of the *Voice* depends less on the quality of its writing than upon the quality of its listings of cultural and entertainment events (which are the best, most comprehensive listings you'll find in any publication, bar none) and upon its classifieds. You can be sure that those people who in the wee hours of the morning stand outside the New Jersey plant where the *Voice* is printed are not there so they can be among the first to read what Wayne Barrett has to say about Harrison Goldin (the city comptroller and frequent target of muckraking articles), or what Nat Hentoff has to say about the First Amendment, or what Jonathan Schwartz has to say about Jonathan Schwartz. They are there to get the *Voice* hot off the press and thus get first crack at the apartments-for-rent listings.

Inveterate *Voice* purchasers readily admit to not having read an article in months. That doesn't matter. We buy the *Voice* each week because its events listings and its ads (and Feiffer too!) fill a giant void left by the city's dailies. Without the *Voice* theater listings, we might never know that a show has opened Off Broadway; certainly not Off-Off Broadway. Were it not for the *Voice* movie listings, only the projectionist would show up for a screening of avant-garde films by Stan Brakhage in some renovated firehouse on Avenue D. Without its listings of summer rentals, we'd have to spend August in the polluted waters of Coney Island rather than on the chic shores of Fire Island. But for the *Voice* personals, the sensual needs of the city's "bi-sexual couples seeking same" might remain unfulfilled.

As a visitor or newcomer to the city, you too should buy the *Voice*. Even if you read none of its articles and attend none of the events it advertises, you will, at least, *know* what's going on. Remember, in New York what counts is knowing about the latest gallery opening, not necessarily attending it. With the *Voice* you can be absolutely *au courant* whether or not you ever leave the house.

Finding enough room to read a newspaper on a crowded New York City subway is a problem. Reading *The New York Times*, which is twice as large as either the *Post* or *News* (both tabloids), can be particularly vexing. New Yorkers have coped by learning the art—and it *is* an art—of folding the *Times* into a quarter of its size. Here is how it's done:

2. Then in half again, and commence reading.

To read, say, the Page One lead article:

1. Fold in half.

3. Flip over to continue reading.

4. Open and fold back to page on which lead article is continued.

5. Fold in half and resume reading.

6. Then, flip over if necessary (if article continues that far) to completion.

Note: You have mastered the art when, like many of us, you are standing on a moving subway holding on to a bar or pole with one hand, and can execute the folding and flipping with your one free hand.

# 12 Restaurants

While other cities might suffer from a paucity of restaurants, here problems derive instead from an abundance of them. With nearly sixteen thousand eating places to choose from,* selecting a restaurant in New York is what it must be like choosing a good table wine in France. Where do you begin? Or, what's more problematical, where do you stop?

It could take years just to sample the restaurants of Chinatown, since that tiny ten-square-block area alone claims something like 350 restaurants. To determine the best Italian restaurants from just those named Alfredo's—of which there seem to be scores—could itself take quite some time. Routinely, New Yorkers take more time deciding where to eat than we spend actually eating.

Though it simplifies matters to first delineate a type of food, then a part of town, and then a price range, even at that the number of possible choices you're left with can be awesome. The East Fifties of Manhattan, for example, probably have as many French restaurants as other cities have doughnut shops or pizza parlors.

The overwhelming number of restaurants creates the imperative that we rely upon one another for restaurant information. When we meet someone for the first time who lives in a part of the city we don't know that well, the first thing we'll ask is, "Do you know of

---

*As staggering as this figure may seem, it is accurate. According to the city's Department of Health, whose responsibility it is to inspect restaurants for Sanitary Code violations, there are 15,700 eating places within the five boroughs; and one might also add, a staff of only sixty to inspect them.

any good restaurants there?" (Actually, if you are looking for a place to live, you would probably ask about rents and apartment vacancies first and about restaurants second.) We exchange information about restaurants the way we suppose people in other parts of the country swap recipes. At parties, comparing notes on restaurants is the number-one parlor game; and knowing of great little neighborhood restaurants that no one else has heard about is the ultimate form of New York City one-upmanship.

Part of the explanation for the city's profusion of restaurants is, certainly, the demand created by out-of-towners—the thousands of tourists, conventioneers, and businessmen who come here each day; and by the hordes of neighboring suburbanites who daily descend upon Manhattan for dinner and a show or, perhaps, for shopping and then lunch.

But the better part of the demand for eating places we create ourselves. The observation has been made that we seem to eat out all the time; and we do. "Man must eat," to be sure, but in New York City it is more accurate to say "Man must eat out."

Eating out is an integral part of the style of living in New York—especially in Manhattan. It is not unusual at all for Manhattanites who are single—or for couples without children—to eat dinner out three, four, five nights a week.

While the rest of America is at church, we're in restaurants having Sunday brunch. While suburban families are out in the backyard barbecuing, New York families are enjoying the food at a Chinese restaurant. While frozen pizzas are being popped into microwave ovens in homes all over the country, we are running out to the nearest pizza place—probably no more than a couple of blocks away—for a slice or two. Whereas elsewhere it is common to resort to eating TV dinners as a matter of convenience, here the equivalent concession to convenience is to order Chinese takeout (and in effect eat in but still eat out). And whereas in most places there is a certain stigma attached to dining out alone—particularly for women—here there is almost none.

When we do eat out, more often than not we'll eat foreign foods. New York supports a tremendous number and range of foreign-food restaurants—and we're not just talking about the standard ones, such as Chinese, Italian, French, Greek, and Japanese. We also support less standard ethnic varieties: Middle Eastern, African, Brazilian, Argentine, Korean, Cuban, Indian, Ukrainian, Romanian, Indonesian, or Thai, and even such hybrids as Italian-Ukrainian, Cuban-Chinese, or Kosher Chinese.*

Sure, the city has its share of coffee shops, luncheonettes, fast-food hamburger and chicken places, and restaurants that serve a most undistinguished American fare. But only foreign-food restaurants are taken seriously. It is no accident that the only four restaurants to receive the highest rating of four stars from Mimi Sheraton of *The New York Times* in the course of a recent year's worth of reviews were places that offered foreign cuisine: Le Cygne (whose rating was subsequently dropped to three stars), La Grenouille, Lutèce, and Vienna '79. No New Yorker earns a reputation for being a food and restaurant maven (expert) by suggesting a great steak restaurant. You establish your credentials by recommending a great Chinese or French restaurant, or any other type of foreign-food restaurant. (Perhaps the one exception to this rule is passing on information about a wonderful neighborhood luncheonette that serves a terrific egg cream and has a stellar collection of magazines.)

And you don't necessarily have to spend a lot of money to indulge in foreign foods here. Without spending much more than one does for a hot dog, you can find hundreds of hole-in-the-wall places which, over the counter, sell knishes, or shish kabob, or souvlaki, or gyros, or crêpes, or cuchifritos, or tacos, or egg rolls, or pirogi. New York City pizza stands, in addition to pizza, offer calzone, zeppoli, rice balls, and sometimes even vastede and panelle—none of which you will find at your basic suburban Pizza Hut.

For these reasons, it becomes impossible to grow up in New York

---

*If you want to know where to find a major concentration of a particular type of foreign-food restaurant, look at the map of ethnic residential communities on page 18. Where there are residential concentrations, there are apt to be corresponding restaurant concentrations.

The notable exceptions to this rule, however, include the following concentrations of foreign-food restaurants located in parts of the city where there is no corresponding residential community: Chinese restaurants on the Upper West Side; Cuban-Chinese restaurants also on the Upper West Side; Korean restaurants in the low Thirties in the vicinity of Fifth Avenue; French restaurants in the Fifties, especially the East Fifties; Japanese restaurants in the East and West Forties and Fifties; Indian restaurants on East 6th Street between First and Second Avenues; and Jewish delis and dairy restaurants on the Lower East Side.

without developing a certain sophistication about ethnic food. By the time New York City kids are ten, they know that at Chinese restaurants Combination Dinner #1—won ton soup, chicken chow mein, egg roll, and fried rice—is strictly the equivalent of *menu turistica*. By the time they're twelve, they've given up spaghetti and meatballs for spaghetti alla carbonara. They are as likely to opt for dim sum as a Burger King; to choose a falafel over a Big Mac; and to prefer Chinese lemon chicken to Colonel Sanders Kentucky Fried Chicken.

Despite the city's abundance of restaurants that are both excellent and affordable, as a visitor or newcomer, you shouldn't expect to light upon them immediately upon your arrival. Especially if you stay close to Midtown, as is the wont of visitors and newcomers, finding the better, more reasonably priced eating places amidst the mass of poor, mediocre, or overpriced ones is no simple task. In the process you almost invariably have to expect to eat at your share of undistinguished, overpriced, tourist-oriented restaurants that make visitors swear they can get the same food back home in Moline, Illinois, for a third the price. And the visitor can't wait to get back to Moline to say so.

These Midtown restaurants include lunch-and-light-snack eateries that offer a rather ordinary $1.00 cup of coffee; $3.00 half grapefruit; $10.00 chef's salad; $6.00 hamburger (undoubtedly called chopped sirloin something or other and invariably garnished with a strip of bacon or two—a hamburger, nonetheless); $7.00 turkey-roll sandwich (but with all the pickles and cole slaw you can eat); $8.00 mushroom omelet (that the mushrooms are canned goes without saying); $3.00 dish of vanilla ice cream with chocolate syrup; and so on.

Or dinner restaurants, which though a notch above ordinary, still never rate even a single star from Mimi Sheraton, and still don't serve food of a quality that will make you feel your $70 for dinner for two was money well spent. These are places that specialize in $20 veal parmigiana, or $20 veal cordon bleu, or $25 Peking duck, or $15 beef teriyaki—à la carte, of course.

If it's any comfort to you, New Yorkers who should know better also get caught eating at these kinds of restaurants from time to time. We're talking now about native or resident New Yorkers who have been eating out for years and who, having separated the wheat from the chaff so to speak, will usually avoid restaurants that cater to the out-of-towner. These are New Yorkers who know about Chinatown's superb restaurants east of the Bowery, away from tourist-infested Mott Street; who know of excellent Chinese restaurants in other parts of the city, particularly on the Upper West Side; and who can tell you the difference between Cantonese, Hunan, Mandarin, and Szechuan cuisines. (Or, as one tourist who asked a New Yorker to direct her to a good Chinatown restaurant said, "Not one of those 'Saskatchewan' places.") These food-and-restaurant-smart New Yorkers will even go as far out as Bay Ridge or Greenpoint in Brooklyn or the Belmont section of the Bronx for good, inexpensive Italian dining, and have discovered the glorious, very reasonable Middle Eastern restaurants along and around Atlantic Avenue in South Brooklyn. If they do decide to spend $150 for dinner for two at a fancy East Side French restaurant, they can walk right up to the best two or three in the city, even if no signs outside reveal their names.

Even these New Yorkers get caught eating in places whose normal clientele is from out-of-town, because there are certain tourist parts of the city where there just aren't many alternatives—certainly not when time is of the essence. For instance, we might find ourselves in the West Forties or Fifties just before or after a Broadway show; or in the West Thirties around Penn Station and Madison Square Garden with just an hour to spare before we catch our train or go to the Knicks game. Otherwise, you can bet we steer clear of such tourist traps. You'd be smart if you did likewise.

Along with the general caveat to avoid Midtown restaurants around the tourist hot spots like the theater district, Rockefeller Center, the Empire State Building, and museums, hotels, and so on, what follows are some additional guidelines that might aid you in distinguishing tourist restaurants from those patronized by a predominantly New York City clientele.

A restaurant is more likely than not to be of the tourist variety if:

• It's a steak house or seafood place. When New Yorkers dine out, it's typically at a foreign-food restaurant. The prevailing attitude here is that you can broil a steak or fish at home.

• Food is served smorgasbord style. Smorgasbords or buffets are for weddings, bar mitzvahs, and Jewish funerals, not for restaurant dining.

• There's a salad bar. Give a New Yorker four leaves of endive any day, rather than all the iceberg lettuce, tomatoes, pickled beets, garbanzo beans, and Thousand Island dressing one can eat.

• There's a spectacular view of the city. Be particularly wary of restaurants situated atop skyscrapers or underneath bridges.

• Windows on the outside contain wax facsimiles of the food served inside. Restaurateurs know better than to try to entice a New Yorker with a plastic rendition of vegetable tempura, customary though it might be in Japan.

• This is your first trip to the city and yet you recognize the name—if you find yourself saying, for example, "Oh my, I've heard of Mamma Leone's."

• Live musical entertainment accompanies dinner. New Yorkers neither expect nor enjoy German folk songs while eating.

• While watching TV in your hotel room you see an ad for the restaurant on Channel 9 or 11.

• Racks of jackets of varying sizes are on hand for male patrons who come without one.

• It's a French restaurant and no reservations are required. New Yorkers go to French restaurants that require reservations days in advance; and for weekends, reservations weeks in advance are often needed.

• It's a Chinese restaurant and the menu includes dishes like "Budha's Delight" or "Peking Potpourri." New Yorkers are more inclined to frequent places where the menu is written entirely in Chinese and where one is reduced to pointing at those dishes one wants to order.

• Tall, rubbertreelike plants rather than hanging plants dominate.

Specific restaurant recommendations are made in the second half of the book, neighborhood by neighborhood.

# 13 **Arts**

## Theater

Although to the tourist, Broadway theater is synonymous with New York theater, to New Yorkers, that's not necessarily so. At least among those of us who consider ourselves serious theatergoers there is the pervasive feeling that Broadway plays—call them shows—are to theater what best-selling books are to literature.

There are exceptions to be sure, but if Judith Krantz novels epitomize contemporary best-sellers, Neil Simon situation comedies capture the essence of prevailing Broadway hits—entertaining, diverting, even witty; acceptable to take your parents to for their anniversary, or cousin George when he's visiting from Atlanta. But great theater that in some way indelibly changes your vision of yourself and the world about you? Hardly.

Thousands of us who attend the theater, therefore, hardly ever attend Broadway theater. Finding a resident New Yorker in a Broadway audience can sometimes be more difficult than finding one on the observation deck of the Empire State Building. Two-thirds of the Broadway audience is composed of non–New Yorkers (about half of whom come from the suburbs and half from outside the metropolitan area altogether). As many New Jerseyans as Manhattanites patronize Broadway.*

In selecting and shaping plays for Broadway, producers unabash-

*These figures come from a study done by the League of New York Theatres and Producers.

edly admit that it is the Long Islander and the Iowan as much as the New Yorker whose taste they have in mind and whose dollars they seek. Tourists are good business for Broadway, and Broadway is good business for business—for hotels, restaurants, bars, cafés, cabs, shops, and stores.

Producers know that entertaining rather than moving experiences are what most out-of-towners seek. Thus, the dominant fare dished out on Broadway includes musicals (accounting for at least a third of the plays on Broadway, designed to be understandable even to non-English-speaking foreign visitors), comedies, and thrillers.

And serious drama—or, as some say, straight drama? Well, fine if you can persuade Elizabeth Taylor to come out of retirement to star in a production of Lillian Hellman's *The Little Foxes*. Otherwise, you try out a dramatic play Off Broadway first and bring it to Broadway only *after* it proves a smashing success. Or else, you bring over a commercial success from London's West End, that city's equivalent of Broadway. That's the level of risk Broadway takes when it comes to nonmusicals.

So where do we who take our theater somewhat more seriously go? To Off Broadway and Off-Off Broadway, naturally. (If you think Broadway means theater, you will be surprised to know that Off and Off-Off Broadway productions together actually outnumber Broadway offerings by about three or four to one—more than a hundred compared to thirty or forty.)

You'll find Off and Off-Off Broadway theaters outside the theater district, which is essentially the Forties and Fifties between Sixth Avenue and Eighth Avenue. Instead they are located all over Manhattan (with heavy concentrations in the East and West Village and in Chelsea) as well as in the other boroughs. But besides just a difference in geography, Off and Off-Off Broadway theaters distinguish themselves from those on Broadway by being smaller and less expensive, and, most significantly, by offering plays that are not always so obviously intended solely to recoup money for their backers.

Count on fewer musicals and more dramas than on Broadway. Look forward to classics, revivals, avant-garde, and experimental plays too; to plays by new black, Hispanic, Asian, and gay playwrights; to plays by Yiddish playwrights and women playwrights. Be prepared for plays that may involve audience participation or plays that could run into the wee hours of the morning. Expect explicit sexual dialogue rather than sexual innuendo; nudity rather than sex jokes; four-letter words rather than double entendre. In other words, unlike the standard Broadway fare, most Off and Off-Off Broadway productions will not boast of "wonderful entertainment that the entire family can enjoy." (Unless, of course, it's *The Fantasticks*, which has been running Off Broadway at the Sullivan Street Playhouse for more than twenty years; it is the *Annie* of Off Broadway, a musical your eight-year-old daughter would indeed enjoy.)

Though Off Broadway and Off-Off Broadway theater tend to be lumped together, there are a number of differences between them— differences that have nothing to do with their distance from Broadway. The Brooklyn Academy of Music, for instance, which is not even in Manhattan, is considered Off Broadway while the Theatre for the New City on Second Avenue at 10th Street in Manhattan is described as Off-Off Broadway.

Size, not location, is what primarily makes one theater Off Broadway and another Off-Off. Fewer than 100 seats, it's Off-Off Broadway; more than 100, but fewer than 500, and it's an Off Broadway theater. (More than 500 seats makes it a Broadway theater, if it is in the Broadway theater district. Otherwise it's officially a "regional theater.")

You can also usually rely on an Off Broadway theater to be a theater, whereas an Off-Off Broadway "theater" can as likely be a church, café, restaurant, basement, apartment building, hotel, storefront, loft, garage, school, settlement house, senior-citizens' center, street, or park. Which is to say that you can't always count on a comfortable seat Off-Off Broadway, but you can always expect to be close to the action.

Then, too, Off-Off Broadway productions don't always use professional actors, whereas Off Broadway productions must. And although Off Broadway might be more uniformly professional than Off-Off, you certainly will pay for that. While ticket prices Off-Off Broadway range from zero to about $6, those at many Off Broadway theaters begin to rival prices you pay on Broadway—$15 to $20 not being unusual, though still a distance from the standard Broadway ticket price of over $30. (The 1981–82 Broadway production of *Nicholas Nickleby* charged $100 for all tickets.)

There is a sense among New Yorkers who follow the theater scene closely that Off Broadway, though spawned as a clear alternative to Broadway theater, is becoming less so. There's the feeling that an increasing number of plays are now produced Off Broadway in lieu of an out-of-town opening. Instead of trying out a play in New Haven, you can now test it right here in the city—say at the Circle Repertory Theater in the Village or perhaps at the Circle-in-the-Square Downtown.

Joe Papp—the David Merrick of Off Broadway—seems to get about every other one of his Off Broadway plays at his Public Theater in the East Village eventually produced on Broadway—*Hair, A Chorus Line, For Colored Girls . . ., Runaways, That Championship Season*, to name but a few. By contrast, Ellen Stewart—the David Merrick of Off-Off Broadway—never does. She clearly does not use her experimental, very innovative La Mama Theatre as a springboard to Broadway, and that now appears to be more true of Off-Off Broadway in general than it is of Off Broadway. It appears that today Off-Off Broadway more consistently fulfills these functions of risk-taking and experimentation than does Off Broadway.

Thus, to complete the analogy of theater to book publishing, if Broadway is the equivalent of mass-market best-sellers by big-name authors that are published by the largest publishing houses, then Off Broadway can be compared to the books of more serious intent— often first novels—that a medium-sized house will put out in a modest first printing, but which then go on to sell one hundred thousand copies and which fetch six-figure advances for the paperback rights. On the other hand, Off-Off Broadway theater is closer to the works of fiction, poetry, essays, short stories, and criticism that academic presses, small presses and, yes, even vanity presses publish in printings of two thousand with not much hope—and, frankly, not that much concern—that even those few copies all get sold.

THE BEST LISTINGS

The Friday and Sunday editions of *The New York Times*, *The Village Voice*, *New York* magazine, and *The New Yorker* magazine all give excellent theater listings—the best you'll find. No publication gives Off-Off Broadway theater as much coverage—reviews as well as listings—as *The Village Voice*. The *Voice* is to following Off-Off Broadway what the *Wall Street Journal* is to following the stock market— indispensable.

# Film

Paris is probably the best city in the world for seeing movies, but New York is not far behind and is certainly number one in the United States. The popular image of New York is as a city with great theater, opera, ballet, museums—all of which is true—but it's also a great film town, though out-of-towners don't normally think of New York in that light. No one comes here from Pittsburgh, for instance, just to see films.

If the serious moviegoer is defined as someone who sees Hollywood and foreign films, talkies and silents, animated films, documentaries, and nonnarrative experimental film, then New York may be the only city in the States where you can be one. It's unquestionably one of the few American cities where you can regularly see good, old films—revivals—in movie houses in lieu of staying up half the night watching the late, late show on television.

Obviously not every New Yorker who goes to the movies more than just occasionally is a serious filmgoer. As happens anywhere else, a lot of New Yorkers consider going to the movies a Friday or Saturday night date; or something to do after shopping at Bloomingdale's (since many of the city's first-run theaters are across the street from Bloomingdale's, in the vicinity of Third Avenue and 59th Street); or an air-conditioned escape if you don't happen to get out to the Hamptons on a July or August weekend.

Yet there are hordes of us who take filmgoing seriously indeed. We think nothing of waiting on line for two hours to be able to see the new Woody Allen movie on the day it opens. We will arrange through a friend of a friend of a friend who works at Lincoln Center to secure tickets to the New York Film Festival, even though we know most of the festival films will open in commercial houses a week or two after the festival closes. We think nothing of spending an entire day in the Museum of Modern Art seeing the three different films the museum will screen in a day. We'll gladly pay $25 to see the four-hour-long 1927 film *Napoleon* by Abel Gance (which, incidentally, sold out the six-thousand-seat Radio City Music Hall for its entire three-weekend run).

Hundreds of us will stand on line to see a midnight showing of *El Topo* by Alejandro Joderowsky. We will sit on hard, straight-back chairs at a showing of Stan Brakhage nonnarrative films in a loft somewhere around the Bowery. We buy series tickets to festivals of Samurai movies, the movies of Brian De Palma or Yasujiro Ozu, Cuban movies, movies by black filmmakers, movies with homosexuality as the theme, Warner Brothers' twenty-five best films by new American directors, or inexpensively made noncommercial films. We also shush anyone around us who dares talk during a film or chews popcorn too loudly.

There is a private film club in Manhattan—called the Cine Club—where movies are screened in a member's apartment and which you can find out about only through word of mouth from inner-circle members. At the Cine Club, not only is talking or eating during a film not tolerated, but neither is laughing—not even if the film is a comedy. And that's how seriously some people in New York take film viewing.

In addition to those of us who are serious filmgoers, or even film buffs, there are a number of New Yorkers who can only be characterized as film nuts. You run into them mostly at the revival houses that daily show double bills of old films—particularly those from the Golden Age of Hollywood, the 1930s and 1940s. There are at least eight revival houses in the city, not to mention the museums, libraries, churches, and colleges that also regularly show old films.

You can recognize New York City film nuts by their yellow pallor, since they spend almost all their time inside movie theaters, coming out for a breath of fresh air only for as long as it takes to get from the Thalia to the Regency, to the Museum of Modern Art, to the Carnegie Hall Cinema, to The New School film series, to the Bleecker Street Cinema, to the NYU Film School. Between films you'll hear them trade movie trivia, name every minor actor in the film just seen, and list every film an actor has ever been in. They'll discuss the quality of the print and of the sound. They all wear glasses.

(There was a guy a couple of years ago who, as the lights dimmed and the film began, would run up to within about four feet of the screen, lie down, and proceed to watch the entire film in the supine position—the only position, he would insist, from which to really appreciate the filmic image. Though rumor has it that he left the city to attend medical school in Miami, he could return at any time. You should look for him.)

There are probably just a relative handful of these film fanatics, and they by no means characterize the typical New York filmgoer. But that New York could support even one of them is the point.

Only in New York are there enough films morning, noon, and night and, more importantly, a sufficient diversity of films so that one could become a film nut if one wanted to be. That choice doesn't exist in any other city where the only notion of diversity is between Cinemas One, Two, Three, Four . . . (somewhere in New Jersey there is actually a Cinema Twelve).

If you've developed an expertise about films, you will have become expert about film lines as well. Though movie lines at popular first-run movies are by no means unique to New York City, what may be is their number, length, and duration.

Not only are lines here likely to be a lot longer than you've seen elsewhere, but there are lines for films you would never expect to attract a crowd. You do expect lines for *E.T.* or *Star Wars* or *The Empire Strikes Back* or *Annie Hall*—particularly if it's a weekend and the film is playing at a first-run Upper East Side theater; but lines for a Thursday afternoon showing of a new film from Yugoslavia or Brazil may come as something of a shock to you.

Part of the reason for this is the power of the city's film critics. If Vincent Canby, film critic of *The New York Times*, says the new Jean-Luc Godard film puts all contemporary Hollywood films to shame, then expect lines. If *Lola Montès* is playing at one of the revival houses, and Andrew Sarris, film critic for *The Village Voice*, says—even just as an offhand comment—that it's his favorite film, then, too, expect lines.

As a final caveat, before you join a New York City movie line, make sure you know what it's for. Films often sell out hours before showtime. If you don't ask, you may find yourself standing in line for half an hour thinking you're going to buy a ticket to the two-o'clock show (which is natural since it is now only twelve-thirty) only to discover that the two-o'clock has long been sold out, and what you're buying now are tickets to the four-o'clock show.

What you have to do is buy your ticket to the four-o'clock show, though it's now only one o'clock, and then kill three hours. This is why as a matter of routine we take books with us to read on line. Or if you're not afraid to give up your place at the front of the line and thereby forfeit the chance to choose where you want to sit, you can go off and spend a couple of hours browsing in bookstores, getting something to eat, getting a drink, or watching people. Take some solace in knowing that at least in New York there are ways to kill time.

Imagine yourself with hours on your hands at some suburban Cinema-Six complex out by the interstate.

## THE BEST LISTINGS

During the week, check the *New York Post*, for it has the most comprehensive movie listings, borough by borough; on Fridays or Sundays, the *Times* is as good.

When it comes to films that are being screened in places other than commercial movie theaters—museums, libraries, churches, schools, film clubs, and so on—*The Village Voice* is the last word. In that respect, the *Voice*'s "Other Movies" section is considered the bible.

# Music and Dance

Aside from finding more of more kinds of live music being performed here than anywhere else you've ever been, what's likely to strike you about the music scene in New York is how seriously we take serious music—defined as classical music and opera.

This is not to say we don't flock to hear all types of music. If you were to go to clubs like CBGB's or Tramps (for rock music), the Lone Star Cafe (for country western and R & B), the Other End (for folk), the West End (for hot jazz), the West Boondock (for cool jazz), or Michael's Pub (where Woody Allen plays Dixieland jazz on Monday nights), the crowds you would invariably find there would be made up essentially of New Yorkers. But whereas the enthusiasm we have toward all forms of popular music doesn't seem to be particularly unique to New York, our enthusiasm for opera and classical music might very well be.

Hundreds of us will stand on line for two days to get tickets to hear the pianist Vladimir Horowitz. Americans stand on line for two days and sleep out in the rain to get Super Bowl tickets; New York classical-music lovers do it to secure Horowitz tickets.

We also willingly pay outrageously high prices for subscriptions to the opera (prices for seven performances at the Metropolitan Opera range from about $500 on down to $100); covet "Mostly Mozart" T-shirts; support several classical music radio stations; and consider Pinchas and Eugenia Zukerman (violinist and flutist, respectively) about as famous as any New York City couple.

During the summertime, 200,000 New Yorkers routinely turn out to hear the New York Philharmonic play in Central Park on a mid-week evening. The Metropolitan Opera performances in the park attract 100,000.

True, the rock singer Elton John did draw a crowd of 400,000 when he gave a concert in Central Park, and Simon and Garfunkel pulled a crowd of more than half a million. True too, the Philharmonic and Metropolitan Opera performances are musical events with a heavy emphasis on the "event." Food abounds and wine flows. (As the tax season is to accountants, so must the Philharmonic park concerts season be to caterers of gourmet picnic dinners.) But still, at the core level, the crowd has come to listen to classical music, and *La Traviata* is not exactly your basic easy-listening music. That 100,000 of us come to hear it seems uniquely New York.

Admittedly, serious music is associated with a certain glamour quite apart from the music itself. Attending Lincoln Center, for instance—home to both the New York Philharmonic and the Metropolitan Opera—is, indeed, stepping out on the town. You can, if you wish, wear an evening gown or a tux to Lincoln Center and not feel a bit out of place; you can sip champagne during intermission; and afterward you can join others in the audience at nearby fashionable watering holes.

Yet, at the same time, thousands will wait on line to get into one of the classical music marathons—twelve or thirteen nonstop hours of just Brahms, or Bach, or Schubert, or perhaps Aaron Copland—at the Symphony Space on Broadway at 95th Street. And unlike Lincoln Center with its fountains, glitter, and glass, the Symphony Space is an old renovated movie house along a stretch of Broadway on the Upper West Side that, politely, can be called "funky." Not so politely, one would say seedy.

Or hundreds of us will spend our winter weekends at the chamber-music concerts at the Brooklyn Academy of Music. (Hundreds more apparently get turned away because the concerts always seem to sell out.) And going to BAM is about as glamorous an experience as dining at Horn & Hardart. To say nothing about its being in Brooklyn—and in a marginal neighborhood, at best, where the most popular after-BAM gathering spot is Junior's delicatessen.

You can be sure that anyone who goes to Symphony Space or to BAM does so solely out of a love for classical music.

As proof of the claim that serious music is identified with New York—the way, say, jazz is with New Orleans, rhythm and blues with Memphis, country western with Nashville, or Motown with Detroit—is the fact that anyone who wants to make it to the pinnacle of the classical-music or opera world would not contemplate going anywhere else. Zubin Mehta left the Los Angeles Philharmonic to take over the directorship of the New York Philharmonic. It could never happen in reverse. Would-be rock stars head for Los Angeles. Would-be violin virtuosi head for New York—more likely than not to study at Juilliard as a beginning.

Though it's important for rock, folk, jazz, and other musicians to perform here, it's imperative for classical musicians to live here. That's why when the Symphony Space holds its thirteen-hour classical-music marathons, almost all the performers come from the immediate Upper West Side neighborhood. (Which, by the way, is where all classical musicians in the city have lived, do live, and always will live. On the Upper West Side, violin cases outnumber attaché cases.)

If it's the case that serious music is identified with New York, then that identification is also true of serious dance. Anyone with aspirations of dancing in other than a Las Vegas chorus line comes to New York. There is no other city you would consider going to. Dance classes around the city are filled with dancers from other parts of the country who have relocated here solely to dance. Perhaps the largest concentration of Midwesterners outside the Midwest is to be found in New York City dance classes.

If you still doubt the claim that New York is the dance capital of the Western world, suffice it to say that whenever dancers defect from the Bolshoi or the Kirov, it is almost always to New York that they come.

It should therefore not surprise you that loads of dance performances go on here all the time (though winter and spring are considered the *official* dance seasons), and that dance is an integral part of the weekend arts-and-entertainment scene. There is, in fact, enough dance to more than justify the dance editors, writers, and columns that the city's papers all seem to have.

What may come as something of a surprise, however, is just how far down the popularity of dance here has filtered. Even among New Yorkers who don't go see dance that much, dance is followed in the papers and dancers are known. Robert Joffrey, George Balanchine,

Paul Taylor, Twyla Tharp, Alvin Ailey, Merce Cunningham, Eliot Feld (among the leaders of the city's major dance companies) may not all be household names but they are very widely known.

Part of the widespread awareness—aside from the prevalence of dance—comes from the fact that the New York press covers dance the way it does sports. Dancers are as much a staple of Page Six (the *Post*'s gossip page) as sports stars. Will the Yankees trade Rick Cerone to the Mets? Will Mikhail Baryshnikov leave ABT (American Ballet Theatre) to return to its arch-rival, New York City Ballet? Which Yankee is not on speaking terms with George Steinbrenner? Is Gelsey (Gelsey Kirkland, principal dancer with ABT) still not talking to Mikhail? Was that Joe Namath dancing at Regine's last night? Was that Cynthia Gregory (another principal dancer with ABT) sitting all alone at O'Neals' pub after last night's performance of *Swan Lake*?

THE BEST LISTINGS

The *Times*, the *Voice*, *New York* magazine, and *The New Yorker* each list more music and dance events than you need know about. For classical music, the Sunday *Times* (in "The Guide" section) is probably the best source. The *Voice*, though weak on classical music (in fact, it hardly covers it at all), is by far the best source of listings for rock, folk, jazz, and pop music—particularly the club-and-café scene.

For dance, *The Village Voice* again excels. Any of the other publications are fine for the top-tier dance companies—the Joffrey, ABT, New York City Ballet, Alvin Ailey, Paul Taylor, Merce Cunningham—but for the lesser-known companies that perform in schools, lofts, and renovated garages rather than Lincoln Center and City Center, the *Voice* listings are nonpareil.

# Museums and Galleries

The average New Yorker may actually know less about the city's museums than the average visitor. Not that we don't go to museums, but rather we tend to go to a certain few of them.

While there are over a hundred museums within the five boroughs, we basically frequent the Big Four—the Metropolitan Museum of Art (also known as the Met), the Museum of Modern Art (a.k.a. MoMA or the Modern), the Guggenheim, and the Whitney. Maybe the list can be stretched to include the Cloisters, the Frick, and the Morgan Library. For those of us with kids, tack on the Museum of Natural History, too. But that would be as far as the list typically goes.

Even as major a museum as the Brooklyn Museum—the seventh largest in the United States—is hardly considered a "must see" for the majority of New Yorkers who attend museums. Probably the first and last time many New Yorkers visited the Brooklyn Museum was only just recently—to see "The Dinner Party" by Judy Chicago, and then only because "The Dinner Party" was a media event. (Thanks to a little help from Hilton Kramer, art critic for the *Times*, who managed to antagonize every woman within four hundred miles of the city by calling the exhibit vulgar feminist propaganda rather than art.) In the amount of publicity—or in this case notoriety—it received, it was the Brooklyn equivalent of the King Tut exhibit at the Met or the Picasso exhibit at the Modern, and it's fairly certain that nothing less could have pried New Yorkers away from the fashionable Upper East Side "museum district" (Fifth and Madison Avenues between 59th and 89th Streets) to Crown Heights in Brooklyn, no less.

This tendency to patronize the Big Four almost exclusively applies equally to those who attend museums all the time as well as to those who go only one or two rainy Sundays a year. One difference is that the former go despite the crowds, while the latter go precisely because of the crowds.

The attitude among serious museumgoers who stick to the Big Four is, Why do you have to go anywhere else when just the Met and the Modern together have more art than any mere mortal could hope to digest—the Met for everything before the twentieth century and the Modern for everything since? My god, three million works at the Met alone! As for the infrequent, rainy-Sunday museumgoer, the feeling is, Where the hell can you possibly have brunch around the Brooklyn Museum?

In either case, the result is the same. It is left to the out-of-towner to support the lesser-known museums—to go just a few blocks north of 89th Street on Fifth Avenue to visit the Museum of the City of New York, or the Jewish Museum, or the Cooper-Hewitt Museum (of design), or the International Center of Photography, or El Museo del Barrio. It is, to be sure, left to the tourist to traipse out to the Jacques Marchais Center for Tibetan Art on Staten Island. Upper Fifth

Avenue museums have in the past even resorted to promotional gim-
micks like music and puppets to attract crowds. And yet, the six hundred people the Museum of the City of New York was able to entice
with a puppet show one evening—a huge crowd for that museum—
pales in comparison to the six hundred people *per half hour* who
attended the Picasso exhibit at the Modern.

Just why visitors go to museums the great masses of New Yorkers
tend to avoid isn't altogether clear. Maybe when tourists come here
to "do" museums, they think that means all museums. Or maybe,
since tourists have guidebooks that list all the museums, they are
aware of ones we aren't. Or perhaps out-of-towners just don't know
that it's chic to go to the Whitney, and not at all chic to go out to the
Richmondtown Restoration and Historical Museum on Staten Island.

Whatever the reasons, for advice about New York's lesser-known
museums—those outside the "museum district" in Manhattan—look
not necessarily for someone carrying a Zabar's delicatessen bag
(surely a New Yorker), but rather someone with a Michelin Guide
(surely an out-of-towner).

If the average New Yorker is not that well informed about the city's
museums, he knows even less about its galleries. There is something
forbidding about them. At least in museums it's okay to be just looking. "Just looking" is a response that doesn't go over very well in galleries, which are, after all, businesses.

Though a lot of us will have absorbed the names of certain galleries through osmosis—the Wildenstein, Sotheby's, Marlborough, Cas-
telli's, and perhaps a couple of others of that level of fame—galleries
here are for the most part the domain of artists, wealthy art collectors
and investors, and visiting strollers.

As someone who might not know your way around the city well,
you shouldn't worry that you may not be able to rely on asking the
man on the street for guidance regarding galleries. There is probably
less need to ask about galleries than almost anything else in New
York. For one thing, you won't have any difficulty discovering where
the bulk of them are. Just ask someone to point you in the direction
of the three smartest commercial neighborhoods in town—57th
Street between Sixth and Park Avenues, Madison Avenue in the Sixties and Seventies, and SoHo—and *Voilà*, you've been directed to 90
percent of all New York galleries.

On and around 57th Street alone, there are something like sixty galleries. Another sixty or so are on the Upper East Side on and around Madison. And as for the number of galleries in SoHo? Well, that would depend on what day the question is asked. That's how fast SoHo galleries come and go.

Nor should you have much trouble figuring out which galleries handle what type of art. It seems the work at a gallery reflects the part of the city where the gallery is. In the old, quiet, subdued environs of Madison Avenue on the Upper East Side, galleries tend to have works of older, established artists—even old masters—as well as antiques and prints. By contrast, 57th Street is more recently developed, noisier, and much more overtly commercial than Madison, and not surprisingly its galleries handle much more contemporary works.

And the galleries in trendy SoHo handle anything that's in. Instead of bronze and marble sculptures, expect kinetic light sculptures; instead of works by old masters, expect art composed by computers; fabric collages rather than tapestries; murals and environmental sculptures that fill an entire room. Rather than a still-life of a bowl of fruit, in SoHo expect broken pieces of the bowl and actual bits of the fruit. Instead of landscapes, you are more likely to find canvases filled with soil, twigs, and leaves.

Lest anyone planning a summer trip to New York to "do" the museums and galleries be disappointed, be aware that although museums are open throughout the summer, galleries tend not to be. In France, all businesses may close down during August; in New York art galleries do (along with psychiatrists).

THE BEST LISTINGS

The *Times*, *The New Yorker*, and *New York* magazine have about equally comprehensive listings of shows at museums and galleries. The listings in the Sunday *Times* (in "The Guide" section) are perhaps the best of the three.

Though *The Village Voice* has good gallery listings, it no longer lists museums. And neither the *Daily News* nor the *New York Post*—supposedly the people's papers—gives much coverage to museums or galleries, lending credence to the notion that art generally has an elitist appeal.

The best guide to museums is a booklet put out by the Cultural Assistance Center entitled "A Guide to New York City Museums." It costs about $1.50 and is available in most bookstores. The guide lists literally every museum in the city and then some—it stretches the definition of "museum" to include zoos and aquariums. It's a superb little book.

# 14 Leisure

## Spectator Sports

To be a sports fan in New York is to be a fan of professional sports, for the world of spectator sports here revolves almost entirely around professional teams: Mets, Nets, Jets, Yankees, Rangers, Cosmos, Giants, Knicks, Islanders, the Arrows indoor soccer team, and just recently the Devils hockey team.

There is some question as to just how many professional teams we can lay claim to. The Nets, Cosmos, and Giants—who all once played in New York—now play in New Jersey. The Devils (formerly the Colorado Rockies) came directly to New Jersey from Colorado, while both the Arrows and the Islanders have always played in Nassau County out on Long Island, and thus have never officially been city teams (when they won the Stanley Cup Championship in 1981, the parade for the Islanders was up Hempstead Turnpike, not Broadway). So some say the city has eleven teams while others insist there are only five. The media, however, do cover the eleven as if they were all New York teams, and whether you count five or eleven, there are still at least twice as many professional teams here as almost anywhere else.

Just about all of the five teams remaining in the city have threatened at one time or another to quit New York—the Knicks and Rangers if the city raises the taxes on Madison Square Garden; the Jets unless the Mets make better arrangements for them at Shea Stadium during the part of the baseball season that overlaps with football; and the Yankees if the city ever decides to end the sweetheart lease with them for Yankee Stadium. Which would leave New York, a town totally oriented to professional sports, with just one professional team—the Mets. And though this scenario has yet to come to pass, it is not really that improbable.

Insofar as media coverage is concerned, college sports are written about only scantily and high school sports hardly at all. For a New York paper to assign one of its sportswriters to cover a college or high school game would be the equivalent of assigning an ace investigative reporter to write obits. Aside from the fact that the professional teams monopolize what space the papers allot for sports (already the sports sections of both the *Post* and the *News* account for about half of those papers' total pages), there's just not all that much fan interest in high school or college sports.

When a city has a hundred high schools—as New York does—it's difficult to identify with any one of them or to consider any of them as *the* city's school. The same is true on the college level. New York is no Palo Alto, Ann Arbor, or Columbus where there is one school, and everyone roots for it (Stanford, Michigan, and Ohio State, respectively).

Besides, New York City colleges aren't very sports-oriented. None, for example, plays hockey; few field football teams, and then typically on a club level; and baseball is played quietly at random fields (as opposed to stadiums) around the city at four o'clock on April afternoons. And although basketball is played at all the colleges, it's not played very well. Some New Yorkers consider St. Johns in Queens a basketball powerhouse, but that's wishful thinking. When St. John's ventures to the South or to the West Coast, even its most avid supporters are reduced to fabricating excuses for its inability to beat teams from other parts of the country.

You might wonder why this happens. Basketball is supposed to be the City Game; and it is. But the whole point of playing the City Game extremely well is so that it becomes your ticket *out* of the city. There are fabulous basketball players to be found on the playgrounds of every borough of New York, but when it comes time to choose a college, the best players won't opt for City College. Instead they head for Kansas, Tennessee, North Carolina, UCLA, and places like that. For a dozen years, 1971–1983, New York University did not even have a basketball team. Here where the best playground basketball in the world is played, Fordham University has in recent years been recruiting basketball players from the Sudan!

Finally, high school and college teams are never likely to compete with the professional teams for fan affection, because city schools lack an essential ingredient. Even if New York City schools played football, played it excellently, and had 100,000-seat stadiums to be filled, they never would be. To fill stadiums requires that a college have a certain spirit—a rah-rah ethos, if you will—and New York schools simply lack that. You need alumni booster clubs, pep rallies, and tailgate parties. Even if anyone here knew what a tailgate party was, hardly anyone would participate. Tailgate parties require station wagons or campers, and there are only about six of those in the entire city.

No, we're destined to remain totally absorbed with our professional teams.

Perhaps it is this preoccupation with professional sports that explains why we're considered to be the most knowledgeable sports fans in the country. It's true; we are, or at least we are when it comes to the major professional sports—baseball, basketball, football, and hockey. This accolade is not just a New Yorker boasting, either. The conclusion was drawn from a poll conducted a couple of years ago by the *Boston Globe*.

To be completely honest, it probably should be mentioned that this same poll also found us to be the most abusive, though it's doubtful that many of us consider that a put-down. Fighting in the stands at a Rangers game doesn't seem that horrible. Talking during a movie or falling asleep watching a play seems considerably more uncouth.

There was a time when it was possible to tell a lot about New Yorkers just by knowing what team we rooted for. The city's professional teams used to have distinct personalities, and the division lines between their respective fans were therefore clear.

The writer Roger Kahn has said of old Brooklyn Dodger fans, for instance, that they were people who loved both the Dodgers and Paul Robeson, the black singer-actor-political-activist. The same could not have been said of Yankee fans of that era, nor, for that matter, of New York Giant baseball fans either.

Later on in the late 1960s and early 1970s, the observation was made that radical students at Columbia University who led the 1968 campus takeover were also fans of the New York Knickerbockers (this even included members of SDS). Nets fans, by contrast, would not even have contemplated occupying a campus building.

But now it's been years since you could tell where we stand on the issues of the day just from where we stand *vis-à-vis* New York's teams. Present-day New York City teams lack the distinctive personalities they once seemed to have, and certainly none of them embodies the character of New York itself the way the old Brooklyn Dodgers did—a team which, though not consistent winners (remember, they were called "dem Bums"), was nevertheless street-smart, spirited, and scrappy. It had panache. It was also an ethnic team and the very first team in baseball to have a black player, and somehow that was befitting a New York team.

(In their song entitled "Mrs. Robinson," Simon and Garfunkel were able to use the former New York Yankee, Joe DiMaggio, to symbolize the quintessential *American* hero. They could not have used Carl Furillo or Duke Snider or Peewee Reese—all former Dodger stars—instead, for they were hardly America's heroes. Only New York heroes.)

Nowadays the only differences between New York teams are their salary scales and their win-loss records, neither of which has anything to do with character. So, who knows how anyone here now chooses which team to cheer? Maybe no one does choose. Today you can't assume a damn thing about us by knowing what team we support. Don't even try.

## Participant Sports

As was already mentioned, basketball is the City Game. That it would be is more or less inevitable. With the square footage of asphalt here far exceeding the square footage of grass, it only stands to reason that basketball prevails. Basketball is also America's most urban sport, and New York is its most urban of cities. Then, too, basketball is dominated by blacks, and no other city has a larger black population than New York.

You'll notice as you walk or take public transportation around the city that you rarely see a black teenage male who is not wearing high-top sneakers—not running shoes and not low-cut sneakers;

only high-tops, for that is *the* basketball shoe. It doesn't matter what else they're wearing. That's because the man's got to be ready to play some b-ball anywhere, anytime.

Elsewhere sports change with the seasons, but at Tompkins Park in the Bedford-Stuyvesant section of Brooklyn or at Crotona Park in the Bronx or on the Frederick Douglass Playground at 155th Street in Harlem or on any number of other playgrounds in the city's many other black neighborhoods, basketball is played summer, winter, spring, and fall. In black neighborhoods, basketball is the main game. Learning to play it well is the main rite of passage.

If there was ever any doubt about this, it was put to rest during the 1977 summer blackout that left us without any electricity for almost a full day. The first night of the blackout was characterized by massive looting throughout the city's poor neighborhoods. And guess what item was stolen more than any other? No, not TVs and not stereos and not radios. Sneakers! In fact, the owner of one radio-television-appliances store admitted that the only reason his store was spared being ravaged was that it happened to be located next to a shoe store. Fifty-dollar Nike sneakers prevailed over $500 TVs. That should tell you something about the position the City Game occupies here.

This doesn't mean you won't find other sports being played here. You'll discover that New Yorkers pursue all sports (in the winter, some even go cross-country skiing in Central Park or Prospect Park or along the frozen, snow-covered beach at Coney Island). When you think about it, maybe stickball and stoopball are also identified with New York and are as suited to being played here as basketball. And perhaps handball is too, since after all, the national handball championships are held here each year at Brighton Beach in Brooklyn. But certainly, no other sports are.

To pursue most other sports here usually requires some unusual effort and expense. No one swims, jogs, or plays tennis, for example, because it's convenient to do so. If you want to swim, you pay to join a health club for the right to swim in a pool that is typically about half the size of any pool you'll find behind any Southern California tract home. In the summer, we have the option of either going to one of the city's beaches (hoping the water is not off-limits to swimming because of pollution, as it seems to be about 90 percent of the time) or deciding to buck beach traffic for five hours to enjoy two hours of fun and sun at one of Long Island's beaches.

Unless one happens to live near a park, jogging entails dodging traffic and pedestrians on the city's streets and sidewalks and inhaling so many exhaust fumes that one has to wonder about the health benefits of jogging in New York. One thing that has to be said regarding the advent of jogging here is that the presence of hundreds of joggers on streets and in parks at hours when they would otherwise be abandoned has done more to make those places safe than any anticrime plan the police department could possibly devise.

As for tennis, you get up at six in the morning to pay $30 to $40 an hour for court time (at the Tennis Club in Grand Central Terminal, members pay $2,000 to $3,000 a year for an hour of court time a week); or you play on a municipal court where the surfaces are anything but all-weather and the waiting times are interminable; or, like a lot of us, you buy your own tennis net and string it up wherever you can!

For kids growing up in New York, playing most sports besides basketball entails adapting the game to the city's peculiar environment. Playing baseball, football, or hockey on the streets or in the playgrounds usually means playing softball instead of hardball, touch football rather than tackle, and roller hockey in lieu of ice hockey. Stoopball, stickball, and curb ball are adaptations—hybrid games really—that result from the city's lack of traditional athletic facilities.

When you come right down to it, ingenuity is probably a more valuable asset here than athletic prowess, and no one is more ingenious than city kids when it comes to using whatever is available. Give New York City kids a ball (typically a pink Spaulding, which we call a "Spaldeen") and ten square feet of asphalt and they'll devise a game. And it won't be a simple game of catch either.

You'll probably see for yourself how city kids incorporate the rungs of fire escapes, parking signs, sidewalk cracks, manhole covers, cars—both moving and parked—stoops, curbs, walls, and hydrants into their games. And if you're anything like us, seeing this will be a warming experience. It should bring a smile to your face, for watching New York City kids *create* street games is thrilling.

To all those who, amid their litany of reasons for not living here, say they could never raise their children in New York because there is nowhere to play, we respond: "True, there is nowhere to play, but that doesn't mean kids don't." Far from it. Furthermore, if the fate of New York City children is having no place to play, the fate of suburban children is having no one to play with. Out there in suburbia you have to organize Little Leagues in order to get more than three kids together. Not here.

BOTH SPECTATOR AND PARTICIPANT SPORT:
THE NEW YORK CITY MARATHON

If you can work it out so that you can be in New York in October for the New York City Marathon, by all means you should. There is nothing quite like it. Whether you're an avid runner or you shun running altogether, you'll love the marathon, for it is both race and event.

Sixteen thousand participants (as compared to seven thousand in the Boston Marathon) and between two and three million spectators (compared to the one million who watch the Boston) make the marathon an experience that transcends just the race aspect. Even at the early stages of the race—say, three to four miles into it—it takes about a full hour for the field to pass. That's how large it is.

No other event in the city engenders the universality of good feelings that the marathon does. It may be the only event in the city that at least some substantial segment of New Yorkers is not cynical about. In that respect alone, the marathon achieves a unique status.

How else does the New York Marathon differ from other marathons? You remember the infamous Rosie Ruiz who was accused of cheating to win the 1980 Boston Marathon, and was subsequently stripped of her title? Apparently she had cheated in the earlier New York Marathon as well, but in a way that could only be accomplished here. Allegedly she started the race, dropped out in the early stages, took a subway uptown, and reentered the race near the finish line. Certainly that could only happen in New York.

## Parks and Beaches

The city's parks seem invariably to disappoint visitors. Visitors expect them to be green—just as they're indicated on the tourist maps. They were at one time, but now the green grass has been reduced to dust or replaced with asphalt. In certain city parks bits of broken glass, rather than grass, provide the major element of green.

Central Park probably provides the biggest shock of all. Not that it's in the worst condition—in fact, it's probably in the best shape of all the city parks—but because it doesn't begin to measure up to the photographs and films that out-of-towners have seen of it.

Upon seeing Central Park for the first time, Eric Heiden, the Olympic speed-skating champion who hails from Madison, Wisconsin, offered the opinion that if Central Park was located in Madison, it would be condemned. "They would just close it down and let it grow," said he. Or something to that effect. He made it sound as though he had journeyed to Agra to see the Taj Mahal only to discover it covered with graffiti.

Well, Eric, we like it. In fact, we love Central Park and, despite its somewhat scruffy, ill-maintained condition, still consider it to be 840 acres of sheer heaven in the city. That it's seen better days does not discourage us from going there even though it does seem to deter you. We would never stop using the park just because the benches needed to be painted more often than they are or because broken or missing slats have yet to be repaired or replaced. (Actually, the city is now installing new benches in the parks. Made of galvanized steel and heavy planks, these new benches, in a three-year test, proved to be "vandal-resistant" if not "vandal-proof.")

Parks in Madison, Wisconsin, wouldn't be in such great shape either if one night 200,000 people descended upon any of them for a concert, as happens regularly in Central Park; or if thousands of cyclists rode through Madison's parks for twenty-four consecutive hours as they do here for Central Park bike marathons; or if on Sunday mornings thirty games of touch football (with players wearing cleats) went on simultaneously alongside twenty rugby matches (with players also wearing cleats), as occurs in Central Park.

The balance in Central Park between park use and abuse is so precarious that park administrators had to turn down the plan offered by the conceptual artist Christo to line 27 miles of Central Park walkways—at 9 foot intervals—with eleven thousand saffron-colored fabric banners. Among other reasons, the thought was that the park simply could not withstand the further wear and tear that would result from the estimated one million additional park visitors who would come to see the exhibit/event/happening just during the two weeks it would be displayed. Those are the kinds of crowds with which Central Park must contend and which parks elsewhere hardly need worry about.

We're the first to admit that neither Central Park nor any other New York City park can begin to hold a candle to any of London's swatches of velvet green. Any park there looks like the Brooklyn Botanic Garden here.

But the difference between London's parks and ours is that in theirs one isn't allowed to do a bloody thing. In some of them one can't even walk on the grass. There is no Frisbee playing, rollerskating, or skateboarding. No softball, football, soccer, lacrosse, or volleyball games. No bike races or road races. No marathons or minimarathons. There is no picnicking and certainly no barbecuing. No rock concerts, symphony concerts, opera-in-the-park, or theater-in-the-park. For sure, there is no horseback riding as there is in Central Park or Prospect Park. All of which take a heavy toll on the parks. Let's face it, about the only activity countenanced in a London park, besides strolling, is lawn bowling. And lawn bowling doesn't exactly attract throngs, nor does it destroy the sod.

Whereas London's parks are visited but not necessarily used, ours are both visited *and* used. In the opinion of most visitors, they're overused, which observation in itself leads to another source of disappointment for the out-of-towner. Visitors expect the parks to be sylvan refuges from the masses and from the hectic pace of city living, only to discover them to be the most crowded, activity-filled places in town.

Out-of-town visitors don't realize that we don't consider the parks as places to escape to, and that rather than go to the park to get away from it all, we go precisely for the reason that we wish to be right smack in the middle of it all. If we wanted to jog alone, we would jog in Brooklyn. If we want to jog along with seven thousand other joggers—or do anything else alongside thousands of others—then we go to Central Park.

Everything happens in the park. The smart visitor or newcomer who wanted a quick lesson in contemporary New York City living would go straight to the park. You can get no better lesson on the recreational, fashion, or musical fads and trends than around Bethesda Fountain in Central Park or around the fountain pool in Washington Square Park in the Village. You'll see the latest roller-disco moves, skateboard techniques, and Frisbee throws. You'll discover if antique clothing is in or out, if punk has come or gone, if folk music still gets played.

And the smart person who wants to escape the city, who wants some peace and solitude? That smart person walks around the financial district on Sunday mornings.

The city's beaches, with the exception of Coney Island, have been a well-kept secret from the newcomer and visitor. Few non–New Yorkers would guess that there are almost 20 miles of beaches in New York City. (Though given all the water in and around New York, one would have to conclude that few cities have done so little with so much.) Certainly no one comes here because of the beaches.

We don't boast about them as we do almost everything else, nor does the typical New York City guide let on to their existence. Instead, under the heading of "Beaches" guidebooks usually suggest the visitor schlep out to Jones Beach on Long Island—30 miles away and at least three hours by car in beach traffic. This as opposed to any city beach which, by contrast, can be reached by public transportation and in about a third the time.

Whether or not you'll be disappointed with our beaches will depend upon the standard you judge them by. Mostly they are large and sandy, though the waters are none too clean nor the surf very high. By Southern California beach standards, you'll likely conclude the condition of New York's beaches is woeful; by European beach standards, decent; and by almost any standard, crowded.

On a single summer day as many as a million people will be on the beach at Coney Island in Brooklyn, three-quarters of a million on the Rockaway beaches in Queens, and half a million at Orchard Beach in the Bronx. Then add on another couple of hundred thousand for Midland Beach on Staten Island. Perhaps "jammed" is a better word than "crowded."

If the typical guidebook doesn't direct the out-of-towner to the city's beaches, it's for the same reason these same books give short shrift to anything outside of Manhattan. All the city's beaches are in the outer boroughs, and that by definition makes them unsmart. Old retired people live out by the beach here. Young professionals would sooner live inside a subway tunnel in Manhattan than in a beach house in the Rockaways.

During the summertime, young professionals and families with money—the Manhattan smart set, the people who take cabs everywhere—head for the Hamptons (Southampton, East Hampton, and Westhampton on Long Island), Fire Island, Shelter Island, Montauk, Sag Harbor, even Jones Beach, before Orchard Beach, Riis Park, Co-

ney Island, or any other city beach. They'd soak in their bathtubs before they'd swim off New York City shores. Upper-income people
who have lived here all of their lives may very well never have been
to a city beach.

Therefore, although you would think that the nearly three million
people on the city's beaches on a summer weekend must represent a
good portion of the city's total population, in fact, they represent
only a sizable portion of the lower-middle class, the working class,
the poor, and the elderly. These are the New Yorkers who stay in the
city during the summer. The city beaches belong to them.

Two caveats before you go. First, if you're intent upon going into
the water, make sure that you can. Because of pollution, the water at
city beaches is often not approved for swimming. Some of the
beaches on Staten Island have been closed to swimming for years.

Some New Yorkers remember when it was possible—maybe fifty
years ago—to swim off Manhattan's shores in the Hudson and East
rivers. Others predict this may be possible again someday. Some predict that within ten years you'll be able to swim in the Gowanus Canal in Brooklyn too! Maybe you will; but for the present, New York's
waters are not to be assumed to be clean. So check newspapers to
see what beaches might be closed to swimmers.

Second, though to the untutored eye any New York City beach
with half a million people looks like any other New York City beach
with half a million people, in truth the beaches differ greatly in terms
of who goes where. The Rockaways are mostly family beaches, as
are the Staten Island beaches. Manhattan Beach in Brooklyn (yes,
that is confusing) is the favorite of teens and young adults. Brighton
Beach has a huge number of elderly beachgoers as well as Russian
Jews, since they live nearby. Orchard Beach in the Bronx is largely
Hispanic. (Taco stands supplement the standard franks-and-burgers
beach fare.) Coney Island? Absolutely everyone goes to Coney Island.

Perhaps the beach that most accurately reflects the city is Riis Park,
which is part of the Rockaways. Though incredibly heterogeneous, it
is also highly stratified. You'll find all kinds of New Yorkers there but
each in their distinct enclave. Starting at the easternmost end and
walking west—that is, starting at Bay 1—the progression will be as
follows: gay men (nude), nudes, black families, white families, and
teenagers and young adults.

# PART TWO

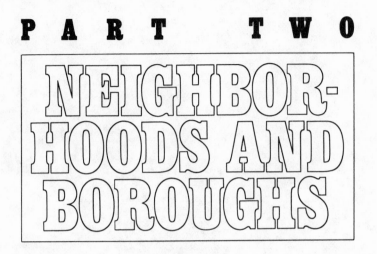

# NEIGHBOR-HOODS AND BOROUGHS

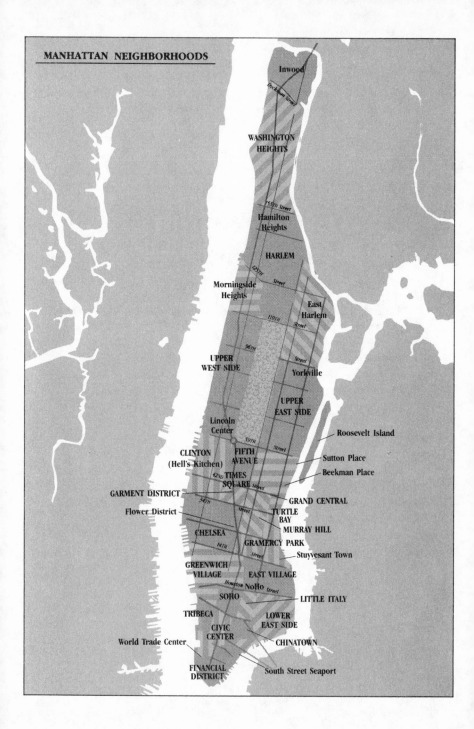

# MANHATTAN NEIGHBORHOODS

Inwood

Dyckman Street

WASHINGTON HEIGHTS

155TH Street

Hamilton Heights

HARLEM

125TH Street

Morningside Heights

East Harlem

110TH Street

96TH Street

UPPER WEST SIDE

Yorkville

UPPER EAST SIDE

Lincoln Center

Roosevelt Island

59TH Street

CLINTON (Hell's Kitchen)

FIFTH AVENUE

Sutton Place

Beekman Place

42ND Street

TIMES SQUARE

GARMENT DISTRICT

GRAND CENTRAL

34TH Street

Flower District

TURTLE BAY

MURRAY HILL

CHELSEA

14TH Street

GRAMERCY PARK

Stuyvesant Town

GREENWICH VILLAGE

EAST VILLAGE

Houston Street

NoHo

SOHO

LITTLE ITALY

TRIBECA

LOWER EAST SIDE

CIVIC CENTER

World Trade Center

CHINATOWN

FINANCIAL DISTRICT

South Street Seaport

# 15 Lower Manhattan

## Financial District: *South Street Seaport / World Trade Center / Battery Park City*

Unlike most of the city, which is bustling day and night, the financial district stays alive during the daytime only. In the evening the area is absolutely dead. Nor is there much life here on weekends. The financial district is one of the few areas of the city oriented almost entirely around working. Relatively few New Yorkers live here; no one comes here to play.

In this respect, the financial district may remind you of Washington, D.C. Five o'clock arrives and the place suddenly empties out. And just as Washington belongs less to Washingtonians than to Virginians and Marylanders, Wall Street belongs more to commuters from New Jersey, Westchester, and other suburbs than to New Yorkers. The average resident of New Canaan, Connecticut, can tell you far more about the financial district than the average New Yorker.

In fact, unless we happen to work there—which means work for a large corporate law firm, a bank, an insurance company, a brokerage firm, or an investment house—the occasions for going to the financial district are rare. Not that it's an uninteresting part of town; quite the contrary. The problem is that, like D.C., the financial district is most interesting during those hours most of us are otherwise engaged.

Thus, it is not unheard of for us who have lived in the city most of our lives never to have been to the Wall Street area. More typically, however, the resident New Yorker does occasionally get down here, but so rarely that we can count the number of times.

For instance, we might have been to the financial district four or five times: once when we played hooky from school back in 1969 in order to attend a ticker-tape parade up Broadway for the Magical Mets who won the World Series that year; then again in the early 1970s to participate in an anti–Vietnam War demonstration (memorable because of violent clashes between demonstrators and hard hats from construction sites in the area); maybe once again, on a whim, to take a Sunday afternoon tour of "Historic Wall Street" led by some professor of urban studies at New York University; and then one time to practice riding our new ten-speed bike, since on weekends the financial district has the reputation for being an excellent place for biking around free of traffic.

Then, if we chose to, we could inflate the number of times we've been here by including trips to the outskirts of the financial district but not into its core—for example, when we took an out-of-town visitor for drinks at Windows on the World restaurant, on top of the World Trade Center, which is on the northwestern fringe of the financial district; or when we took the Staten Island Ferry from the southern fringe; or when we attended a free outdoor jazz concert on Pier 16 of the South Street Seaport Museum along the eastern fringe. All of these excursions are *officially* within the financial district, but not really. It's like saying you've been to Chicago, when you've actually only been to Chicago's O'Hare Airport.

To characterize the financial district as only a place to work may not be accurate in another five or ten years. Changes are in the wind. Some have already begun.

For one thing, the city's financial community, once located here and here only, has started to disperse to other parts of the city or out of New York altogether. Already numerous major Wall Street law firms have left for Park Avenue in the Forties and Fifties, giving rise to the phrase "Wall Street–*type* law firm." The American Stock Exchange seems constantly to be threatening to relocate to either New Jersey or Connecticut. Other firms already have.

Two projects could irrevocably alter the character of the financial district. One is an immense marketplace complex of shops and restaurants (as many as one hundred eating places) at the South Street Seaport; and the other is Battery Park City just to the west of the

World Trade Towers (whose excavation, incidentally, provided the landfill upon which Battery Park City is being built). The latter will include a Rockefeller Center–type complex of office buildings, stores, restaurants, and even a skating rink, three high-rise luxury apartment buildings (with nearly two thousand apartments), plus nine additional acres worth of housing to be built by six different developers (most of which will also be luxury housing).

The strategy to "revitalize" the financial district appears to be two-pronged. On the one hand, you attract tourists to the area by providing tourist attractions, such as places that make Belgian waffles or snow-cones, as opposed to what now exists, which are merely exquisite examples of nineteenth- and early-twentieth-century architecture. On the other hand, you attract residents by offering luxury housing close to work. This, of course, serves to encourage businesses to locate in the financial district and dissuade those already there from leaving.

When this influx of tourists and residents comes to pass—probably by the late 1980s—the financial district will no longer sleep at night and on weekends. We may also come to rue the fact that it doesn't and pine for these days when it still does.

## OF INTEREST

There is no way that you could possibly miss the World Trade Towers or the Stock Exchange or Federal Hall or the Customs House or any number of the other major, and large, attractions within the financial district. But you could quite easily miss the following sights, all of which are jewels, and not to see them would be your great loss:

**1) Mural at Peck Slip**    (at Front Street on the northern edge of the South Street Seaport area). Painted on the side of a monolithic brick structure belonging to the Consolidated Edison Company, the mural depicts, among other things, an arcade and what you would actually see through the arcade—the Brooklyn Bridge—if the building really did have one. The World Trade Towers will awe you; the Stock Exchange will confuse you. This mural will simply make you smile. It's among the city's most whimsical sights.

**2) Cocoa Exchange Building**    (127 John Street at Water Street). This is probably the city's best example of architecture as gimmickry. Entering the building is like entering the funhouse at an amusement park—mirrors, winding tunnel, neon lights, and so on. From the street you see pipes, heating ducts, and other mechanical apparatus exposed and painted à la Beaubourg Museum in Paris. Wall Streeters who can look down at the building from neighboring skyscrapers report that on the outside landing about six stories up, mosaic bird tracks encircle the building and lead to a mosaic depicting a bird's nest. If this building were located, say, in Midtown, it would be among the most controversial and talked-about structures in the city. As it is, relatively few of us even know it exists—proof of the fact that New Yorkers don't pay much attention to this part of town.

**3) Downtown Branch of the Whitney Museum of American Art**  (26 Wall Street at Nassau Street). The museum is located on the mezzanine floor of the Federal Hall National Memorial. The smallish crowds, and hence the quietude, are a welcome alternative to the large crowds and babble that you encounter at most of the uptown museums, including the uptown Whitney. Also, the downtown Whitney has noontime programs of music, dance, and film at least one day a week.

**4) Nevelson Plaza**  (Maiden Lane at William Street, just behind the Federal Reserve Building). Give us a few benches in the middle of the street so we can sit and watch the people and the traffic, and we're happy. Not only do we have that here, but this little pocket park is also graced with *seven* huge sculptures by Louise Nevelson.

**5)** Noontime cultural activities at **Trinity Church** and **St. Paul's Church**  (Broadway at Wall Street and Broadway at Fulton Street, respectively). You would think that the city's most community-minded and active churches would be located where there was a community. But instead, they are right smack in the middle of the financial district, where there is no resident community. Be that as it may, these two churches, aside from their architectural interest, offer almost daily noontime programs of music, talk, film, dance, and the like. Prayer too.

**6) Bowling Green Subway Station**  (on IRT Lexington Avenue line, at the bottom of Broadway near Battery Park). That's right, you are encouraged to visit a subway station. This one happens to be tiled, bright, well lit, and clean, which, of course, makes it an aberration within the New York City subway system. After seeing this station, the notion of what subways should look like is not left to the imagination, or to visiting Paris, Munich, Mexico City, or Moscow. The station's excellent lighting and solid orange background also provide optimal conditions—museumlike, really—for viewing the graffiti that covers the exterior of every subway car.

## EATING PLACES

There is no dearth of eating places in the financial district; inside the World Trade Center alone there must be twenty-five or thirty separate dining establishments. Yet it is not a part of town known for its great restaurants.

Generally, the restaurants fall into one of two categories: those that cater to the expense-account crowd and offer $20 lunches (mostly, these are restaurants that serve food of a quality comparable to hotel coffee shops but at room-service prices—believe it or not, $5.00 for half a cantaloupe, $10.00 for a chef's salad, $7.00 for a turkey-roll sandwich, and so forth); and the inexpensive but ordinary luncheonettes, coffee shops, sandwich shops, and fast-food places that cater to the non-expense-account crowd.

To be sure, this is not a part of the city where you go for ethnic food. The fare at the average restaurant here is about as ethnic as the staff of your average investment banking firm.

Not surprisingly then, you don't often hear us say we're going to Wall Street to eat. New Yorkers do go to **Windows on the World** restaurant atop the World Trade Center—at least for drinks—and you do hear New Yorkers talk about eating at **Sloppy Louie's** (92 South Street), a very unpretentious, austere seafood restaurant near the Fulton Fish Market (or what's left of the Fulton Fish Market, which is now mostly in the Bronx).

Most restaurants throughout the financial district are closed in the evening and on weekends. Every article ever written about the financial district, therefore, mentions the cafeteria inside the **Seamen's Church Institute** (15 State Street) across from Battery Park—open evenings and weekends and open to the public—as being a good place to eat should you discover all other restaurants closed.

# Civic Center

The Civic Center, like the financial district upon which it borders, is a part of the city we tend to ignore unless we actually work in the area.

Most of us couldn't tell you where the financial district ends and the Civic Center begins. To many, the Civic Center is simply where the courts are, somewhere down around Wall Street, though the courts are actually a good fifteen blocks north of Wall Street. The division line between the financial district and the Civic Center is where three-piece suits from Brooks Brothers all of a sudden turn into polyester slacks and sports jackets from Syms.

New Yorkers can sooner tell you where to find Hong Fat's Restaurant in Chinatown, upon which the Civic Center also borders, than we can direct you to City Hall. (To those of us with cars, the Civic Center is merely where we park when we go to Chinatown, since we can never park *in* Chinatown.) Probably not more than one in five New Yorkers even knows that the Municipal Building is *not* City Hall.

Most of us confuse the former with the latter, though City Hall is a hundred years older and twenty stories shorter than the Municipal Building and bears no resemblance to it whatsoever. City Hall looks like a French mansion; the Municipal Building resembles an exceedingly tall wedding cake. Confusing the one with the other would be like a Londoner mistaking the Tower of London for the Houses of Parliament. Not knowing where City Hall is also makes fighting it that much more difficult.

It would be one thing to ignore this section of the city if it were just a bunch of city, state, and federal buildings. But there's more. As one of the oldest parts of New York, the Civic Center is historically and architecturally one of the richest quarters.

Among its buildings are some of the city's first "skyscrapers." The Woolworth Building, for example, reigned as the world's tallest building for nearly two decades—from 1913 until 1930, when the skyscraper construction boom took Midtown by storm and gave us the Chrysler Building and the Empire State Building.

The commercial streets west of Broadway—west of the courts and the major concentrations of municipal buildings—contain perhaps as many good examples of cast-iron buildings as SoHo, though relatively few New Yorkers know the Civic Center area for this reason. These same streets, which tend to merge into TriBeCa, also contain many of the last vestiges of Manhattan's light manufacturing, warehousing, and produce industries; though here, as in neighboring TriBeCa and SoHo before that, these businesses are fast being displaced by their conversion to residential loft buildings. The galleries, cafés, tasteful but overpriced restaurants, gourmet food shops, and music clubs can't be far behind.

Unbeknownst to many New Yorkers, in and around the Civic Center is also one of the city's best, most lively shopping areas. Church Street and West Broadway and all the cross streets in between abound with bargain stores: bargain clothes, bargain books, bargain appliances, bargain food and spices.

The real novelty of the shopping area, however, is the dozens of places that sell electronic equipment and parts, hardware, tools, or any manner of other potentially useful junk. These stores have bins out front piled high with gadgets that appear to have come from dismantled TVs and computers, or boxes filled with just hand shovels, or pieces of plastic of various sizes, shapes, and hues, or rolls of Mylar, or rasp handles, or old army canteens, or gaskets from old refrigerators. (Such stores used to be standard fare all along Canal Street, until Canal Street began catering to the new residents of TriBeCa and SoHo—residents who buy oil paints before house paints.) Some places actually auction off their wares, and bargaining on price is often the rule; all in all, the atmosphere is bazaarlike. Very European; very crazy.

## OF INTEREST

**1) The Woolworth Building**   (233 Broadway at Barclay Street across from City Hall Park). Once it may have been the city's tallest building, but it still is New York's most elegant office building, even if its lower Broadway address is *déclassé*. Don't overlook the intricate stonework near the top of the Woolworth Building (best viewed from the Brooklyn Bridge) or the tilework inside the lobby.

**2) The Municipal Building**   (1 Centre Street at Chambers Street). Simply so that you'll know it's not City Hall.

**3) New York City Civil Court and Criminal Court**   (111 and 110 Centre Street, respectively). Though visitors to London routinely visit the Old Bailey to watch trials, tourists to New York City hardly ever think to visit our courts. You should. Not that you can't visit courts in your own city, but it's doubtful they would match ours for hysterics and histrionics.

Civil Court is anything but civil. It includes the Housing Court, where New York City tenants do battle with their landlords, as well as Small Claims Court, where consumers take on merchants and entrepreneurs. (Since it begins at around 6:30 P.M., Small Claims Court provides one of the few nighttime entertainment activities within the Civic Center.) Then, of course, there are arraignments or trials to observe in Criminal Court. What you'll discover, perhaps in a more graphic way than you would care to, is that all the unfortunate clichés about the beleaguered American criminal-justice system are true.

**4) Mashugana Ike's** (111 Chambers Street between Broadway and Church) and **Mr. Auction**  (90 Chambers, same block). Both these establishments more or less typify the slew of discount stores in the downtown Civic Center area. Mashugana Ike's (spawned in response to Crazy Eddie's) specializes in radios, TVs, stereos, and other electronic equipment. Mr. Auction, by contrast, specializes in nothing since it sells everything. The performance of Mr. Auction himself, who indeed does auction off the merchandise, is not to be missed. It's not to be believed either.

**5) McAuley Mission**  (90 Lafayette Street at White Street). Because you should be aware that just five blocks away from SoHo's Dean & Deluca's (one of New York's most overdone, overstated, overstocked, and overpriced gourmet food stores), some New Yorkers are lining up for the distribution of bed tickets so they'll have a place to sleep that night.

**6) White Street**  (between Broadway and Church). Perhaps the best example of the converting of commercial buildings to residential loft dwellings in the Civic Center neighborhood. These buildings on White Street also happen to be excellent examples of cast-iron architecture.

**7) The Brooklyn Bridge**  (entrance at Park Row). Whether or not you're interested in the financial district or Civic Center, the Brooklyn Bridge is reason enough to journey down to this section of the city. It's everyone's favorite bridge. Aside from its own elegance, it offers one of the most sensational views of lower Manhattan's skyline.

While you're admiring the Gothic arches upon which the bridge sits, you should know that after the completion of the bridge, it was discovered that inside the vaults formed by these arches, a constant year-round temperature of 65 degrees was maintained—the perfect temperature for storing wine. Therefore, for years wine sellers stored their wine under the bridge. Why that's no longer done is not clear.

If, as you gaze down from the bridge, you're wondering what that 2-mile-long string of red brick buildings along the East River is, it's almost all public housing. These projects extend from the Brooklyn Bridge, past the Manhattan and Williamsburg bridges, and right up to 14th Street. But more about that in the discussions of the Lower East Side and East Village.

## EATING PLACES

You don't encounter the expensive restaurants here that you do in the financial district. The difference is probably explained by the fact that bankers, lawyers, and insurance executives there eat on expense accounts; civil servants don't.

In any case, cheap eating places proliferate throughout the Civic Center—sandwich shops, coffee shops, luncheonettes, and delis mostly. One especially nice restaurant for a light, pleasant, inexpensive lunch is the **Wine & Cheese Restaurant** (153 Chambers Street) connected to, but above, the store Cheese of All Nations. Also, the **Delphi Restaurant** (109 West Broadway) is an extremely popular, extremely packed cheap Greek restaurant. Or if the possibility of seeing City Comptroller Harrison Goldin, or any number of other City Hall luminaries, excites you, you might want to eat at **Ellen's Cafe** (270 Broadway), a favorite eating place of New York City politicos.

Otherwise, quality eating establishments aren't in great demand in the area. Most workers here seem to spend their lunch hour shopping rather than eating anyway. Those more interested in food can go over to Chinatown. The Civic Center's proximity to Chinatown may indeed be the greatest inducement to work for the City of New York. It is no coincidence that mayors of New York have always adored Chinese food. In terms of major negotiating and decision making, the restaurants of Chinatown are to New York City government what the cloakrooms of Congress are to Washington.

# TriBeCa

If you want to know what SoHo was like ten or twelve years ago, visit TriBeCa. Just keep in mind that the comparison is to SoHo ten or twelve years ago—once it had already been "discovered" by the upper-middle class and by tourists—and not fifteen or twenty years ago when SoHo was still almost exclusively industrial and commercial; when the only residents were struggling artists living illegally in the commercial loft buildings either cheaply or for free; when the only visitors to SoHo were those who were lost. In this respect, TriBeCa has lost its virginity, so to speak, and quite a while ago.

But unlike present-day SoHo, where most traces of an industrial-commercial past have been obliterated, TriBeCa still claims a substantial number of manufacturers, warehouses, and produce wholesalers, all of whom coexist with the growing numbers of residential loft dwellers. Moreover, TriBeCa as compared to SoHo is a chic place to live, not super-chic; expensive rather than outrageously expensive; visited by tourists but not overwhelmed by them. Food and art have certainly made their presence known in TriBeCa, but they don't yet dominate the area as they do in SoHo. In other words, TriBeCa still belongs to the people who live and work there, while SoHo now seems defined, at least on weekends, more by aging couples from the suburbs who neither act nor dress their age.

No, TriBeCa has not yet been completely gussied up and homogenized. It still maintains a substantial mixed-use character in the uniquely urban sense of the term. Thus you can't automatically assume people live in every building, as you can in SoHo today. You really have to look for signs of residential life, or at least you do in the area of TriBeCa west of Hudson Street, which is still largely industrial and commercial.

Indeed, what makes TriBeCa still such a fun neighborhood to explore is that the residential lofts aren't all obvious to the street-level observer. Here you find people living in the most unlikely of places—say, in a building you would swear was completely devoted to coffee wholesaling and distribution. But then, up near the top of the "warehouse," you suddenly spy some sign of people residing within—a hanging plant, or flowers in a windowbox, or a bookcase, or a cat, or someone sitting out on the fire escape reading a book. Or you hear live jazz emanating from the third floor of a trucking firm. Or outside a huge metal fire door you observe twelve buzzers with names of occupants alongside.

You can still consider the residents who live in TriBeCa "urban pioneers," for they are living in a part of the city and in buildings where no one has ever lived before. You have the feeling that these are the sort of people who if they didn't live in a city, would live in the country—never in the suburbs. You don't necessarily have that same feeling about many present-day SoHo residents.

But the question is, How long will this last? Is it just a matter of time before all the spaces now devoted to cheese and egg distributors become art galleries? Frankly, at the rate at which co-op conversions seem to be taking place in TriBeCa, things do not augur well for the industrial-commercial community. Every time one visits TriBeCa, it seems another commercial building is being renovated for dwellings. And these include really massive buildings that will provide hundreds upon hundreds of apartments and lofts.

As a residential neighborhood, TriBeCa has already overgrown its original boundaries—the triangle formed by Canal Street, Hudson Street, and West Broadway (TriBeCa derives from the *Tri*angle *Be*low *Ca*nal). It has expanded eastward, westward, and southward, subsuming much of the area west of the Civic Center. The once small triangle of TriBeCa is becoming a rather large trapezoid. It could very well become an extension of SoHo. (*So*SoHo? *So*uth of *So*uth of *Ho*uston?)

Go see it before it does.

## OF INTEREST

**1) Duane Park**    (Duane Street just west of Hudson Street). Perhaps the best vantage point in TriBeCa from which to observe what TriBeCa was (food wholesaling establishments), what it is (commercial and residential tenants sharing the same building), and what it's becoming (expensive residential co-ops, such as the Duane Park Lofts—canopied entrance and all).

**2) No. 2 White Street**    (at the corner of West Broadway). Thought to be one of the oldest buildings in all the city still standing. About two hundred years old.

**3) No. 157 Hudson Street**    (just north of Hubert Street). The headquarters of the Nice Jewish Boy Moving & Storage Co., surely a company that could only be found in New York City.

**4) No. 135 Watts Street**    (between Greenwich and Washington Streets). Without doubt one of the loveliest old—built in 1891—commercial buildings in Manhattan. It looks as if it belongs in Amsterdam. Today it has apartments above and a new, trendy restaurant below.

**5) The Film Forum**    (just above TriBeCa at 57 Watts Street just west of Sixth Avenue). This movie theater located in what had been a truck garage is one of the longest surviving movie places in the city devoted to noncommercial, independently made film (that is, film made without major commercial or studio backing). As a center for serious film, it is well on its way to becoming to New York City what the Cinemathèque is to Paris.

Started in a second-floor apartment of a brownstone on the Upper West Side in 1970, the Film Forum moved to Greenwich Village in 1975 and to its present location in 1981. Its history is also the history of neighborhoods changing. In 1970, the Upper West Side was about the most logical section of the city in which to find an audience to support an alternative theater. (In 1970, TriBeCa as a residential neighborhood did not even exist.) In the 1980s, TriBeCa rather than the Upper West Side is the congenial location for such a movie house.

## EATING PLACES

A few years ago the major sources of food in the area were the food trucks that pulled up to the commercial buildings each morning and afternoon to dispense coffee, doughnuts, danish, and sandwiches. That has changed. Along with residents to TriBeCa have come restaurants. Along with fancy residents have come fancy restaurants. Thus, there is no shortage of eating places here, though restaurants and food-related stores don't yet seem to be quite the obsession here that they are in SoHo.

One of the best places to eat in TriBeCa is **Sheba Restaurant** (151 Hudson Street), which serves Ethiopian food at fairly moderate prices. And one of the most interesting places to eat is the **Square Diner** (33 Leonard Street at West Broadway). For one thing, it's your classic American diner, and there are but a few of those, as opposed to coffee shops or luncheonettes, in Manhattan. The food is not bad as far as diner food goes, and the menu has been enhanced by a Greek-Spanish influence.

But what makes the Square Diner particularly interesting is that it serves as a barometer by which to measure change within the neighborhood. As long as the Square Diner continues to offer dishes like rice pudding, Jell-O, bacon and eggs, or egg creams, you can assume TriBeCa is still in the state of transition from industrial-commercial to

residential. Once the diner becomes a fine restaurant that offers spinach salad, quiche, wine, or nouvelle French cooking (when it becomes what the Empire Diner in Chelsea is), you'll know TriBeCa is
no longer in transition. It will have occurred.

## Chinatown

For out-of-town visitors, Chinatown is a place for looking around
and eating. For us New Yorkers, who have already looked around
Chinatown dozens of times, it is a place to eat only. When we say
that we know Chinatown well, what we mean to say is that we know
of several excellent restaurants there.

It's hard not to view Chinatown as a tourist attraction only. This
impression is probably what prompted one out-of-towner, as she attempted to sidle through the throngs of visitors along Mott Street,
Chinatown's main thoroughfare, to say, "They should have made
Chinatown bigger," as if it was created in the manner of Disneyland
precisely as a tourist attraction.

Actually, "they" did make Chinatown bigger. Until fairly recently,
Chinatown's northern boundary was Canal Street, its eastern boundary the entrance to the Manhattan Bridge. But the Chinese community has since grown and flowed over Canal Street into Little Italy, and
past the Manhattan Bridge into what used to be the Jewish Lower
East Side. Still, the center of Chinatown—where the restaurants and
hence the tourists are concentrated—remains on and around Mott
Street. So, although Chinatown has indeed grown, the growth
doesn't make Chinatown any less crowded for the tourists. They still
have to sidle through the Mott Street throngs.

In truth, Chinatown does have a life of its own apart from tourism;
it only appears not to. Well over 100,000 Chinese reside in Chinatown, which is equal to the number of Chinese living in all other
parts of the city. (Outside of Chinatown, most Chinese in New York
live in Queens.) But aside from observing them shopping for food
or placing bets at OTB (Off-Track Betting), you're not really likely
ever to be privy to much else that goes on within the Chinatown
community, above and behind the restaurants.

The 100,000 Chinese of Chinatown are able to go about their business more quietly and, if need be, more surreptitiously than any other
community of 100,000 people on earth. We can go to Chinatown fif-

ty times and never see even one of the five hundred garment shops—mostly nonunionized sweatshops—that apparently operate there. Apparently, because we only read about them.

There are reportedly scores of illegal gambling parlors located throughout Chinatown, but again, we never see them. Nor do we ever see any evidence of the Chinese youth gangs that operate as a kind of Chinese Mafia, extorting "protection" money from merchants and other businessmen. We know they exist because from time to time we read about "gangland style" executions in Chinatown.

Rather than try to find the "real Chinatown," which you never will, accept it for the tourist attraction that it is, and be comforted by the knowledge that as far as tourist attractions go, it's one of the best. We who otherwise scrupulously follow the dictum that one doesn't go where tourists do, nevertheless go to Chinatown all the time.

We can rationalize coming to a touristy part of the city by confining our visits to that part of Chinatown that relatively few tourists frequent. That is, we get away from Mott Street and venture into Chinatown east of the Bowery. And then we also seek out restaurants where no tourists go; or, better yet, where the clientele is almost all Chinese.

Moreover, even though Chinatown is one of the city's leading tourist attractions, we go there because, unlike other tourist traps, Chinatown's restaurants still maintain a very high quality at not very high prices. Chinatown is truly the place where you get the best Chinese food in the city. We go to neighborhood Chinese restaurants for convenience. We come to Chinatown for the real thing. Its food is the standard by which to judge *all* Chinese food.

## OF INTEREST

**1) Chinatown east of Bowery** (East Broadway, Catherine Street, Henry Street, Madison Street, and so forth). Though this part of Chinatown isn't exactly free of tourists, it certainly is freer of them than the other side of Bowery around Mott Street. Here, at least, stores, markets, and restaurants do cater to a primarily Chinese clientele. Here, particularly during the mornings and afternoons of a weekday, you do get some idea of what Chinatown would be like without tourists.

If you travel east along East Broadway, you see businesses other than those related to food—printing firms, construction companies, real-estate offices, insurance firms, and the like. You see Chinese businesses alongside Jewish and Hispanic enterprises, and signs outside them all are often written in three languages.

Catherine Street, considered the best shopping street in Chinatown, is where you see markets that have assorted animals in the windows—dead and alive—including pigs and turtles, as well as vegetables you have never seen before. When you ask where they come from, you're told they come from New Jersey, as does much of the city's produce. But somehow, they look far more exotic than that.

**2) Off-Track Betting Office**    (7–8 Chatham Square). This OTB office is interesting because it is here that you can observe scores of eighty-year-old Chinese men who have not assimilated to American life one bit except to bet on horses. You can bet (not at OTB however) that they don't read English, yet somehow they do read the *Racing Form*. Incidentally, this small OTB outlet is said to take in more money daily than the OTB located at Penn Station.

**3) Lack of Graffiti**    Chinatown's most interesting nonsight. MTA (Metropolitan Transportation Authority) officials should talk to some Chinatown leaders.

## EATING PLACES

There are some 350 restaurants in Chinatown. For an area that plays to an essentially captive tourist market, the number of excellent— even superb—Chinese restaurants is unusually high. Therefore, it wouldn't be totally unthinkable to pick a restaurant at random. It would, however, be a bit ill-advised, and you would probably do a lot better to follow some guidelines, or better yet, have those who know whereof they speak recommend specific places.

As for some guidelines, we tend to avoid those Chinatown restaurants where: people are waiting on the sidewalk to get in; signs in the window say "Cocktails"; signs in the window say "Tour Groups Welcome"; colored photographs or wax or plastic mock-ups outside show the food served inside; or the menu includes dishes called such things as "Mongolian Beef" or "Shanghai Special." Another clue: Though elsewhere around the city a newspaper review posted in the window means the restaurant has been discovered and thus ruined, that does not apply to Chinatown. There is no Chinatown restaurant that has not been reviewed a hundred times. All Chinatown restaurants have been discovered; many survive that fate.

Given a choice between a small restaurant and a large one, we'll opt for the small. If we have to choose between a place you walk down into and one you walk up to, we'll usually wind up walking down. And finally, we never enter a restaurant before applying what we consider to be the acid test. How many Chinese patrons are there inside? Under no circumstances would we eat where no Chinese eat. A clientele that is half Chinese and half not is considered optimal. The bravest among us will sometimes eat where the clientele is 100 percent Chinese. Which requires that when you order, you *point* to what other people are eating.

Though the following restaurants don't by any means represent a definitive listing, they are among the restaurants that New Yorkers who often go to Chinatown eat at and recommend to others: the restaurant at **No. 3 Doyers Street**, which specializes in noodle dishes and has no name outside; **Foo Joy** (13 Division Street), because aside from being excellent, it's the only Fukienese Chinese restaurant in New York (cuisine of Fukien Province, which accounts for the numerous fish dishes, since Fukien is a coastal province, as well as for the many braised meat and fish preparations); **Gim Beck** (70 Mott Street), because even though it is on touristy Mott Street, it's so small tourists overlook it anyway, and since lots of cops from the 5th Precinct eat there, it must be good; **Hong Fat** (63 Mott Street), even though it too is on Mott and even though people do line up outside, because it is still considered a Chinatown institution; **Hwa Yuan Szechuan** (40 East Broadway); **Phoenix Gardens** (inside the mall entered at 46 Bowery), since it is so hard to find and since Mayor Koch used to eat there regularly; and **Yun Luck Rice Shoppe** (17 Doyers Street) because *The New York Times* food experts swear by it.

## Little Italy

Little Italy is the center of New York's Italian community only in the minds of those people who write tourist guides and fail to update them—the same people who still refer to Greenwich Village as a bohemian quarter, which of course it hasn't been for about twenty years.

Little Italy may still be the symbolic center of the city's Italian community, but as far as being an actual population center, it definitely is not anymore. By 1970 the Italian population of Little Italy had already dwindled from about 150,000 to only about 5,000. By now there can't be more than 2,000 or 3,000 Italians who live there. Its southern portions near Canal Street are now occupied by substantially more Chinese than Italians, its northern part near Houston Street by more Hispanics than Italians, and its core (Mott and Mulberry Streets between Broome and Hester) by more tourists than Italians.

The tip-off that few Italian residents remain here is the fact that Italian restaurants abound. This may seem paradoxical, but you'll see that it's not. If you were to visit any of the city's larger, more authentic Italian neighborhoods (more authentic in the sense that residents rather than tourists make them viable)—Carroll Gardens, Coney Island, Bensonhurst, or Bay Ridge in Brooklyn, Astoria or Ozone Park in Queens, or Belmont or Tremont in the Bronx—you would see that there are relatively few Italian restaurants. There are loads of pizza parlors, bakeries, and other Italian food-related shops, but in terms of actual, sit-down restaurants, there are few. Which makes eminent sense, for the attitude of first-generation Italians is "I can make better Italian food myself."

If you don't accept this theory as proof that Little Italy has lost its Italian residential community—lost its Italian soul—there is additional evidence. When the film director Martin Scorsese made his film *Mean Streets*, which is about Little Italy, he didn't film it in Little Italy at all, but in the Belmont section of the Bronx. Ditto for *The Godfather*.

## OF INTEREST

**1) Old Police Headquarters Building**    (240 Centre Street between Grand and Broome). This beautiful landmark building, modeled after London's Old Bailey, was at last report slated to be converted into a luxury hotel. If and when this comes to pass, it will be only the second major hotel to be built in Manhattan below Canal Street in about 150 years. The first was the hotel at the World Trade Center, and that was only recently built. Which tells you how this part of town has blossomed as a tourist center—primarily due to the emergence of SoHo as a tourist hot spot in the last five years or so, rather than Little Italy or Chinatown, which have been favorite tourist centers for years and years.

Also, the fact that the plan to make this building into a hotel won out over the competing proposal by community groups to convert it into an Italian Cultural Center may be an indication that Little Italy's days as even the symbolic center of New York's Italian community are numbered.

**2) Handgun Center**   (behind the old police headquarters). Though everyone knows about the city's garment district, diamond center, theater district, flower district, publishers row, and so on, few New Yorkers know about the handgun district. But here it is, logically situated where the police headquarters used to be. The street is lined with small shops that sell guns—including custom-made models—bulletproof vests, ammunition, knives, and other such things. The question is, what becomes of the handgun center once the old police headquarters becomes a posh hotel?

**3) PS (Public School) 130**   (143 Baxter Street between Hester and Grand). Though this school is located in the heart of Little Italy, you'll nevertheless notice in the school's playground that all the students are Chinese. You can conclude one of two things: either Little Italy has, indeed, become Little Chinatown, or else all Italian kids really do go to parochial school.

## EATING PLACES

The Italian restaurants of Little Italy, as a group, are very good, but not great. Little Italy does not set the standard for Italian food in the city as Chinatown does for Chinese food. Many neighborhood Italian restaurants are on a par with, or even better than, ones in Little Italy. On the whole, the Italian restaurants in Coney Island, for example, are probably as good as those of Little Italy. (Yet few New Yorkers other than Brooklynites patronize Coney Island's restaurants; no one from out-of-town does.)

New Yorkers who eat in Little Italy seem to be typically from Queens and in their early twenties. One surmises this from the preponderance of Queens accents and college T-shirts one observes among the people waiting on line to get into places like **Puglia** (185 Hester Street) or **Luna's** (112 Mulberry Street)—considered two of the best, most reasonably priced, and most lively restaurants in Little Italy.

**Umberto's Clam House** (129 Mulberry) should be mentioned for both its culinary and historical importance—historical in that this is where Joey Gallo of Mafia fame was gunned down, and the restaurant about which Bob Dylan sings in his song titled "Joey."

Incidentally, **D&G Bakery** (45 Spring Street) sells the best Italian bread, bar none, in all of New York.

## Lower East Side

Once a predominantly Jewish quarter, the Lower East Side today is far more Hispanic and Chinese than it is Jewish. The number of Hispanics (mostly Puerto Ricans and Dominicans) and Chinese (mostly from Hong Kong)—maybe even blacks as well—living in the tenements and low-income housing projects that characterize the area far exceed the number of Jews who still live here (most of whom live in middle-income housing).

In the Essex Street Retail Market, there are now as many concessions selling sugar cane, platanos, or bacalao as those selling marzipan, corned beef, or lox. Along Grand and Delancey Streets, Chinese restaurants and Puerto Rican restaurants surround the Jewish delis. On Henry Street, Jewish synagogues have been joined by Hispanic *synogogas* and *iglesias*, a Buddhist center or two, and a black Baptist church. Nowadays cockfighting—illegal though it is—is a major after-hours form of entertainment on the Lower East Side. Cockfighting is not a very Jewish pastime.

Yet, as far as everyone is concerned—that is, everyone but the people who actually live here—the Lower East Side still means the Jewish Lower East Side. When New Yorkers say "We're going down to the Lower East Side" (we say "down" even if the actual direction is up, as it would be if we were coming from, say, downtown Brooklyn), we mean the part which, because of the hundreds of Jewish stores and scores of Jewish restaurants that remain, retains an essentially Jewish character. This is the area that, for the most part, lies between Houston and Delancey west of, and including, Essex Street. Or more simply defined, Orchard Street and vicinity.

Lower East Side still means Jewish Lower East Side, and shopping and eating are still the two activities that draw us here. There is certainly no dearth of things to buy at Bloomingdale's, but not at the bargain-basement prices you find on the Lower East Side. Everyone loves a bargain, which explains why you'll see shoppers who come down here in their Mercedeses and Cadillac Sevilles to hunt through the stores along Orchard Street (for clothing) or on Eldridge (for fabrics and textiles) or along Grand (for drapes, towels, linen, and other dry goods) or on the Bowery (for lamps and lighting fixtures).

We can buy things at discount prices here because stores have reduced their overhead by eliminating interior design (and by taking designer labels out of designer clothes), unless you consider stacks of cardboard boxes and floor-to-ceiling rows of shelving to be interior decorating. Actually, most merchandise is displayed on the street—on racks and in bins. And true to the Middle Eastern–bazaar atmosphere that exists down here, bargaining on price is not only permitted, it is expected. Which is another thing that you just can't do at Bloomingdale's.

Similarly, though we can get Jewish-style food all over the city, too often it lacks a real Jewish *tam* (loosely defined as taste, or what's missing whenever chicken soup with matzoh balls is made by anyone other than a Jewish grandmother). So we come down to the Lower East Side for the real thing.

Former New York City dwellers who now reside in the suburbs may no longer be hooked on the city, but they remain hooked on Jewish food. Thus, they come here for their periodic "fix." They come down from Scarsdale to have a combination corned beef, tongue, and pastrami sandwich on rye with a Dr. Brown's Celray Tonic; or to have lox and eggs or a vegetarian "cutlet" made of protose at a dairy restaurant; or just to have a knish or load up on pickles, whitefish, nuts, halvah, and extremely dark pumpernickel, which one can find at any number of the Jewish appetizing stores that are located throughout the Lower East Side.

And then, besides coming here ourselves to eat or shop, we love to take out-of-town guests to the Lower East Side. We particularly like to take visitors from places like Tennessee who have never met a Jew, who believe all Jews live in New York City, and that everyone here is Jewish.

They come down here to the Lower East Side and get yelled at by a Jewish merchant on Orchard Street for "just looking"; or barked at by a Jewish counterman in a deli for not speaking up; or treated by a Jewish waiter as if he were their Jewish mother, telling them to order brisket of beef, *not* chopped liver, and then chastising them for not eating everything on their plate.

They go back to Nashville and tell everyone that New York is just what they thought it would be. In other words, they go home to

Nashville satisfied because we've shown them the New York they wanted to see—exotic, Jewish New York.

The Lower East Side has never experienced the typical cycles of most New York City neighborhoods, which have tended to go from good to bad to good to bad and so on. It was always—and still is—a neighborhood of poor housing and poor people—once poor Jews, now poor Hispanics, Chinese, and blacks.

And the way things look, it will remain a poor neighborhood—albeit a tourist attraction and a family one at that. This is another way of saying the Lower East Side is not being gentrified as is every other Manhattan neighborhood south of 96th Street. You see a few fancy loft dwellings on East Broadway or even on the Bowery, but very few. For the most part, the gentry would not consider living here; certainly not before Dean & Deluca's (the SoHo gourmet food shop) opened a branch.

The absence of gentrification is a mixed blessing. On one hand, tenements remain. On the other hand, there is no immediate threat of Orchard Street—a street which resembles a bustling outdoor bazaar—becoming an enclosed mall of genteel boutiques. New York without Orchard Street? Impossible! Well, that's what they said about Ebbets Field and the Polo Grounds too.

## OF INTEREST

**1) Orchard Street.**   Sunday is its busiest day, and thus, is considered the best time to see Orchard Street. But you should also see it during the week (most stores are closed on Saturday, the Jewish Sabbath) when you'll get a completely different look and feel for the place. Without the crowds, you'll have a better chance to actually see the stores, go inside, even get service. Without the hordes of visitors and shoppers, you're also more likely to be aware of a life that goes on above the stores—a life in tenements for poor Chinese and Hispanics.

**2) Urban Garden**   (on Eldridge Street at Stanton, just down and around from Yonah Schimmel's). Here in the midst of urban rubble sits a quite extraordinary garden. If you're the sort of person who notices flowers growing in the cracks of sidewalks or appreciates prison art and literature, you'll like this garden. It bespeaks a certain urban spirit and optimism.

**3) Schapiro's Kosher Wines**    (124 Rivington Street). This is not just a wine store; it's a winery too—the only one in New York City and the only place in the city where you can buy wine on Sunday. For that reason alone, Schapiro's is a good place to know—for all the times you have dinner parties to attend on Sunday but forgot to buy the wine the day before.

**4) Seward Park High School**    (350 Grand Street). This is where the actors Walter Matthau and Bernie Schwartz (who grew up to be Tony Curtis) went to high school. Students here no longer have names like Matthau and Schwartz, since no Jews attend Seward Park these days—rather, blacks, Chinese, and Hispanics do.

If you've never seen a New York City public high school, you should know that Seward Park is a typical-looking one. Where's the football field? What "field" there is consists of the fenced-in area you'll observe on the roof of the building.

**5) Public Housing Projects**    (between the Brooklyn and Williamsburg bridges). About two miles worth of public housing projects fill the space between these two bridges (actually the projects extend beyond the Williamsburg Bridge right up to 14th Street). And they say no poor people live in Manhattan anymore.

Though these low-income projects are among the first ones built in the city—during the late 1940s and early 1950s—they still remain the model. Like all public housing in New York City, they are built of red brick, have yellow shades on the windows, and are totally devoid of air-conditioners. The combination of these three traits is how you distinguish public housing from all other types of housing in the city.

## EATING PLACES

Though you can do almost no wrong in choosing eating places on the Lower East Side—that's how good they generally are—what follows are eating and food establishments New Yorkers seek out time and time again.

For the sheer quality of its food, **Bernstein-on-Essex Street** delicatessen (135 Essex Street) rates very high. (The deli menu, that is, *not* its Kosher Chinese food.) *New York* magazine says its pastrami is the best in the city. **Katz's** (205 East Houston Street) can't compare with Bernstein's for quality, but it can for atmosphere. Katz's is where the caricature of the Jewish deli counterman was invented: one part gruffness, one part Jewish mother, and one part wise-guy.

Among dairy restaurants,* **The Grand Dairy Restaurant** (341 Grand Street) and **Ratner's** (138 Delancey Street) are analogous to Bernstein's and Katz's—the Grand for sheer quality and Ratner's for sheer atmosphere.

For a more expensive, less boisterous place, **Sammy's Roumanian Restaurant** (157 Chrystie Street) is recommended. (It's really Roumanian-Jewish cooking.) The waiters are sure to give your out-of-town guests something to talk about back home. The seltzer in siphon bottles too.

**Russ & Daughters** (179 East Houston Street) is one of the Lower East Side's best appetizing stores; **Kossar's Bakery** (367 Grand Street) has no competition as far as bialies are concerned (consider them onion rolls, but that really doesn't do bialies justice); and any place that specializes in pickles as does **Hollander Pickle Products** (35 Essex Street) certainly warrants a visit.

Finally, the place that alone justifies a trip to the Lower East Side (which is probably why you always see cabs pulling up in front) is **Yonah Schimmel's** (137 East Houston at Forsythe Street). Its specialty, of course, is knishes—potato, kasha (buckwheat groats), and cheese—but you can also get cheese bagels, homemade yogurt, borsht, *muhn kichel* (call them poppyseed cookies), potatoniks (call them potato pudding), and wonderful, wonderful strudel—cheese, apple, poppyseed, and more.

Perhaps other places can match Yonah Schimmel's knishes (many knish *mavens*, for instance, say Mrs. Stahl's in Brighton Beach in Brooklyn has the best knishes in the city), but no other place can match its ambience. Except for the microwave oven that recently

---

*Dairy restaurants serve no meat dishes. Dairy restaurants, however, bear little resemblance to vegetarian restaurants in general, for dairy restaurants are specifically Jewish vegetarian restaurants. Typical dairy restaurant fare includes: "roasts" and "cutlets" made of protose; fish dishes such as gefilte fish and boiled carp; egg dishes like onion, lox, and green-pepper omelets; kasha varnishkas (buckwheat groats and bowtie noodles) and noodles with pot cheese; hearty soups (mushroom barley, yellow split pea, etc.); assorted breads (always including Russian pumpernickel); various sour-cream dishes such as blintzes with sour cream, potato pancakes with sour cream, herring with sour cream, boiled potatoes with sour cream, pirogen with sour cream, etc.; and assorted desserts like prune danish, pound cake, noodle pudding, rice pudding, baked apples, stewed prunes with sweet cream, strudel, and cheesecake.

supplanted the oven downstairs—and in the process made using the dumbwaiter obsolete—Yonah Schimmel's probably looks much as it did when it first opened more then seventy years ago.

## SoHo: *Canal Street*

SoHo is a major tourist attraction pretending to be just a quiet residential neighborhood. It's true that a lot of New Yorkers do live here; but it's also true that residents alone cannot sustain art galleries, gourmet food stores, nouvelle French restaurants, cafés, and clothing boutiques that specialize in such things as alligator pants and feather ties. And if there is any doubt that SoHo caters to tourists, all you have to do is count the number of cars with Jersey plates down here each weekend. (Tourists, as distinguished from residents, are the ones wearing the aforementioned alligator pants and feather ties.)

As for those New Yorkers who do reside here, contrary to popular belief, they are *not* mostly artists. Fifteen years ago, or even ten years ago, they were. That was when the commercial loft buildings were still occupied mostly by light manufacturing, warehousing, packing, and other businesses; and in each building some few artists lived cheaply (and illegally since living in these commercial buildings was then forbidden) while being able to work in spacious surroundings.

This is hardly characteristic of SoHo today. Most of the commercial enterprises have since either moved to the less expensive suburbs or gone out of business altogether. Buildings once filled with commercial lofts now contain almost exclusively residential lofts (which are now legal). Many are fancy enough to have doormen, and not only are rents no longer cheap, renting itself has almost become an anachronism. One no longer rents a loft in SoHo; one now purchases it, and in SoHo a loft can easily cost $200,000 or more, on top of which one must pay a $1,500 or more monthly maintenance fee.

This is all to say that few artists can afford to live here anymore. About the only artist who could is Andy Warhol, and he doesn't. Scores of artists have left SoHo to live in inexpensive lofts in other parts of the city, like in Brooklyn in the area *D*own *U*nder the *M*anhattan *B*ridge *O*verpass, otherwise known as DUMBO.

Though precious few artists remain in SoHo, loads of galleries do, and it is probably the prevalence of these galleries that prompts people to still think of SoHo as an artists' quarter. But that's like thinking of Madison Avenue in the Sixties and Seventies as an artists' quarter just because of the plethora of galleries there. Madison Avenue is certainly not where artists live, nor is SoHo.

The more typical resident is the person recently described in a *New York Times* article upon his appointment to a high government position: registered Republican, graduate of Yale College and Columbia Law School, highly successful Manhattan lawyer specializing in commercial litigation. Impeccable credentials, to be sure, but not for an artist. The article concludes by saying, "Mr. C., who is divorced, moved from Manhattan's Upper East Side to SoHo, where he enjoys cooking for guests in his spacious loft."

SoHo implies a life-style that is more youthful, more arty, more exciting, more with-it, more what's-happening, more high-stylish, more tasteful, which explains its allure. It also explains why when someone mentions a SoHo loft, SoHo crowd, SoHo restaurant, SoHo anything, he is not only indicating its location—*So*uth of *Ho*uston (pronounced "Howston," not "Hyooston")—but also describing it as being implicitly youthful, arty, exciting, with-it, and so forth.

The chances are you'll either love SoHo or hate it. Few people react to SoHo neutrally. How you do react may depend upon how you perceive SoHo's evolution from a primarily commercial and artists' neighborhood to an area predominantly for upper-income professionals and tourists. In other words, did the conversion to residential lofts force out the commercial tenants and artists? Or did the conversion save an area businesses and artists would have left anyway, thus preventing empty, abandoned buildings from taking over this part of town?

In any case, SoHo is an important part of the city to see and understand, for every city has a SoHo. Every city has former commercial and industrial areas that have been gentrified. SoHo may be an example of gentrification in heavier doses than you're likely to see elsewhere—you may even decide it's an example of gentrification gone amok—but it will be extremely instructive for you to see, nevertheless.

## OF INTEREST

**1) Dean & Deluca's**    (121 Prince Street). This is the gourmet food store that seems quintessentially SoHo. If you like Dean & Deluca's, you'll love SoHo. If not, you'll hate it. Here you'll find more gourmet food more tastefully displayed—and more expensively priced—than just about anywhere else in the city. By surpassing almost all other gourmet food stores (it makes Balducci's in the Village seem like a mom-and-pop grocery), Dean & Deluca's epitomizes the urban good life associated with living in this part of town.

**2) Children's Energy Center**   (174 Prince Street). Anywhere else this would be called a day-care center, which it is. In SoHo it's called an energy center. This, of course, reflects a certain attitude one finds here, a certain reluctance to call a spade a spade. What else could account for SoHo restaurants referring to lox as "saline smoked salmon"?

**3) Mural at No. 141 Prince Street**   (Greene Street side of building). On what would otherwise be a blank wall is the painted façade of an apartment building—windows, air-conditioners, a cat in a window. It was done by the same person who painted the mural at Peck Slip in the South Street Seaport area. This is one of the few examples of SoHo not taking itself seriously. It's also one of the few examples of genuine street art here.

**4) Urban Archaeology**   (137 Spring Street). A unique store. Basically, it collects and sells items salvaged from the exterior and interior of old city buildings—gargoyles, lintels, cornices, balustrades, fireplace mantels, doorknobs, and so forth.

**5) Canal Street.**   Though not really SoHo, Canal is located just below SoHo. Also, SoHo has obviously had its influence on Canal Street. Stores once characterized by selling whatever "junk" they would get from close-out sales have now spruced up a bit, and rather than sell just random items, they consciously stock what might appeal to the SoHo gentry. In other words, now the stores will sell refrigerators, not just the parts to refrigerators.

**6) Cast-Iron Buildings**   (throughout SoHo but especially on Greene Street, West Broadway, and Broadway). What with all the vintage-clothing boutiques, galleries, restaurants, and cafés, it's easy to forget that SoHo is first and foremost a historic, cast-iron district. As hard as it may be to imagine, there was a time when people came down to SoHo solely to see the cast-iron buildings. They're quite beautiful, and under no circumstance should you miss them.

# EATING PLACES

There are loads of eating places in SoHo. Most of them have come into existence in the past few years, so it's hard to talk about old, reliable standbys.

As a group, SoHo restaurants tend to be expensive, to specialize in brunches, and to have a huge number of desserts made with whiskey or some other alcoholic beverage. Beyond the compulsory hanging or potted plants, restaurants all seem to have a gimmick which, of course, never has anything to do with the quality of the food: chamber music in one, a catwalk balcony in another, wood-burning stove in another, and the like.

How good are they? Well, when the *Times* recently reviewed a dozen SoHo restaurants, on a zero-to-four-star scale, it gave two stars to two places (The Elephant & Castle on Prince Street and The SoHo Charcuterie on Spring Street). None received more than two stars.

Should you tire of "salmon sausage over seaweed" or "roast quail with chestnut mousse"; or want cheese in your omelet rather than caviar or plain French toast rather than brioche French toast; or should you want a 40¢ cup of coffee rather than a $1.00 cup, remember that **Dayton's Cafeteria** (454 Broadway) and **Dave's Luncheonette** (71 Canal Street) are nearby.

# 16 The Villages

## Greenwich Village: *West Village*

To say that the Village (called Greenwich Village only by those who don't know any better) is a bohemian quarter—mecca to writers, artists, poets, and intellectuals—is about as accurate a statement as saying that Berkeley, California, is a center of student radicalism. Berkeley may have been such a place. Similarly, the Village *was* a bohemian sector, but hasn't been since two tiny rooms "that need work"—if you can even find them—started renting for $800 a month.*

Nowadays systems analysts, lawyers, editors (not writers), various and sundry other professionals, and NYU students from upper-income families live in the Village. Would-be writers, artists, poets, and intellectuals only wait on tables in the Village. They live elsewhere— in the East Village all the way over between Avenues A and D; or in parts of the Upper West Side where there are still apartments large enough for five people to share; or in still relatively inexpensive neighborhoods in South Brooklyn, such as Boerum Hill, the south end of Park Slope, or underneath the Manhattan Bridge.

This is not to say the Village has become the Upper East Side. The Village still enjoys the mystique of having been a bohemian quarter, even if it no longer is. To many, that mystique is even more palpable

---

*News of this obviously has not traveled to West Springfield, Massachusetts, where a high school class recently proposed a trip to Greenwich Village to "observe people who live outside the norm free from harassment." The West Springfield School Board quickly nixed the idea. Unanimously.

than the reality of what the Village now is. Thus, writers from out-of-state who come to New York with a half-finished novel or play still head immediately for the Village to look for a place to live, though ultimately they might wind up living in a studio apartment in Woodside, Queens.

That mystique gets perpetuated by the continued existence, even proliferation, of cafés, bars (straight and gay), art-movie houses, Off and Off-Off Broadway theaters, bookstores that specialize in homosexual or lesbian literature, unique clothing boutiques, jazz clubs, and more vegetarian restaurants than anyone could begin to count. Also, every unemployed eccentric who lives within 30 miles of the Village is still attracted to it, thus assuring that its street life, if not its residential community, remains as lively and as colorful as ever.

And though today's Village residents don't exactly enhance the bohemian mystique, they don't completely destroy it either. Though far more bourgeois than bohemian, Villagers at least distinguish themselves from residents of other neighborhoods by never voting for Republicans and by not being afraid to live in buildings without doormen.

The Village manages to be more things to more people than any other neighborhood in the city. That half its residents live there because it's quiet and half because it's so lively is just one indication of the kind of multiple appeal the Village has.

It is far and away the city's most popular neighborhood. The Village enjoys the kind of attraction that Berkeley, the North Beach section of San Francisco, Cambridge, Massachusetts, and the Left Bank of Paris do, only multiplied at least threefold. It is a favored area in which to live, hang out, eat out, stroll, see movies, go to plays, listen to live music, browse in bookstores, sit in cafés, go to school, and shop for food and clothes. And that one can do all these things in a single neighborhood makes the Village New York's most self-contained—and hence most convenient—neighborhood. Its residents never have to leave except to go to work. Village residents consider 14th Street uptown.

Its low buildings, narrow streets, and small stores make the Village feel like one of the city's most livable neighborhoods, even if in actuality it might not be. The Village stays up later than almost every other part of New York, and has the grace and decency to sleep later too.

The Village is also relatively safe, which certainly enhances its popularity. It is one of the few parts of the city where parents allow their teenaged daughters to go unaccompanied at night.

The only New Yorkers who seem not to like the Village are those of us who characterize it as a scene, or more accurately, as scenes. There is nothing subtle about the Village. Whatever it has it has a lot of. There are not just a few cafés, but scores of them. Other neighborhoods have a few charming little restaurants; the Village has dozens of them. The Village doesn't just have a sizable gay population, but a mammoth gay community. There are not merely several historic buildings; rather, the entire Village has been designated a historic district.

What in another neighborhood would amount to a quiet diversion, in the Village is elevated to the status of being a very identifiable, very fashionable scene that attracts hundreds to it. There is, therefore, the café scene, the charming-little-Village-restaurant scene, the gay scene, and the historic-Village-walking-tour scene. Washington Square Park is a scene itself. Even the quiet residential West Village manages to be a quiet-residential-West-Village scene. New Yorkers who don't like such scenes live in Murray Hill or in the outer boroughs.

## OF INTEREST

**1)** The few stores on **West 8th Street** (between Fifth and Sixth Avenues) that are not shoe stores. It is generally agreed that West 8th is the Village's most commercial, most tawdry strip. Though it has been that way for years now, it recently has been commercialized in a peculiar direction: It now proliferates with shoe stores. The genesis of this trend is not clear, but the results are. There must be at least twenty shoe stores on this one block.

One bright note on West 8th has been the recent conversion of Nathan's fast-food deli on the corner of West 8th and Sixth Avenue into a B. Dalton bookstore. This is perhaps the only example in the Village—maybe in the entire city—of a fast-food place becoming a bookstore and not vice versa.

**2) West 4th Street Playground** (Sixth Avenue at West 4th Street). For years now blacks from all over the city have been coming here to play basketball. The games go on all day long (including tournaments during summer evenings), and the play really is quintessential

New York City–style basketball—high skill, lots of scoring, loads of dunking, little passing, and much arguing.

**3) 18 West 11th Street** (between Fifth and Sixth Avenues). You'll have no trouble spotting this town house, since it is the only one on the block with a modern façade. Some of us know it for that reason. Others know it as the house built on the site of the town house used as a Weathermen's "bomb factory," which was destroyed in a 1969 explosion. Some New Yorkers probably also know it as the house next to the one where Dustin Hoffman used to live. He has since moved to the San Remo on Central Park West.

**4) Balducci's** (424 Sixth Avenue at 9th Street). This gourmet food store is to the Village what Dean & Deluca's is to SoHo and Zabar's is to the Upper West Side. A visit to this bustling, overpriced store will tell you as much about who lives in the Village—and how—as a visit to those other stores will reveal about the life-style of their respective neighborhoods.

However, if what you want to see are the cozy little Village stores where customers are known by name (Balducci's is clearly not such a place), go to **Zito's** at 259 Bleecker (a bakery that's been in the Village since the beginning of time); **Ottomanelli's** at 281 Bleecker (a meat market with a lamb wearing glasses in the window); **Murray's** at 42 Cornelia Street just above Bleecker (a food market with the lowest prices for cheese in Manhattan); **McNulty's** at 109 Christopher Street (a coffee and tea shop that not only mixes special blends for its regular customers but keeps the customers' preferences on file); **Li-Lac Chocolates** at 120 Christopher Street (makes homemade chocolates on the premises); or **Raffetto's** at 144 West Houston Street (where fresh pasta was being made fifty years before Bloomingdale's ever got the idea).

**5) Jefferson Market Library Garden** (Sixth Avenue at 10th Street). Here is another secret to maintaining a beautiful lawn and garden in the city. Enclose them inside a 15-foot-high cyclone fence and keep the public out.

**6) The West Village** (west of Seventh Avenue). Here is the part of the Village that tourists who stay close to Washington Square Park, West 8th Street, and Sixth Avenue often miss. The West Village is known primarily for two things: for its quiet, elegant residential streets; and for being the most gay part of the Village. It is also the part of the Village where West 4th Street somehow manages to end up north of West 12th!

The farther west one goes, the quieter and gayer the West Village becomes. That is, until one reaches West Street and the gay bars of the motorcycle-leather-crowd variety, where it is not quiet at all.

**7) Christopher Street**   (west of Seventh Avenue and Sheridan Square). Christopher Street is both the symbolic and actual center of the Village's gay male community. And now you know why the national gay magazine, *Christopher Street*, is so named. **Gay Street**, incidentally, a little comma of a street that cuts off Christopher just west of Sixth Avenue, was so named long before the Village became gay.

**8) Abingdon Square Park**   (intersection of Hudson and Bleecker). Abingdon Square epitomizes the quiet side of the Village, as Washington Square Park reflects its most noisy, busy face. Unlike Washington Square, Abingdon Square is not a three-ring circus of activity. Nor is it filled primarily with visitors and tourists. Village residents themselves go to Abingdon Square Park with their children; rarely do they take their children to Washington Square Park anymore.

**9) Bedford Street.**   The location of some of the city's weirdest, yet most lovable, buildings. **No. 75½** is said to be the narrowest house in New York (also, as every tourist guide points out, the former home of Edna St. Vincent Millay and then John Barrymore); while **No. 77½** is supposed to be one of the oldest houses still standing (built in about 1800), if, indeed, it is still standing, which at last look seemed tenuous at best. The roof of **No. 100** comes not to a peak but to two peaks; hence it is called Twin Peaks.

There is nothing strange about **No. 102**; but this lovely wood frame house is worth seeing if you're in the neighborhood. **No. 86** is Chumley's Restaurant, most famous for not having any sign that says it is Chumley's.

**10) No. 121 Charles Street**   (near the corner of Greenwich Street). Guaranteed to be your favorite house in New York City. It may be the city's smallest edifice. Call it a cottage.

**11) Westbeth**   (436 West Street at Bank Street). Westbeth might be one of the few places in the Village where a community of artists actually does exist. This complex, once the Bell Telephone Laboratories building, was converted into housing for artists and their families in 1970, probably one of the first buildings in the city to be converted from commercial to residential use.

**12) The West Coast Apartments** (Washington Street between Horatio and Gansevoort Streets). One of the more recent examples in the Village of renovating a once commercial structure to co-op apartments. Also, one of the more recent examples of a mural being painted on a building. The mural of a hundred-foot-long train is in the approximate place where trains once did pass through the building when it was the Manhattan Refrigeration Company. The trains ran along the elevated tracks, portions of which still stand on either side of the building.

**13) Cadet General Store** (523 Hudson Street near Charles Street). The only store in New York devoted to clothing for short men. That is, 5 feet 8 inches and under.

**14) Quinion Books** (541 Hudson Street). A bookstore that sells only drama books and cookbooks. These two categories probably sum up the interests of contemporary Village residents as well as anything else.

Hudson Street, by the way, is Jane Jacobs's (author of *The Death and Life of Great American Cities*) example of the ideal mixed-use urban street; though the particular mix of uses on Hudson has changed since she wrote her book.

## EATING PLACES

One goes to some parts of the city for a particular kind of food. The Village, however, offers *every* kind: Italian, French, Greek, Mexican, Israeli, Brazilian, African, Middle Eastern, to say nothing of innumerable burger-quiche-omelet places and vegetarian restaurants. So, one goes to the Village to eat for a particular kind of ambience. Somehow eating at La Crêpe in the Village is more satisfying than eating at La Crêpe on West 44th Street.

As for price? Upper East Siders come down to the Village for what they consider a cheap meal. On the other hand, couples from Brooklyn come into the Village to eat on their anniversary, because by their standards, Village restaurants are expensive and thus appropriate for celebrations.

Generally, West Village restaurants are smaller, quieter, and less tourist-oriented than those east of Seventh Avenue. West Village eating places are more neighborhood-type restaurants, though a Village "neighborhood restaurant" is not exactly the same as one in Jackson Heights, Queens, which really does cater to an exclusively neighborhood clientele.

Village eating places that are extremely popular with New Yorkers—and places you might not happen upon—include: **The Pink Tea Cup** (310 Bleecker Street) for inexpensive homemade Southern-style cooking—ribs, greens, black-eyed peas—where one can get things like pecan pancakes for breakfast (also grits), corn and apple fritters, homemade pies, and fresh vegetables; **Chez Brigitte** (77 Greenwich Avenue), a hole in the wall, where coffee still costs 35¢ and omelets only about $3.00 compared to the standard $6.00 or $7.00 Village omelet; the three **Alfredos** (maybe the best Italian restaurants for the price in Manhattan), which include **Tavola Calda da Alfredo** (285 Bleecker), **Trattoria da Alfredo** (90 Bank Street), and **Caffe da Alfredo** (17 Perry Street), located in a town house and probably the most "Village glamorous" of the three; **Janice's Fish Place** (570 Hudson), which is run by Janice, who once worked with Hisae of the famous fish restaurants.

In the burger-quiche-omelet genre, **Elephant & Castle** (68 Greenwich Avenue) is certainly among the most favored places, and the same is true of **Arnold's Turtle** (51 Bank Street) among vegetarian restaurants. For pizza there are only **Ray's Pizza** (465 Sixth Avenue), the best-known pizza place in all the city, and **John's Pizzeria** (278 Bleecker Street), where you can't buy pizza by the slice.

Many New Yorkers swear **La Tulipe** (104 West 13th Street) is better than most of the French restaurants in the East Fifties. They also swear you pay East Fifties prices.

An alternative to those cafés that line Bleecker Street—Café Le Figaro, Café San Marco, Café Borgia—is the **Cornelia Street Café** (29 Cornelia Street). The Bleecker Street cafés attract tourists and kids from suburban high schools. The Cornelia Street Café attracts Village residents.

## East Village: *NoHo*

The East Village bears little resemblance to Greenwich Village (or the West Village). It's not quite the case of comparing apples to oranges, but it is, at the least, like comparing eating oranges to juice oranges. The East Village, of course, has the seeds in it.

This is another way of saying the East Village is considerably scruffier—more funky—than Greenwich Village. To East Village residents, this characteristic is its major attraction. It keeps rents down to a half or even a third of what they are in Greenwich Village, keeps tax lawyers and successful clothing manufacturers out, and keeps tourists in Washington Square Park and out of Tompkins Square Park.

All of this makes the East Village a more authentic residential neighborhood in the sense that it really does belong to the people who live there. Greenwich Village, by contrast, is shared equally between residents and visitors.

Whereas tourists inundate Greenwich Village, the visitors who do come to the East Village usually have a specific purpose, typically to attend the many theaters (which, by the way, outnumber the theaters in Greenwich Village and are also considerably more experimental and offbeat), or to hear rock music, since the East Village is the major center for rock (including punk rock) in the city.

But even then, someone who comes to the East Village to see a play at the Public Theater or at the La Mama Theatre Club, for example, will just as likely eat in Greenwich Village beforehand and drop down to SoHo for a drink afterward. This is despite the fact that the East Village teems with a variety of excellent, very inexpensive ethnic restaurants, terrific cafés, and colorful bars.

These eating and drinking places, then, remain patronized mostly by East Village residents; they are truly neighborhood establishments. And East Village residents couldn't be happier that couples from Great Neck who are always coming into the Village to dine would never think of eating in the East Village.

Part of the reason why visitors—or certain New Yorkers for that matter—tend to ignore the East Village is related to its image problem. The East Village hasn't yet completely shed the image created in the late 1960s and early 1970s of being the Haight-Ashbury of New York—home to hippies, yippies, flower children and freaks, runaways, psychedelic drugs, acid rock, and Hell's Angels.

Though the East Village remains the Manhattan neighborhood with the most authentic counterculture institutions, personages, and life-styles, it's by no means the hippie haven it was in the early 1970s.

The East Village has been cleaned and scrubbed and washed behind its ears.

Aside from the East Village being a very vital, inventive, and resourceful part of the city, it could quite possibly be Manhattan's most mixed residential neighborhood as well—mixed economically, ethnically, racially, and by age. This is because it remains one of the few Manhattan neighborhoods that still retain a mixed housing stock. Almost every other neighborhood is by now either totally gentrified or totally poor.

But housing in the East Village runs the gamut from luxurious town houses along Stuyvesant Street to public-housing projects along Avenue D, to middle-income Village View Houses on First Avenue, to fairly expensive rental and co-op apartments in recently renovated buildings along the cross streets between First and Third Avenues, to relatively inexpensive housing in not-yet-renovated buildings along those same streets, to "bombed-out" buildings between Avenues A and D, either occupied by squatters or abandoned altogether.

Housing is so varied that, unlike most other sections of the city where the quality of housing may differ drastically from block to block, here dramatic differences can exist between one end of the block and the other. This is why ads for housing elsewhere in Manhattan might stipulate "good neighborhood" or "good block," but in the East Village ads often say "good building" only. Which tells you something about the building next door.

Of course, the housing situation is destined to change, and to an extent already has. As recently as five or six years ago, the East Village was the one "undiscovered" Manhattan neighborhood in that it had cheap housing and yet was not a slum. Anyone intent upon living in Manhattan, but who otherwise couldn't afford to, came to the East Village to find inexpensive housing, and usually did. It just meant having your bathtub in the middle of your kitchen, but in a strange way that was considered appealing.

To be sure, the East Village has now been discovered. Rents have increased, already many buildings have "gone co-op," much old, cheap housing has since been renovated into new, more expensive housing, and so on. Still, one suspects that as long as mammoth public-housing projects remain in the East Village, the neighborhood will always remain a little rough around its edges. This will assure the East Village of never being completely homogenized and of never becoming as expensive as the West Village. East Village residents couldn't be happier about that either.

## OF INTEREST

**1) First Houses**    (East 3rd Street between First Avenue and Avenue A). This is the first public-housing project built in the United States (1934). Still used as public housing, the project looks more like garden apartments than low-income housing. It really is quite nice; particularly the courtyard inside the project. The one sad note is that this project makes one realize that all public housing built since is worse.

**2) Jacob Riis Houses**    (Avenue D from 6th Street to 14th Street). A more contemporary example of New York City public housing. This massive project—three acres' worth—is an example of what low-income housing is rather than what it could have been. Jacob Riis Houses are rather oppressive looking, despite the project's plaza-playground, which has won more architecture awards and prizes than the Citicorp Building and the Guggenheim Museum put together. Though given the present condition of the playground, you may wonder how.

**3) East 3rd Street**    (between First and Second Avenues). The fact that the Hell's Angels and the Catholic Workers (Maryhouse, the residence of this Catholic social-activist organization, is at 55 East 3rd) can be neighbors makes East 3rd Street one of the city's more ecumenical blocks. Incidentally, East 3rd Street (just east of here between Avenues B and C) has recently been the center of the Lower East Side's drug trades, where much of the city's trafficking in cocaine occurs.

**4) East Village Theater District.**    The East Village is to Off-Off Broadway theater what Greenwich Village is to Off Broadway. Experimental theaters of all shapes and sizes populate the East Village, mostly in buildings not originally constructed as theaters, such as garages, warehouses, churches, storefronts. Clusters of theaters are located along East 4th Street between Second and Third Avenues (New York Theater Ensemble, La Mama Theatre Club, Dramatis Personae, Truck & Warehouse Theatre, etc.); along Second Avenue (Theatre for the New City, Entermedia Theatre, Orpheum, etc.); and around Astor Place (Public Theater, Astor Place Theatre, Colonnades Theatre, etc.).

**Phebe's Place** (361 Bowery at 3rd Street, just below the East 4th Street string of theaters) is considered the Sardi's of Off-Off Broadway—a favorite after-theater gathering place.

**5) NoHo** (area *N*orth of *Ho*uston between Broadway and the Bowery). This is more what SoHo looked like when it was still more an industrial and warehouse area than a residential enclave. Residential lofts are abundant here too—and the number keeps growing—but it's still a substantially commercial section. Boutiques and hordes of tourists have not yet arrived.

Kate Millet of *Sexual Politics* fame, who is a sculptor as well as a writer, has her studio down here. **CBGB** (315 Bowery)—one of the city's best-known rock clubs—is located here too. It has been known for punk rock and new-wave rock, but, of course, that changes.

**6) Astor Wines & Spirits** (12 Astor Place between Broadway and Lafayette Street). It's really a wine-and-liquor supermarket—shopping carts and all. It is to wine and liquor what Barnes & Noble is to books. Coming here is not like going to your little neighborhood liquor store. People come to Astor Wines from all over the city and from out of town to buy by the case. It has both great wines and great bargains.

**7) Stuyvesant Street** (diagonally between East 9th and 10th Streets). It is perhaps the only really fashionable address in the East Village.

**8) The Strand Book Store** (828 Broadway at 12th Street). This is the largest secondhand bookstore in the United States—maybe the world. Its shelves hold something like 2 million books. Strand customers not only buy books, but they read them too.

The Strand is located in an area once known as the secondhand-book district of New York. Fourth Avenue was known as Book Row, and it once boasted thirty or so used-book stores. As rents rose, bookstores left, and now but a handful of them remain.

**9) McSorley's Old Ale House** (15 East 7th Street between Second and Third Avenues). McSorley's, one of the oldest and most famous bars in New York, was in the news ten or twelve years ago when it was sued by a group of feminists for its men-only policy. McSorley's lost. Previously, women couldn't go in and didn't. Now they can but don't.

**10) M. Schacht Appetizing**   (99 Second Avenue between 5th and 6th Streets). As the neighborhood's premier food store, it is the Balducci's of the East Village, which means it is nothing at all like Balducci's—an expensive, chic, and overly crowded food store in Greenwich Village. It is as low-key as Balducci's is high, which in itself suggests a major difference between the East and West Villages. M. Schacht lacks Balducci's pretentiousness and it smells better too.

**11) East 6th Street**   (between First and Second Avenues). This is an example of a mixed-use block to the *n*th degree. This one short block has half-a-dozen Indian restaurants, a Japanese restaurant or two, one or two macrobiotic restaurants, a health-food store, Odyssey House (drug rehabilitation program and residence), a Jewish synagogue, clothing stores, secondhand stores, and housing that runs from excellent to poor.

**12) Little Ukraine**   (the area around East 7th Street and First and Second Avenues). This is what's left of the city's Ukrainian-American community, which at one time was the predominant ethnic group in the East Village. Mostly what remains now are some wonderful Ukrainian restaurants.

**13) St. Mark's-in-the-Bowery Church**   (East 10th Street and Second Avenue). More poetry gets read at St. Mark's in a week than gets read in Greenwich Village in a year.

**14) Theater 80**   (80 St. Marks Place near First Avenue). Aside from showing some of the best old films ever made—mostly films from the 1930s and 1940s—Theater 80 is the only movie house in the city where the projector is in back rather than in front of the screen. (Ask at the ticket window for an explanation of how the rear-projection technique works.) Theater 80 is also one of the few movie theaters left that still serves freshly brewed coffee.

**15) St. Marks Place**   (between First Avenue and Avenue A). This block was the central issue in a child-custody suit a few years ago. The father, from upstate Kingston, New York, was seeking custody of his nine-year-old child, who lived on St. Marks with his mother, solely on the grounds that the neighborhood was not a fit one for raising a child. The case was known as "the quality-of-life suit." The father claimed the neighborhood was a "mean place" characterized by crime, pollution, and burned-out buildings. The mother countered by insisting the neighborhood was "rich with great cultural and ethnic diversity." And that, in a nutshell, more or less summarizes the differing attitudes of New Yorkers about the East Village. Judge for yourself.

## EATING PLACES

No part of the city has a greater collection of good, inexpensive— even cheap—restaurants than the East Village. Yet, with the exception of the **Second Avenue Deli** (158 Second Avenue), hardly any of them enjoy a citywide reputation. Essentially they serve an East Village crowd. East Village eating places fall into four major groups: Indian or Pakistani; Ukrainian; dairy; and macrobiotic.

By now there must be a dozen or more Indian restaurants here. In the West Village, a brick wall is exposed and *voilà*, a cozy French restaurant. In the East Village, some fabrics are hung on the wall and *voilà*, a cozy Indian restaurant.

At least half the Indian restaurants are along East 6th Street between First and Second Avenues. Since most of them are run by various members of the same family—who pool their supplies, chefs, help, and profits—the quality and prices at all of them are fairly comparable. **Kismoth** (326 East 6th Street) is among the original East Village Indian places, and is worth a visit just to see how colanders can be used as light fixtures. More establishment-looking restaurants— and a bit more expensive—are **Oriental Indian** (151 Second Avenue) and **Mitali's** (334 East 6th Street).

Among the Ukrainian restaurants, **Veselka's** (144 Second Avenue) is superb (don't overlook the dining room in back). The **Orchidia** across the street (145 Second) is interesting in that it combines Ukrainian and Italian cooking. This is where you can get Ukrainian pizza.

The **B & H Dairy Restaurant** (127 Second Avenue) is an East Village institution. When Abbie Hoffman was underground, he surfaced just to come to the B & H for a meal. Once it was considered *the* dairy restaurant in the East Village, but then it closed, and before it reopened, the **Kiev Restaurant** (117 Second Avenue) was started. Now they compete with each other. Try the Kiev for its outstanding challah. Or at least look in if for no other reason than to see a cross-section of who lives in the East Village.

Started in the 1960s by hippie types, the **Cauldron** (308 East 6th Street) began as a macrobiotic restaurant. It has since been sold to

Orthodox Jews who now run it as a Kosher macrobiotic restaurant. The combination of "typical East Village crowd" and Orthodox Jews who together make up the Cauldron's clientele creates a strange effect, to say the least.

**Hisae's Place** (35 Cooper Square, or Third Avenue between 5th and 6th Streets) is one of the original Hisae restaurants, which are now located all over the city. It serves fish dishes primarily.

**The Cloisters** (236 East 9th Street between Second and Third Avenues) is one of the best cafés in New York if best is defined by lovely outdoor courtyard (with fountain, fish, and turtles), by quiet, and by café au lait served in bowls.

**Caffe Kabul** (32 St. Mark's Place) is an absolutely terrific and cheap café and Afghani restaurant.

Anyone who says there aren't any good, inexpensive restaurants in Manhattan just doesn't know anything about the East Village. And people who pay $10 for meat loaf, powdered mashed potatoes, canned string beans, and chocolate-cream pie made with imitation chocolate and imitation whipped cream in an Upper East Side coffee shop—rather than come down to the East Village—deserve what they get.

# 17 Chelsea and Vicinity

## Chelsea: *Flower District*

Chelsea is one of the better known but least-talked-about neighborhoods in Manhattan. This probably has something to do with the fact that most of us don't know what to say about Chelsea. It lacks typicality. There is nothing you can call quintessentially Chelsea. (Chelsea residents themselves, however, insist that a sense of neighborhood is what is quintessentially Chelsea.)

With almost all other neighborhoods we can make references that are understood by other New Yorkers to have a particular meaning. For example, you'll hear us talking about a typical Upper West Side apartment (old, large, high-ceilinged, dark apartments along Riverside Drive, West End Avenue, or Central Park West); a typical Upper East Side swinging singles bar or a West Village gay bar; West Village types and East Village types; a typical Madison Avenue gallery; and so forth.

None of these references requires any elaboration. There is a kind of consensus as to what is meant—whether or not it's accurate.

But when we try to think of a typical Chelsea apartment, or restaurant, or resident, or architecture, store, block, or anything else, the mind draws a blank. Not that Chelsea lacks personality or character, only that it lacks a unifying or pervasive one.

There are gorgeous brownstone blocks, for instance, in the low-Twenties between Ninth and Tenth Avenues, but not enough of them so that they really characterize the area. There are huge public-housing projects in Chelsea, but nothing on the magnitude of those on the Lower East Side. Chelsea is a commercial and manufacturing center, yet not overwhelmingly so. Chelsea has lots of poor residents (though considerably fewer than it did pregentrification), yet it's not thought of as one of the city's poorer neighborhoods. Chelsea has loads of wealthy residents, and yet it is not considered one of the wealthy neighborhoods either. And so it goes.

The problem with Chelsea may be that it's too diverse for its own good. This makes it difficult to have a sense of Chelsea as a distinct neighborhood—to know where you are when you're there, as you do in other neighborhoods. About the only thing that always gets associated with Chelsea is the Chelsea Hotel, and that's only because of its name.

None of this is meant to derogate from the attractiveness or interest of Chelsea. The inability to sum up Chelsea in the tight, neat way we do other neighborhoods means it escapes stereotyping and clichés, which many feel is a positive thing. It also means that Chelsea must be appreciated according to its parts rather than as a whole.

## OF INTEREST

**1) Marxist-Leninist Bookstore**   (West 15th Street between Seventh and Eighth Avenues). Unlike B. Dalton, Barnes & Noble, Waldenbooks, or any of the other chain bookstores you'll run into on every other block throughout the city, Marxist-Leninist bookstores are few and far between. So when one does exist, you should at least know where.

**2) West 21st Street**   (between Seventh and Tenth Avenues). Here you get a chance to see three different sides of residential Chelsea. Between Seventh and Eighth, 21st Street is in the throes of being gentrified (which is happening throughout Chelsea now). In other words, it's still a mixed residential block, but renovations are fast and furious.

By contrast, 21st between Eighth and Ninth seems to have escaped gentrification thus far; which probably has something to do with the public school in the middle of the block. And then there is 21st Street between Ninth and Tenth Avenues, which may be the most uniformly beautiful town-house block in Chelsea. It's the sort of block the actor Anthony Perkins—a Chelsea resident—might live on.

**3) General Theological Seminary**    (20th Street between Ninth and Tenth Avenues). The seminary and its pastoral setting is Chelsea's centerpiece—its Gramercy Park, so to speak. Yet aside from Chelsea residents and people who write about parks or architecture, maybe one New Yorker in five hundred has even heard of the seminary, let alone knows where it is. Maybe one in ten thousand has ever visited it and its extraordinarily beautiful grounds.

**4) Chelsea Hotel**    (222 West 23rd Street between Seventh and Eighth Avenues). As is true of Chelsea in general, though most of us have heard of the Chelsea Hotel, few have actually bothered to go see it. When we do, we're shocked to discover that it's pink!

Once famous as a residential hotel for writers (people like Eugene O'Neill, Dylan Thomas, Thomas Wolfe, and Arthur Miller lived there at one time or another), it's now probably far more infamous than famous. This is a consequence of its attraction in recent years to rock singers rather than to writers. Its infamy was secured when Sid Vicious, at the time a member of the punk rock group the Sex Pistols, stabbed and killed his girlfriend-manager at the Chelsea where they had been living. (Sid Vicious subsequently died of a heroin overdose while out on bail, so he was never actually convicted of the murder.)

**5) The Joyce Theater**    (Eighth Avenue between 18th and 19th Streets). To many New York City film buffs, this was the site of one of the city's most beloved movie houses—the Elgin Theatre, its barbershop chairs in the lobby a more indelible image than the multitiered balconies of Radio City Music Hall. The Elgin was also one of the first movie theaters in New York to have midnight film showings.

But alas, the Elgin exists no longer as a movie theater. It has since been converted into a dance theater for medium-sized companies—a link between dance in downtown loft buildings and at City Center. Maybe they've kept the barbershop chairs in the lobby nonetheless.

**6) The Flower District**    (just to the east of Chelsea). Sixth Avenue, particularly between 26th and 29th Streets, is the center of the city's wholesale flower district. It is to flowers what the garment district is to clothes. But while the best time to visit the garment district is during the day, the best time to see the flower district is in the early-morning hours when the fresh flowers are being cut and prepared for distribution.

## EATING PLACES

For a neighborhood that does not immediately come to mind as an obvious place to eat out, Chelsea has many and varied restaurants. Most are cheap to moderate in price. It's hard to think of a Chelsea restaurant that is as expensive as those French restaurants in the East Fifties.

Among the Chelsea restaurants best known among New Yorkers are: the **West Boondock** (114 Tenth Avenue at 17th Street), where you can eat soul food and hear live jazz; the **Empire Diner** (210 Tenth Avenue at 22nd Street), whose Art Deco design, desserts, and hours (it never closes) recommend it to neighborhood residents and rock stars alike; and **Hisae's Chelsea Place** (174 Eighth Avenue), which is another of the Hisae restaurants that populate Manhattan (though Mimi Sheraton, the restaurant reviewer for the *Times*, thinks it's not as good as the other Hisaes).

Among the lesser known but best eating spots in Chelsea are the numerous Spanish-Chinese and Cuban-Chinese restaurants. They are scattered throughout Chelsea just as they are on the Upper West Side. The Chinese menu is distinct from the Latin fare, though you can mix and come up with such unusual combinations as egg foo yung with a side order of plantanos. **Chinita Spanish-Chinese Restaurant** (Eighth Avenue at 19th Street) and **Asia de Cuba** (190 Eighth Avenue at 20th Street) are both mainstays for Chelsea residents. Both are cheap enough so that it's possible to eat there for less than it would cost to cook at home. And you do get the feeling that a good number of the patrons at the Cuban-Chinese restaurants do, indeed, eat there every day.

Not to be upstaged by the Cuban-Chinese combination, **Joseph's Middle Eastern Restaurant** (198 Eighth Avenue) has come up with some unique combinations of its own—Middle Eastern, Jewish, and Hungarian. One can order shish kabob, blintzes, or gefilte fish and schnitzel.

One excellent eating place in the Flower District is the **Beaubern Café** (42 West 28th Street), a bar and restaurant. It offers an American fare of burgers, chops, and sandwiches along with a quiche here and there and some Greek dishes thrown in as well. The Beaubern is not the kind of restaurant that will ever get reviewed anywhere, which is probably what makes it so attractive to visit. It is truly a neighborhood bar-restaurant that only New Yorkers who live or work in the immediate neighborhood would ever know about or patronize.

# 18 Gramercy Park– Murray Hill and Vicinity

## Gramercy Park: *Union Square / Lower Broadway / Madison Square / Stuyvesant Town*

Most New Yorkers who say they live in Gramercy Park—one of the city's most exclusive addresses and the part of the city which most resembles an upper-class London residential neighborhood—only wished they had. If questioned more thoroughly, they will usually admit to living a good six to eight blocks away. Part of the motivation for saying one lives there is social climbing, pure and simple. But aside from that, there is the real problem of living near Gramercy Park—but certainly not on it or even that near it—and not knowing what else to call the neighborhood.

In fact, that is a problem with this entire area, from 14th Street to about 27th Street between Fifth Avenue and the East River. This section of Manhattan—a mixture of commercial loft buildings, residential lofts, office buildings, town houses, and high-rise apartment buildings for either upper-income or middle-income residents—has no commonly accepted neighborhood name. Nor, for that matter, does it have any common neighborhood identity.

It is neither downtown nor Midtown. Chelsea, which basically covers the same area *west* of Fifth Avenue—not downtown nor Midtown either—may not have a clear overall identity, but at least it has an overall name. This area has neither.

## OF INTEREST

**1) Union Square**    (bounded by 14th and 17th Streets and Broadway, University Place, and Park Avenue South). Though you couldn't tell by the looks of it today, Union Square was once the center for radical political activities in New York City. During the early 1900s, political speeches and demonstrations went on here daily. Emma Goldman (the anarchist-feminist referred to as "Red Emma") practically camped out in Union Square in those days; that's how often she spoke here.

There are still demonstrations by the Left in Union Square from time to time—seemingly for nostalgic reasons—and there are a number of union offices still located around the square as a reminder of bygone days as well. But for the most part, New Yorkers respond to Union Square as a sort of grungy park we'd prefer spending fifteen minutes to walk around than two minutes to walk through. (This could all change since major renovations are planned for Union Square, scheduled to begin in Spring 1983.)

Apropos of nothing, one of the more interesting stores around Union Square is **Klepper Folding Boats** (35 Union Square). How many stores can there be in New York that sell canoes?

**2) Lower Broadway**    (below 23rd Street). This may not yet be as famous a residential loft area as SoHo, but it's well on its way to becoming that. The fact that the artist Andy Warhol and the theatrical director-choreographer Michael Bennett (who did *A Chorus Line*), for example, have lofts here certainly bodes for a future of fame.

Some New Yorkers know Lower Broadway only as the part of Broadway where it suddenly winds up running *east* of Fifth Avenue (which it does starting at the **Flatiron Building** on 23rd just east of Madison Square). Others know it only as the location of **Paragon Sporting Goods** (867 Broadway), *the* sporting-goods–camping-supply store in the city.

**3) Barnes & Noble**    (both sides of Fifth Avenue at 18th Street). There are now loads of Barnes & Noble bookstores in and outside the city, but this is where it all began. The Barnes & Noble Annex on the west side of Fifth Avenue is easily the best place in the city for discount-priced books. The Annex, you should know, defies browsing, however. It requires delving, probing, plunging, and upturning in order to find what you want.

**4) Stuyvesant High School**    (15th Street between First and Second Avenues), **Washington Irving High School** (16th Street at Irving Place), and **Friends' Seminary** (16th Street between Third Avenue and Stuyvesant Square). These three schools, all located within a few blocks of each other, reveal the options open to high school students in New York City. Stuyvesant may not look like much, but it is *the* most prestigious public high school in New York—more difficult to get into than Bronx Science. Most of its students commute from the outer boroughs, but its reputation warrants an hour-and-a-half commute by subway each way, each day. In 1981, about thirty of its graduates were accepted by Yale, about twenty-five by Harvard. Washington Irving, on the other hand, doesn't look like much, and, in fact, it isn't a very good school. It's where poor kids who don't get into Stuyvesant wind up going. Friends' Seminary, a private school, is where wealthy kids who don't get into Stuyvesant go to school.

**5) The Little Synagogue**    (127 East 20th Street between Park Avenue South and Broadway). Billed as neither Orthodox, Reform, Conservative, or Reconstructionist—but rather "just a Jewish Synagogue for Jewish people"—it is undoubtedly the smallest synagogue in New York; probably the only one located in a town house; and certainly the only synagogue located above a locksmith.

**6)** The beautiful condition of **Gramercy Park**    (20th to 21st Street at the foot of Lexington Avenue). Here is the secret for maintaining a beautiful park in New York City. Restrict its use to a handful of rich people who have their own set of keys to gain entrance (the acid test for anyone claiming to reside *on* Gramercy Park), make sure kids are attended by a nanny, and don't allow anyone to walk on the grass.

Gramercy Park is a private park, so you'll have to settle for looking through its gates along with the rest of us who don't have keys. That is, unless you come here on Christmas Eve, when as a gesture of incredible magnanimity, Gramercy Park is open to the public for caroling. To the public!

If you've ever wondered about the genesis of the cooperative-apartment phenomenon, you can stop wondering. It all started at **34 Gramercy Park**, the oldest co-op apartment building in the city.

**7) Madison Square**    (23rd Street to 26th between Fifth Avenue and Madison Avenue). Could a London park ever look so bad? Madison Square has seen much better days, like when the original Madison

Square Garden stood across the street (which explains how the new Madison Square Garden is so named even though it's now located on Eighth Avenue in the Thirties), or when the arm and torch of the Statue of Liberty were displayed here before its other parts arrived and the whole thing was moved to Liberty Island.

**8) Single Room Occupancy Hotels**    (Lexington Avenue in the Twenties). Just above Gramercy Park, one of the most exclusive addresses in New York, are several SRO's for transients and welfare recipients. These hotels are among the most nonexclusive addresses in the city.

**9) Stuyvesant Town** and **Peter Cooper Village**    (First Avenue from 14th Street to 23rd). These may look to you like your basic New York City low-income public-housing projects, but they're not. They are, in fact, middle-income projects (Stuyvesant Town runs to 20th Street and Peter Cooper Village from 20th to 23rd). The way you can tell is by the air-conditioners in the windows and by the almost totally white tenant population.

Metropolitan Life, which built these projects, was accused of discriminating against black families when, in the mid-to-late 1960s, it was discovered that of the almost 9,000 apartments in Stuyvesant Town perhaps 50 were rented to blacks; and of about 2,500 apartments in Peter Cooper Village, maybe 10 were rented to blacks. Supposedly Metro Life did something about this, but from the looks of whom you see in and around Stuyvesant Town and Peter Cooper Village, you can't be sure.

**10) Waterside Apartments**    (East River between 25th and 29th Streets). There is no way that this can be mistaken for public housing. The indoor swimming pool (which can be seen from the FDR Drive and taunts drivers stuck in traffic in front of Waterside), indoor ice-skating rink, and proximity of the United Nations School (next door) eliminate all doubts.

You can get to Waterside by walking over the FDR Drive at 25th Street, and if you're lucky, you'll get to see a classic New York City traffic jam.

**11) River Walk**    (East River waterfront between 16th and 24th Streets). This is still a nonsight, in the sense that the planned waterfront community called River Walk has been selected for development by the city but has yet to be built. If and when it is, what will result is a waterfront community of restaurants, apartments, theaters, stores, a hotel, and a boat marina. The inspiration for it, apparently, is Marina Del Rey in Los Angeles.

## EATING PLACES

If you're a lover of coffee shops, you've found your Eden. This has to be the coffee-shop center of the city. The avenues in particular (First, Second, Third, Lexington, and so forth) overflow with them.

There is at least one restaurant in this part of town that is a New York City institution: **Brownie's** (21 East 16th Street), which bills itself not only as New York's first health-food restaurant, but the first in the country.

Not yet institutions, but well on their way, are: **Amy's** (210 East 23rd Street), a kind of fast-food Middle Eastern restaurant, of which there are more outlets around Manhattan than McDonald's; **The Front Porch** (119 East 18th Street), which has at least three or four other branches around the city, and which used to specialize in soups, salads, and sandwiches but now has a much expanded menu (chicken in pastry, fresh pasta, fish and meat dishes, and so forth); and **Z** (117 East 15th Street), one of Manhattan's better Greek restaurants.

**Joanna** (18 East 18th Street) looks as if it belongs in SoHo, but it's here in the middle of the Lower Broadway commercial loft district, which tells you that commercial lofts are fast becoming residential lofts. **La Colombe d'Or** (134 East 26th Street) is an expensive French restaurant where Union Square and Madison Square publishers go for publishing lunches in lieu of the East Fifties French restaurants frequented by their Midtown counterparts. And there is **Hubert's** (102 East 22nd Street), which is relatively new to Manhattan but not to New York. For a number of years, Hubert's was situated in the Boerum Hill section of Brooklyn. It was one of the very best places in the city to eat then, and apparently still is. You'll be inclined to call Hubert's cuisine French. They call it New American Cuisine. Alas, Hubert's is *not* cheap.

Then, if you want, you can walk up Lexington into the high Twenties and low Thirties—which is officially Murray Hill—and find a string of ethnic restaurants of varying sizes, types, and quality (many Indian, Turkish-Middle Eastern-Armenian, and Italian restaurants).

## Murray Hill

It would be perfectly reasonable if, upon hearing of Murray Hill, you were to ask "Murray who?" for Murray Hill is not one of the better known, so-called glamour neighborhoods. If anything can be said to be concentrated in Murray Hill, it would have to be private, nonprofit social-service agencies—hardly the stuff of *New York* magazine articles. Unless you live in New York, there is no reason why you should have heard of Murray Hill. Unless you work there, there are precious few occasions to go to Murray Hill.

Though office buildings, hotels, consulates and missions to the United Nations, and restaurants of the sort that have large ads in the "restaurants" section of the Yellow Pages pervade Murray Hill, it is essentially a residential neighborhood (a predominantly white middle-to-upper-income residential neighborhood, and one that thus manages to feel completely devoid of ethnicity despite the great number of ethnic restaurants there). New Yorkers who live here bill it as a "quiet residential neighborhood," though what is meant by "quiet" probably is not so much a lack of noise as a lack of attention. It has no definable life-style; no obvious type of Manhattanite lives here. Indeed, there is the distinct sense that Murray Hill attracts precisely the sort of people who eschew things like "definable life-style"; the kind who make charitable donations in the name of "Anonymous."

Murray Hill does not grab many headlines. For that reason, its most famous tourist attraction—the Morgan Library (a museum)—is probably New York's most obscure tourist attraction. And because of its rather low profile, from a security point of view, it was a stroke of sheer genius to locate the Cuban Mission to the U.N. in Murray Hill. You cannot attack or demonstrate in front of a place if you don't know where it is.

Even among New Yorkers, there are legions of us who will admit to knowing where Murray Hill is only by virtue of the movie theaters, coffee shops, delis, cigar shops, and various other establishments that were accommodating enough to use "Murray Hill" as part of their business name. Even at that, there is still considerable debate as to Murray Hill's boundaries. Consensus seems to indicate that Murray Hill runs from about 27th Street to 40th Street between Madison and Third; but only your postman knows for sure.

# OF INTEREST

**1) The Little Church Around the Corner**   (29th Street west of Madison). Anything in Manhattan called the little anything around the corner is worth visiting. This is a charming church, though a bit out of place, it seems, in New York City. It claims that more weddings have been performed here than in any other church in New York. (The Little Church Around the Corner is *not* related to the Little Synagogue described in the Gramercy Park section.)

**2) The Third Avenue Organic Garden**   (Third Avenue at 31st Street). This may not be as impressive as the vineyard in Montmartre, smack in the middle of Paris, but the garden is Midtown Manhattan's only one, and deserves to be seen.

**3) 31st and 32nd Streets**   (between Second and Third Avenues). These are probably the two loveliest blocks in Murray Hill (actually, Kips Bay, which is just east of Murray Hill). They look more like West Village blocks than Murray Hill. (These two blocks seem to have the highest concentration of architects and graphic designers in the city. Milton Glaser, the designer of *New York* magazine and many other publications—and probably the city's best-known designer—works out of the town house at 207 East 32nd Street.)

**4) Norman Thomas High School**   (33rd to 34th Street just east of Park Avenue). That the City of New York would name a public high school after a socialist seems to distinguish it from most other American cities. Try to think of another city that would similarly honor a socialist.

**5) The Complete Traveller**   (199 Madison Avenue at 35th Street). The only bookstore in the city entirely devoted to travel books. (If they don't have at least ten copies of *Street Smarts* in stock, ask them to order the book.)

**6) Sniffen Court**   (152 East 36th Street just west of Third Avenue). This is an absolutely wonderful little mews, with a cobblestone walk and about ten converted carriage houses. It's every bit as effective an urban oasis as any of the Village mews—MacDougal Alley, Washington Mews, Grove Court, Patchin Place, and so on. Yet, unlike the Village mews, which almost every New Yorker has heard of, hardly any of us have heard of Sniffen Court.

**7) The Cuban Permanent Mission to the U.N.** (315 Lexington Avenue at 38th Street). If you do pass the mission, there is no chance whatsoever that you could miss it. The police barricades, security booth, electronic cameras attached to the building, and cops out front are dead giveaways.

**8) Third Avenue at 39th Street.** All over the city, neighborhoods change dramatically from one block to the next. Here is another example of the phenomenon. On the south side of 39th are Murray Hill residential buildings, marking the end of Murray Hill. On the north side are office towers, marking the beginning of the Midtown business district. New York City does not have enough room for buffer zones between neighborhoods.

## EATING PLACES

Murray Hill is inundated with restaurants—ethnic restaurants along Lexington Avenue and Third Avenue from the upper-Twenties through the Thirties, and restaurants specializing in brunch up and down Second Avenue.

Murray Hill is considered a center for both Middle Eastern (Turkish and Armenian) and Indian restaurants (as well as Indian food stores and sari shops). In addition, you'll find a score of Italian restaurants, several Japanese, Chinese, and Spanish restaurants, a Mexican restaurant or two, of which there are relatively few in the city, and even a Louisiana Cajun restaurant (on Lexington Avenue between 28th and 29th Streets).

The problem in Murray Hill, however, is trying to figure out which of the slew of restaurants are better than just so-so. A few guidelines: Avoid restaurants that have reviews from weekly community newspapers in Queens rather than Mimi Sheraton's reviews from *The New York Times*; avoid any place whose review in the window is dated 1976 or earlier; avoid places that participate in two-for-one dining coupon plans, which an unusually large number of Murray Hill restaurants seem to do; avoid restaurants that advertise on Channel 9 TV; avoid Indian restaurants that are more expensive than other Indian restaurants generally are, or that offer champagne among the beverages served: and if you should ask someone on the street to recommend a good restaurant, avoid any referred to as "the Spanish place," "the Japanese place," and so on, as opposed to those referred to by name.

Two very small and therefore easy-to-miss places are: **Francesca's** (129 East 28th Street), a tiny Italian—bring your own beer and wine—restaurant; and **Tibetan Kitchen** (444 Third Avenue), a store-front restaurant said to be the only Tibetan restaurant in the United States.

One Murray Hill restaurant—an institution really—that you unfortunately won't see is the Belmore Cafeteria (formerly at 407 Park Avenue South at 28th Street). After some fifty years as a wonderful, inexpensive cafeteria and hangout for New York City cab drivers (the Belmore was featured in the movie *Taxi Driver*), the Belmore was sold to a developer who is putting up a thirty-story condominium on the site.

# ⑲ **Midtown**

## Garment District: *Herald Square*

No less crowded, no less frenetic, and seemingly no less anarchic, the street activity in and around the garment district (34th to 42nd Street between Eighth and Sixth Avenues, but whose spine is Seventh Avenue) is actually a lot more explicable than elsewhere in Midtown. It is because anyone who comes to this area does so for some fairly obvious reasons.

Thus, if you add together the number of New Yorkers who work in the garment district—the most visible being those who push racks of clothing up and down Seventh Avenue—the commuters streaming toward Penn Station, the travelers spilling out of the Port Authority, the shoppers hopping from Macy's to Gimbels to the other 34th Street stores, and the tourists visiting the Empire State Building along 34th Street, you will have accounted for almost all of the daytime street activity.

Nighttime activity can be explained by whatever is going on at Madison Square Garden. And weekend activity is even easier to account for: shopping at Macy's or Gimbels (open Sundays) or at the camera stores around Herald Square (many, run by Orthodox Jews, are open Sundays) which form the city's "photographic equipment district."

You don't have to ask yourself whether people on the street might live in this part of Midtown, because they don't. No one lives here. It's entirely nonresidential (unless you consider down-and-out New

Yorkers who "live" in the Port Authority bus terminal residents of the area).

Nor do you have to wonder whether these might be New Yorkers out strolling, for no one just strolls here. We stroll up and down Fifth Avenue, throughout Midtown on the East Side, and even around the theater district. But you will never hear us say "Let's go for a walk around the garment district." Nor do we come here just to kill time.

This may explain why people seem to walk just a bit faster here than in other parts of the city. It's a purposeful walk. Of course, to out-of-towners who think all New Yorkers walk at a terrifically fast pace all the time and everywhere, to say that we tend to go at a somewhat faster speed here than elsewhere in the city may seem like splitting hairs.

## OF INTEREST

**1) Fur District, Millinery District, Button and Zipper District,** and so forth (around the fringes of the garment district). The heart of the garment district is Seventh Avenue and 38th Street, but all around its core are subdistricts related to it: hats in the Forties, furs from 27th and 30th Street between Sixth and Seventh Avenues, and below that, districts for ribbon, thread, buttons, zippers, corrugated boxes, sewing machines, and sewing machine parts. Each of these mini-industries is concentrated as an enclave on a particular street or streets, giving some order to what at first blush seems like undifferentiated chaos. Adding to this sense of order is the fact that the housing project just below the garment district—between Eighth and Ninth Avenues from 24th to 28th Street—was built by the International Ladies' Garment Workers Union for ILGWU members, many of whom work in the garment district.

Speaking of the chaos here—the incredible crunch of people, moving racks of clothing, and trucks that never seem to be able to move—you might wonder what, if this is a supposedly declining New York garment industry, must the thriving "garment districts" of Hong Kong or Taiwan possibly be like.

**2) General Post Office** (Eighth Avenue between 31st and 33rd Streets). Some people can't imagine how large the population of New York City is until they see how extraordinarily thick the directories for each borough are. Others don't have any perspective on the size of the city until they see the General Post Office, which is gargantuan—to say nothing of all the branch post offices throughout the city. (And as all guides hasten to add, you should note that the General Post Office is said to have the world's longest inscription, in feet, on a building. It reads: "Neither snow nor rain nor heat nor gloom of night stays these couriers from the swift completion of their appointed rounds.")

**3) Macy's** and **Gimbels**    (at Herald Square). These are particularly interesting to visitors or anyone else who hasn't been to Macy's or Gimbels in the past ten years. If you remember them as bargain alternatives to Bloomingdale's, Saks, Lord & Taylor, Bergdorf's, and other high-class East Side department stores, you'll be shocked to see how much things have changed. Though Macy's (still the world's largest department store) and Gimbels are not yet in the same league with those East Side stores, it seems clear that those establishments are perceived as their competition. Both Macy's and Gimbels have gone the designer-clothes route with a vengeance. Many New Yorkers insist that Macy's Cellar—its food and housewares emporium—surpasses the food and housewares department at Bloomingdale's.

## EATING PLACES

This part of town is not considered a particularly rich eating-out area. In fact, many of us think of it as one of the worst parts of Manhattan for dining. We will eat here only if we have to—because we work in the garment industry or because we're going to see the Knicks play at the Garden, and we have only twenty minutes before game time to grab a bite to eat. Selecting a place here is really a matter of choosing among the lesser of the evils. Which coffee shop will it be: Squires or Chock Full O' Nuts?

If you do find yourself in the neighborhood and hungry, however, try one of the better and more interesting Jewish and/or dairy restaurants that remain from the time the garment district was filled with predominantly Jewish workers. Now the typical worker here is more likely to be Hispanic than Jewish, and the number of Spanish restaurants far exceeds the dairy or Jewish eating places. **Dubrow's Cafeteria** (515 Seventh Avenue) is a dairy restaurant and delicatessen, while **Hershey's Dairy Restaurant** (167 West 29th Street) is, as its name implies, a dairy restaurant only, which means, actually, dairy-vegetarian (see the section on the Lower East Side for details of typical dairy restaurant dishes). **Lou Siegel's** (209 West 38th Street) is a more for-mal, more expensive restaurant. Lou Siegel's is also Kosher, which means, among other things, that since meat is served, no dairy prod-ucts are. On a practical level, this will require that you resist the in-credible urge to order a glass of milk with your chocolate seven-layer cake.

## Times Square: *Theater District / West Fifties–Carnegie Hall Area*

Though the area of Times Square and the theater district (42nd Street to the low Fifties between Sixth and Eighth Avenues) is one of the city's leading tourist centers, it's also one of Manhattan's tawdriest, sleaziest sections. For every legitimate theater located here, there are at least five illegitimate ones, that is, porn houses. Sex shops, peep shows, pornographic bookstores, massage parlors, and prostitutes overshadow the Broadway theaters (which are actually just off Broadway, primarily to the west). They, far more so than the legiti-mate theaters, set the tone for this part of the city.

In truth, Times Square and vicinity is a kind of pockmark on the face of Manhattan. And it's a particularly troublesome one, for unlike other pockmarks throughout the city, this one happens to be very prominently placed. Visitors don't always see other pockmarks. On the other hand, no visitor to the city has ever missed seeing Times Square.

Thus, it should be perfectly understandable why we tend to be on the defensive when you mention Times Square. We constantly have to explain to out-of-towners that Times Square is Times Square and not New York City; that its sleaziness is peculiar to it, and that its denizens make up a unique subculture that you won't come across in most other parts of the city.

We are always in the position of explaining that if one were to live in New York, it would not mean living in the middle of Times Square. Few New Yorkers live in Midtown to begin with, and hardly a soul lives in the Times Square area. In fact, compared to many oth-er neighborhoods, unless you go to see a Broadway show, Times Square is one of the easiest areas in Manhattan to avoid altogether—and many of us do so assiduously. We may find ourselves coming within its fringes for one reason or another, but if we wish, we can usually manage to avoid coming into its center. We almost never, for instance, *have* to walk on Eighth Avenue through the Forties—perhaps the area's raunchiest stretch—in the course of our normal comings and goings about the city.

Yet, all the explanations and qualifications notwithstanding, Times Square remains an embarrassment to a lot of New Yorkers. For twenty or thirty years now politicians, realtors, and businessmen have been trying to clean up Times Square. The division of the City Planning Department assigned to the Times Square redevelopment project works overtime. In the past several years literally hundreds of proposals for the restoration of the area have been put forward. They range from the ridiculous to the sublime, with the overwhelming majority falling into the former category.

There have been proposals to create a giant family-oriented amusement park in the middle of Times Square, to build a mammoth exhibition center, to bring trolleys back into the area, to create a huge pedestrian mall, to use special lighting effects on the tops of buildings, to reclad the Allied Chemical Building (built on the steel framework of the original New York Times Building) in a new "skin" to cover the one that was put on to cover the original skeleton. More recently, the strategy seems to be to infuse Times Square with massive numbers of new "high-class" establishments, such as luxury hotels, apartment buildings, office buildings, and legitimate theaters. A major redevelopment plan just adopted by the city and state entails the construction of four office towers, a hotel, and a merchandise mart (for the garment industry), and the renovation of several theaters into legitimate ones—on and just north of 42nd Street between Broadway and Eighth Avenue. And, of course, old structures now housing so-called low-life establishments (pornographic bookstores and X-rated movie theaters) would come down to make room for the new buildings, as the city and state exercise their powers of eminent domain in an unprecedented way.

To many of us this appears to be wishful thinking. The strategy doesn't seem to recognize just how pervasive the sleaze really is. Nor does it acknowledge the legacy or ethos of Times Square as being the kind of place it is and attracting the kinds of businesses and people that it does. One or two luxury hotels and four or five office towers do not the East Fifties make.

The powers that be should either accept Times Square for what it is (after all, since Broadway seems to set attendance records almost every year, tourists apparently can't be that offended by the area), or else simply knock *everything* down and start all over from scratch. But to talk about things like lighting effects and trolleys is truly absurd.

Anyone who thinks the problem of street crime can be solved easily should know something about street crime in Times Square—which has one of the highest crime rates in New York City. For one thing, the Times Square area demonstrates that street crime in desolate areas will not be solved simply by encouraging more people to be on the streets. Something like eight thousand people *an hour* walk the block of 42nd Street between Seventh and Eighth Avenues, and yet it is the worst crime block in the city.

Nor is the answer to street crime merely increasing the number of cops on foot patrol. This same block is the most-patrolled block in Manhattan—foot patrol, mounted patrol, and plainclothesmen—and still has more crime (particularly robberies) than any other block.

## OF INTEREST

**1) Women Against Pornography**   (579 Ninth Avenue). This is an organization founded a few years ago by a group of feminists to fight against the proliferation of pornography everywhere and in Times Square in particular. Unlike politicians and realtors, for whom the concern is that pornography is bad for business, Women Against Pornography is concerned with the fact that pornography is bad for women—that it uses and abuses women, encourages sexual crimes against women, and promotes a generalized societal attitude of woman as object. Among the group's consciousness-raising activities is a guided "pornographic tour" of Times Square.

**2) Out-of-Town Newspapers**   (42nd Street and Broadway). If you're from Kansas, Florida, New Mexico, Paris, Rome, or anywhere else and can't live without your local paper, you should certainly know about this stand. It sells papers from all over the country and world.

**3) Sidewalk Chess**   (northeast corner of Broadway and 42nd Street). One is prepared to find anything and everything in Times Square, except serious chess playing. Nonetheless, serious chess is played here—on the street during the summers—and has been for the past several summers. Seven or eight chessboards are set up and players who man them challenge all comers. Serious betting, of course, goes along with the serious chess playing.

**4) Times Square Motor Hotel**    (Eighth Avenue at 43rd Street). Just so you'll know that Manhattan, which supposedly has everything, has motels as well.

**5) New York Times Building**    (229 West 43rd Street between Seventh and Eighth Avenues). No one would suspect that the country's most respectable paper would be located in the middle of the city's least respectable section.

**6) Actors Equity Building**    (1560 Broadway at 46th Street). If you want to see working stars of the stage, see a Broadway play. But if you're more interested in seeing nonworking, would-be stars of the theater, stand outside the Actors Equity Building.

**7) High School of Performing Arts**    (120 West 46th Street between Sixth and Seventh Avenues). The High School of Performing Arts was the subject of the movie *Fame*, though the film was actually shot in another building—apparently because the Board of Ed wouldn't allow the film's makers to use Performing Arts because of four-letter words in the script.

In any case, this is the school that doting parents encourage their obviously talented children to attend in the hope that they too will grow up to be Liza Minnelli or Al Pacino, both of whom graduated from Performing Arts. The reaction of parents who are not New Yorkers will probably be, "How could anyone send their kids to school in Times Square?" (This is actually a moot question, for the High School of Performing Arts is planning to move to new quarters at Lincoln Center in 1983.)

**8) West Fifties**    (just above the theater district). Like the theater district below it, the West Fifties between Sixth and Eighth Avenues are absolutely crawling with tourists and are rife with tourist-oriented establishments—hotels, overdecorated and overpriced restaurants, nightclubs, supper clubs, and shops that sell "I Love New York" underwear and other souvenirs.

Tourists find this an ideal Midtown location—near the park, just above the theater district, a hop away from Rockefeller Center and Fifth Avenue shopping. It is precisely for that reason that New Yorkers tend to avoid it. We come here to see films, to go to Carnegie Hall, to attend the ballet at City Center, to take classes at the Art Students' League, to buy books at Coliseum Books, to take an out-of-town friend to the Russian Tea Room for coffee and dessert. Otherwise we have not much reason to come here.

A few places in the West Fifties that should be pointed out include: **Studio 54** (254 West 54th Street), the famous discothèque, though in light of the fact that its original owners went to jail for tax fraud and the disco fad has faded, by the time you see it, the building may be the *former* site of the once-famous Studio 54; the **Bombay Cinema** (225 West 57th Street), which shows only Indian films and, though one never sees lines out front stretching the length of 57th Street, the theater has existed for a number of years; and the **Carnegie Hall Cinema** (883 Seventh Avenue just below 57th Street), one of the best film repertory houses in New York, which shows old films and changes its program of double bills daily; in addition, it is one of the only movie houses in New York with a café inside, and one of the few theaters where refreshments include yogurt rather than popcorn.

## EATING PLACES

Few New Yorkers eat out around Times Square and the theater district. We know that restaurants here are mediocre, overpriced places that prey upon the captive market of out-of-town theatergoers who don't know any better.

There are a number of indications that prove restaurants here look solely to the tourist trade. In the theater district, for example, you'll find the only one or two Polynesian restaurants in the city. And you can be sure New Yorkers do not eat in Polynesian restaurants. Here too you find Chinese-American restaurants, and that is obviously meant to attract the tourist, for New Yorkers go to Chinese restaurants for Chinese food and not for chopped sirloin steaks and French fries. And speaking of steaks, the theater district has one of the city's largest concentrations of steak houses.

Even a place like Mamma Leone's looks primarily to tourists. No restaurant in New York which seeks a New York City clientele will advertise buffet dining, for that's just not something we find enticing. Buffets are a turnoff we associate with expediency rather than with good food. And, to be sure, it's no accident that the restaurants along 46th Street between Eighth and Ninth (called Restaurant Row by some) have parking lots. New Jerseyans, not New Yorkers, drive to restaurants.

The West Fifties above the theater district aren't much better insofar as finding nontourist places. Basically, the West Fifties have Chinese restaurants for tourists who wouldn't bother to go to Chinatown, Italian restaurants for those who wouldn't make the effort of finding a small neighborhood Italian place, and delis like the Stage, Carnegie, or Lindy's for tourists who wouldn't deign to visit the Lower East Side. And thus, as many New Yorkers do, you would do well to eat in some other part of the city when you come to this area of Midtown for a show. You can walk west to Hell's Kitchen, where there are a number of new eating places, particularly beneath and near the Manhattan Plaza Apartments on 42nd Street between Ninth and Tenth Avenues; or walk north to Columbus Avenue in the Seventies, which is now lined with about fifty restaurants and, at least compared to the West Fifties or theater district, is considered somewhat off the tourist path; or walk east to the Fifth Avenue area where you'll pay through the nose for a meal, but at least there's the chance of it being excellent.

Or, if you're intent upon staying in the theater district, a few very acceptable alternatives include: **Bangkok Cuisine** (885 Eighth Avenue) for very good, very inexpensive Thai food. Among the many Brazilian restaurants in the area, **Cabana Carioca** (123 West 45th Street) serves authentic Brazilian dishes at moderate prices. And **Molfetas** (307 West 47th Street) or any other of the Greek restaurants in the upper Forties near Eighth Avenue. At Molfetas and the other Greek places the food is hearty if not necessarily great, and prices are low. You'll be well fed and won't come away feeling you've been ripped off as so often is the case at restaurants in the area.

# Hell's Kitchen *(a.k.a. Clinton)*

Jewish politicians running for office in New York City trace their roots back to the Lower East Side in order to establish their ties to "the people." Similarly, politicians of every other ethnic stripe trace their roots to Hell's Kitchen (the West Thirties, Forties, and Fifties west of Eighth Avenue)—historically, home to poor Irish immigrants, then Germans, Italians, Greeks, and Hispanics. Authentic *West Side Story* territory.

When Senator Daniel Patrick Moynihan ran for the U.S. Senate in the late 1970s, in the most transparent though obviously successful effort to establish his working-class credentials and thus gain the blue-collar vote, he based an entire campaign on the fact that he grew up in Hell's Kitchen above his family's bar, or something to that effect. He would then talk about how he went on to City College, a public institution. (He conspicuously failed to mention that he spent just one year there and went on to graduate from Tufts, a private institution; or that he subsequently spent most of the rest of his adult years in Cambridge, at still other private and privileged institutions—first getting a Ph.D. from Harvard and then teaching at MIT.)

However, Pat Moynihan may have been one of the last politicians to be able to use Hell's Kitchen as a catch reference to mean "having ethnic, working-class roots." Unlike the Lower East Side, which is still overwhelmingly poor, though no longer predominantly Jewish—and in that respect is among the least changed neighborhoods in Manhattan—Hell's Kitchen has changed considerably in recent years, albeit more slowly than elsewhere around Manhattan.

The first dramatic change occurred when Hell's Kitchen was renamed Clinton, a name that will get someone seeking elective office exactly zero votes. To say that you grew up in the Clinton section of Manhattan would probably cost you votes, because most New Yorkers wouldn't have the slightest idea what you're talking about.

The biggest change, however, came with the completion of Manhattan Plaza Apartments on Ninth and Tenth Avenues between 42nd and 43rd Streets and the ensuing infusion of young, mostly white, middle-class people into the neighborhood. New restaurants, stores, theaters, and other establishments followed, and more white, middle-class residents followed them.

You now see buildings throughout the West Forties between Ninth and Tenth Avenues being renovated. And if you speak to old-time residents of this area, all they can talk about is how rents have skyrocketed in recent years and how poor people are being pushed out of Hell's Kitchen.

There are still many of us who would under no circumstances consider living west of Ninth Avenue; nor would we walk there at night. But there are just as many of us who would, though as recently as five years ago we wouldn't have been comfortable doing so.

Hell's Kitchen remains a kind of rough, multi-ethnic, socioeconomically mixed neighborhood, but it certainly has been pointed in the direction of *becoming* more uniformly white, middle- and upper-middle-income. In the vernacular of New York City, it is an "emerging neighborhood." It remains to be seen what effect the completion of the new convention center in 1984 (on Eleventh Avenue between 34th and 39th Streets) will have on Hell's Kitchen.

## OF INTEREST

**1) Manhattan Plaza Apartments** (Ninth and Tenth Avenues between 42nd and 43rd Streets). If there is any one apartment complex that is almost singly responsible for changing a neighborhood, this is it. When Manhattan Plaza was first completed, the developers couldn't give apartments away to middle- and lower-middle-income people for whom the project was built, and for which purpose federal housing grants had been secured. The complex was just too close to Times Square, and Eighth Avenue (pornography row) in particular.

To save their investment, the developers convinced HUD officials to allow them to rent to people of moderate means in the performing arts, who because of their profession would want to be near the theater district. And now, a swimming pool, tennis court, health club, and half a dozen restaurants later, you can be sure there is a waiting list to get an apartment here.

**2) Theater Row** (42nd Street between Ninth and Tenth Avenues, on either side of Dyer Avenue). This is a complex of seven small theaters, which together make up the single largest concentration of theaters on any one block in the city. They are nothing like Broadway theaters just a block or two away. As Off or even Off-Off Broadway theaters, they are much more experimental than those on Broadway. One theater in the complex, for instance, specializes in plays by and about Hispanics, another in plays by and about blacks. Additional theaters and a recording studio are located in the former West Side Air Terminal Building on the same block, just west of Dyer Avenue.

**3) The Actors Studio** (432 West 44th Street between Ninth and Tenth). This is where the likes of Paul Newman, Marlon Brando, Jane Fonda, Dustin Hoffman, Robert De Niro, and Jill Clayburgh first learned their craft. Apparently, Hollywood and Broadway stars still come back to the Actors Studio for lessons. The late Lee Strasberg was its artistic director.

**4) Ninth Avenue** (the high Thirties and the Forties). Ninth Avenue is not really a restaurant center as much as just a food center: meat, fish, vegetable, fruit, and spice markets, bakeries, and so on. Half the restaurants in New York get their meats, vegetables, and other food provisions on Ninth Avenue. It's always been dense with Italian and Greek food shops, and in recent years Ninth Avenue has also become a center for Filipino and Thai food.

Every spring there is a Ninth Avenue International Festival, which is the only time some New Yorkers venture here. If you really want to see Ninth Avenue, you should come other than on the weekend of the festival. There will be about half a million fewer people on Ninth Avenue when the festival is not going on.

**5) Film Center**   (the Forties and Fifties on Ninth Avenue and west of Ninth). This is not a film center in the Hollywood filmmaking sense, but rather it is the center for buying and renting filmmaking equipment, projectors, and screens; for film editing and distribution; and for film processing—developing, soundtracking, and so forth.

**6) Hare Krishna Center**   (340 West 55th Street just east of Ninth Avenue). This is a new twist to the population mix of Hell's Kitchen—Hare Krishna. The center occupies an entire building and includes a boutique of Hare Krishna imports and a health-food restaurant.

**7) Parking Garages and Parking Lots**   (throughout Hell's Kitchen). The parking-lot center of Manhattan. Apparently, while real-estate values remained relatively low in the area, parking lots were the best, most profitable way to utilize property. Now that Hell's Kitchen is coming up in the world—which means real-estate values are coming up in the world—don't be surprised if more and more parking lots become apartment buildings.

**8) The New York Exposition and Convention Center**   (34th to 39th Street between 11th and 12th Avenues). The Convention Center is probably a project more interesting to see in the construction stages than it will be as a completed building. To see how a five-block-long building is constructed is truly awesome, so go get a look before mid-1984, the projected completion date.

**9) Big Apple Miniature Golf**   (12th Avenue at 44th Street). Manhattan's only miniature-golf course warrants being mentioned.

## EATING PLACES

Since the completion of the Manhattan Plaza Apartments at Ninth Avenue and 42nd Street and Theater Row just across 42nd Street from them, there are now a lot more restaurants in the area. There must be four or five restaurants of the "tastefully appointed" variety within the Manhattan Plaza complex itself. There is even a restaurant on Ninth Avenue and 43rd Street called Hell's Kitchen Restaurant & Bar, a name no one would have dared use before Hell's Kitchen was renamed Clinton.

The **Food Workshop** (424 West 43rd Street), one of the new restaurants within the Manhattan Plaza complex, is an excellent health-food café and restaurant, though it is not particularly cheap; call it moderately priced. And a block away is **El Taquito** (402 West 44th Street), which could very well be the best Mexican restaurant in the city. The fact that it accepts no credit cards indicates that El Taquito makes no attempt to capture the tourist trade—a point in its favor.

There are a couple of Thai restaurants on Ninth in the mid-Fifties, and, of course, some of the old Italian standbys like **Manganaro's** on Ninth at 37th Street. But this part of Manhattan still remains better known for food stores than for restaurants.

One reasonable alternative to restaurant dining here is to collect sandwich or picnic provisions from the Italian, Jamaican, Polish, Filipino, Spanish, Greek, and African food stores that line Ninth, and then make your own meal. And under no circumstances should you miss getting dessert from the **Poseidon Bakery** (629 Ninth Avenue). Half the stores and restaurants in New York try to pass off the Greek pastry they've gotten from Poseidon as their own.

# Fifth Avenue Shopping District:
## *Rockefeller Center / 57th Street / Central Park South*

Fifth Avenue in the Fifties (actually, starting at around 47th or 48th Street, just below Saks)—including Rockefeller Center and the cross streets on either side of Fifth—is the city's most glamorous, most exclusive, most photographed, most visited area. This description once applied to the Thirties and Forties along Fifth as well, but not since they've come to look more like West 34th Street than Fifth Avenue— a blur of camera, record, Oriental rug, shoe, and optical stores (save for the distinguished B. Altman's and Lord & Taylor, and the New York Public Library).

If someone who is not from New York knows but one part of the city, this is it—Rockefeller Plaza, St. Patrick's Cathedral, Gucci, Tiffany's, Bergdorf's. Fifth Avenue is the universal image of New York City. It is the one place in the city in which Prince Charles and Lady Diana contemplated having a New York apartment—on top of the Trump Tower at 56th and Fifth. The Plaza Hotel at 59th Street and Fifth is the one New York building that has been featured in every movie ever made about the city. Residents of rural, dirt-road towns in the South can recognize the Plaza.

Fifth Avenue is what New York tourists come to see, and with the exception of the ice-skating rink at Rockefeller Plaza turning out to be somewhat smaller than they imagined, Fifth Avenue never seems to disappoint anyone. (This contrasts with Times Square, which seems to disappoint everyone.) Who cares if so many of the department stores once synonymous with fashionable Fifth Avenue and New York City—Saks, Lord & Taylor, Altman's, Bonwit's—now have branches in Westchester, Long Island, and New Jersey as well? To untold numbers of visitors, as well as to people who have never come to New York and maybe never will, Fifth Avenue *is* New York.

The irony is that for us New Yorkers, Fifth Avenue, probably more than any other part of Manhattan, can make us feel like tourists in our own city. This, of course, doesn't apply to that handful of wealthy matrons who come here weekly to shop and lunch, as opposed to those of us who come to Fifth Avenue to shop twice a year—Christmas and on our spouse's birthday—if that often. Nor does it apply to those of us who work in the area, walk Fifth Avenue almost daily, and thus take it for granted.

But almost all other New Yorkers come here infrequently, and when we do, we basically react the same way tourists do. We gawk.

We gawk at the line of limousines lined up in front of St. Patrick's—one of the few places in the neighborhood where cars can park as long as they're attended—with the chauffeurs inside waiting for their employers to finish up doing whatever one does at Elizabeth Arden's. We marvel at the fact that Fifth Avenue can be so crowded it makes Broadway seem deserted by comparison. Mostly we stare at the most elegantly, stylishly, and expensively dressed women in the city going into Bergdorf's to buy still more elegant, stylish, and expensive clothes to be worn for future clothes-shopping excursions.

Then we go back whence we came. We go back to New York.

Part of what makes Fifth Avenue seem so unlike New York to so many of us is that its atmosphere is far too cosmopolitan, too international. There's Gucci, Cartier, Bulgari, Vuitton, Cardin, Buccellati, with stores in Rome, London, Palm Beach, Hong Kong, and Düsseldorf. There are the ticket offices of all the international airlines. There are now Arab sheiks living in all the new apartment towers being built on and near Fifth. And as is the nature of cosmopolitanism, national characteristics—or in this case, New York City traits—become lost.

Cosmopolitanism turns all shops into Italian and French boutiques; transforms all ethnic food into international cuisine; makes everyone seem as though he or she obviously has a second home in Switzerland. One suspects, therefore, that Fifth Avenue in the Fifties shares more things in common with the Via Condotti in Rome or with any other major capital city's international glamour zone— where one goes to buy $500 boots, $1,000 dresses, $50 lunches, and $1 million condominiums—than it does with Seventh Avenue just two blocks away.

## OF INTEREST

**1) Mercantile Library**    (17 East 47th Street between Fifth and Madison). There are but a handful of quiet oases in Midtown, and this is one of them. Though it is a private library whose facilities are available to members who pay a yearly fee, the guess is that if you quietly enter and make your way to the very beautiful and very plush second-floor reading room, no one will notice or mind. There you'll find big, comfortable chairs, tables and desks, magazines, newspapers, coffee and tea (25¢ a cup), bathrooms, and extraordinary peace and quiet. And you will have seen a library that few New Yorkers—not even people who have worked in the area for thirty years— know about.

**2) Diamond District**    (West 47th Street between Fifth and Sixth). Diamonds certainly belong in this section of town, but the particular ambience of this street is wonderfully out of sync with Fifth Avenue elegance. That is to say, this district where diamonds are bought, cut, set, and sold—mostly by Hasidic Jews—has more the feel of the garment district than of Tiffany's.

**3) Scribner's**    (597 Fifth Avenue at 48th Street). This is one of the best-stocked bookstores in the city and one of the few

Fifth Avenue bookstores (Rizzoli is another) that still caters to the so-called carriage trade (which, one supposes, today means limousine trade). This is as opposed to the chain bookstores that now line Fifth—Barnes & Noble, Doubleday, B. Dalton—which depend more on street traffic. Bookstores, in fact, are probably the only stores in the Fifties along Fifth that do depend on street traffic. Actually, we shouldn't knock Fifth Avenue bookstores, since books are about the only things most of us can afford to buy on Fifth Avenue.

**4) Paley Park**   (East 53rd Street just east of Fifth). Most New Yorkers know about this little pocket park with its waterfall. What most don't know is that the waterfall was built for its aural rather than visual effect. In other words, its purpose is primarily to block out the noises from the street.

**5) Hunting World**   (16 East 53rd Street just off Fifth). Though no Fifth Avenue store in the Fifties sells what can be characterized as the necessities of life, Hunting World somehow seems to go to a ridiculous extreme. It could very well be New York's most decadent store: the store for the man—in this case, he-man—who has everything. Not to be taken too seriously.

**6) Films at the Museum of Modern Art**   (West 53rd Street just west of Fifth). No one need tell you about the art collection at the Modern, but less well known to visitors and newcomers is MoMA's film program. Its three films per day, which change every day, all for the price of museum admission make this the biggest film bargain in town. For New York City film freaks, MoMA is home away from home.

Outside the Modern, look up and you'll see the apartment tower recently built atop the museum. Seventeen million dollars were paid just for the air rights to build the tower, where a one-room studio apartment sells for $200,000.

**7) The New Residential Apartment Towers**   (on and just off Fifth Avenue). The tower above the Modern just mentioned, Olympic Tower (at 51st and Fifth), the tower above Saks (at 49th and Fifth), and the like indicate two trends here. One: the building of residential apartments on top of already existing buildings, since there is no room left in this part of Midtown to erect anything anywhere else. The alternative is to knock down perfectly good buildings—as was done with the old Bonwit Teller department store at 56th and

Fifth—and construct another one in its place. Hence, the Trump Tower where Prince Charles and Lady Di once considered paying $5 million for a twenty-one-room condominium. Two: the construction of residential apartments—condominiums all—in this part of Midtown where heretofore no one at all lived.

**8) 57th Street**   (east of Fifth Avenue). This could be the most international, jet-setty strip in New York—more so than Fifth itself. It's lined with French and Italian boutiques, French restaurants, and scores of art galleries. Fifty-seventh Street is *the* gallery block, even more than Madison Avenue or SoHo.

See what you want to see, but one store you must see is **Hammacher Schlemmer** (147 East 57th Street). It's really an adult toy store. Here you'll find a feather renovator, a five-foot-high pepper mill, a motorized surf board, a $3,000 copper roast-beef cart, a clock that gives the time in response to a clap of the hands, an automatic vacuum record cleaner, and so on. Perhaps New York's one unique store.

**9) Central Park South.**   New Yorkers will walk ten blocks out of their way to get to Central Park South, for it is one of the very few places in the city where we can always count upon being able to find and use a public bathroom. Most of us have never stayed at any of the fancy hotels on Central Park South—the St. Moritz, Park Lane, Plaza, for instance—but we can walk into any one of them and know exactly where the restrooms are located. We even have our favorites. Few New Yorkers can pass the Plaza without thinking of Scott and Zelda Fitzgerald frolicking in its fountain and of all the times we've used its bathrooms.

**EATING PLACES**

See the next section, since eating places in the Fifth Avenue shopping district overlap those in the Grand Central business district just to the east of Fifth Avenue.

# Grand Central and Vicinity
## *(Through the mid-Fifties)*

Consider the area just north of Grand Central as the heart of corporate America. Or, if you have a less sanguine view of big business, think of it as the belly of the beast.

In either case, the clusters of office towers here—from which we derive both our famed skyscraper "canyons" and much of our sky-line—represent the most prestigious business addresses in the city (include Sixth Avenue in the Fifties in this category as well, though that is a fairly recent development). Any corporation worthy of a Fortune 500 ranking has headquarters here. This is also where you'll find the large Madison Avenue advertising firms and the city's and country's largest publishing, public-relations, and communications firms.

More Brooks Brothers suits, wing-tipped shoes, attaché cases, and romantic novels find their way to this part of Midtown each day than anywhere else in the city. Which is to say, more New Yorkers who are professionals, white-collar workers, receptionists, and secretaries earn their living here than in any other part of town.

Upper-income suburbs surrounding New York owe their very existence to this East Side business district, for it is here that "the man in the gray flannel suit"—the suburban commuter—comes to earn his livelihood. (Unless he works for a financial institution—a bank, brokerage firm, investment house, insurance company, or the like—in which case he works in the Wall Street area.)

As a business district, it is as highly concentrated as the one in Los Angeles is spread out. If the image of Los Angelenos going to work each morning is that of being *dispersed* to points hither and yon, the image of New Yorkers is that of being *funneled* from points hither and yon into this one section of Midtown.

This in itself would make Grand Central and vicinity the most congested part of Manhattan, which it is. But in addition to being the major business district, this is also the major East Side hotel district (the conversion of the famed Biltmore Hotel into an office building notwithstanding), to say nothing of its proximity to the Fifth Avenue shopping district. Traffic moving across 42nd Street near Grand Central and the Hyatt Hotel, for example, supposedly moves at an average rate, over the course of a day, of something like five miles an hour. This means that during the rush hours, traffic moves hardly at all.

Heavy traffic is only one of the reasons we'll avoid this area unless we work or have business here. The heavy concentration of large buildings on small streets, which has the effect of creating the so-called canyons, also has the effect of capturing the fumes from vehicle traffic so that you can actually see, smell, and taste the air. On sunny days the canyon walls block out the sun. On breezy days they create veritable wind tunnels. Not an ecologically pleasant part of town.

Also, though there are probably no more physically imposing parts of Manhattan, there are certainly more interesting sections. Compared to shopping, entertainment, or even residential districts, there is less texture to the street life here—mostly people going to work or lunch or tourists coming from their hotels or dinner. There is nothing here that you might want to watch for hours on end as you might, for instance, want to for an entire afternoon in Washington Square Park in the Village. The East Side business and hotel district, unlike Washington Square Park, is conspicuously lacking in colorful characters.

Even the architecture in the area is considerably less interesting than it is awesome. For everyone but people who write about architecture, it seems the rectangles of glass that now dominate the area create the effect, at least, of architectural sameness. We have often overheard visitors comment that the buildings "all look alike." Many of us are inclined to agree.

Yet, for anyone who wants to know what it's like to live in New York—or in this case work here—it's imperative to visit this particular section of Midtown Manhattan. To do it right, you should visit during either the morning or the evening rush hour when tens of thousands of New Yorkers and commuters bedecked with attachés pour through the doors of the massive office towers and Grand Central. It is at that time only and in this part of Midtown primarily that one can share the feeling of wealth and power and the sense of importance that is uniquely associated with working in Midtown Manhattan.

Though not every New Yorker resides in a high-rise apartment building, that image, nevertheless, epitomizes living in the city. Similarly, though not everyone works in a Midtown office tower, that particular slice of New York life, more than any other, captures the essence—certainly people's fantasy—of working in New York.

Although the East Forties and Fifties have for decades been the most overbuilt section of the city, they still manage to be the location for about 80 percent of the new construction going on in New York at any given time. We can't imagine where developers could possibly find room to put up another sixty-story office tower, but up they continually go. There is never a time when we can come here and not have to walk around the makeshift sidewalks skirting some construction site. These impermanent obstructions are a permanent East Side Midtown feature. If one happens not to come to this area for, say, six months, one is always flabbergasted by the new buildings begun during that brief absence.

The reason the most overbuilt part of Manhattan continues to be the focal point of still more construction is simple. From a developer's point of view, this is the most desirable, potentially lucrative section of the entire city. No real estate is more valuable, brings higher rents, and is less risky as a speculative venture.

That is why, when during the 1960s hardly any new construction could be found anywhere in the city, there was new construction galore here. When in the mid-1970s the City of New York teetered on the edge of bankruptcy and development projects everywhere were shelved, here in the East Forties and Fifties—the "golden Fifties" primarily—new construction went on uninterrupted. And that is why St. Bartholomew's Church at Park and 50th was offered $100 million for the land on which it sits so that an office building could be constructed on the site.

## OF INTEREST

**1) Vanderbilt Avenue**   (just west of Grand Central). Vanderbilt is Midtown's least-known street, sandwiched as it is between Madison and Grand Central, running only from 42nd Street to 46th.

The banner emblazoned with a huge "Y" which hangs from a building at 44th Street and Vanderbilt is not the YMCA. This is the **Yale Club**, conveniently located next to America's largest corporations where so many of its graduates work, and next to Grand Central, through which so many of Yale's graduates commute to their homes in the Connecticut suburbs. Not surprisingly, the rest of the Ivy League have their alumni clubs close to the center of corporate America too: Dartmouth, which shares the Yale Club; Harvard and Princeton just west of Fifth Avenue on 44th and 43rd Streets, respectively; and Cornell on 50th Street east of Lexington.

**2) Brooks Brothers**   (346 Madison Avenue at 44th Street). If you notice a particular preppy, WASP, Ivy League, corporate-executive look in and about the business district and you wonder how that look was cultivated, step inside Brooks Brothers.

Though it is most commonly associated with conservative, tweedy, preppy men's clothing, Brooks Brothers has a women's department as well. What is revealing about the women's department is that its size is just about proportional to the extent of the inroads women have made into the higher echelons of corporations—still a whole lot smaller than men's, but certainly larger than the corner it was just a few years ago.

In any case, whether for its sociological revelations, for its clothing, or just for the wood-paneled elegance and splendor of the place, you'll enjoy Brooks Brothers. Perhaps you'll discover how its customers decide to shop there as opposed to the nearby J. Press, F. R. Tripler, or Paul Stuart, which together with Brooks Brothers comprise a kind of "corporate-look row."

**3) St. Bartholomew's Church**   (Park Avenue at 50th Street). Is it worth $100 million? If you're interested, after weeks of debate, the board of the church decided not to sell the church itself for $100 million but to lease the land on which the adjoining community house sits for $10 million a year. God is bread!

**4) Park Avenue Plaza**   (entered from either 52nd or 53rd Street between Madison and Park). The building, among the newest glass structures in the area, has a public space inside which combines the features of the tree-filled atrium of the Ford Foundation Building and the waterfall of Paley Park. Indeed, it's a rainy-day alternative to drinking, sitting, reading, or doing whatever one does in Paley Park (two blocks away), since Paley Park provides no cover and this indoor park with waterfall does. Still, in terms of the manifold public uses to which space in office buildings can be devoted, on a scale of one to ten, Park Avenue Plaza rates only about a four or five. On the same scale, the **Citicorp Building**, with its dozens of stores and restaurants and the musical performances given in its atrium, ranks a ten.

**5) St. Peter's Church**   (Lexington Avenue at 54th Street in the shadows of the Citicorp Building). Unlike St. Bartholomew's, which didn't sell its church building itself to a corporation, St. Peter's did. It allowed Citicorp to raze the original St. Peter's for the construction of the Citicorp Building on the condition that a new church would be built on the site. The result is one of the more striking examples of modern church buildings you're likely to see anywhere. The interior may put some people off a bit, since it looks more like someone's newly furnished loft than a church. The pews, for example, look as if they came from Norsk (Danish modern) and the fabric from Marimekko (bold, bright, stark designs).

When St. Peter's isn't busy being a church, it's a theater. Many of us know it best as the Off-Off Broadway theater where *The Elephant Man* and other plays were first produced before going on to bigger and better theaters.

**6)** Small residential buildings along **Third Avenue** (sporadically here and there, with a cluster on either side of 53rd Street). Their interest to you is primarily as an indication of what planners contemplated building size to be in this part of the city when the streets were first laid out. In other words, five-story buildings rather than forty-story towers were planned for Madison, Park, Lexington, and Third, and even smaller buildings for the cross streets. Forty-story buildings on streets laid out for five-story ones goes a long way in explaining the present congestion on the East Side.

## EATING PLACES

The East Side business and hotel district together with the Fifth Avenue shopping district don't provide many candidates for *The Underground Gourmet* guide to New York. Rather you'll find restaurants here in *New York on $500 a Day*.

This is fancy, *very* expensive restaurant territory—the Fifties especially. French restaurants dominate; Japanese restaurants run a close second (55th Street between Fifth and Sixth, with at least seven or eight French restaurants on that one block, is a French restaurant row; 56th, also between Fifth and Sixth, is the Japanese equivalent).

What are considered to be the city's absolutely finest restaurants— the pantheons of excellent dining—are located in this part of Midtown: La Grenouille, Le Cygne, Le Chantilly, La Caravelle, The Four Seasons, Christ Cella, and Lutèce, which is just on the outskirts of the business district. We don't necessarily know this from firsthand experience, for the above are not dining establishments for the average New Yorker—not even the average New Yorker who eats out frequently—as the restaurants of Chinatown, for example, are.

We know about these restaurants more likely than not because we've read about them. They are of the sort that get reviewed constantly and have feature articles written about them interminably: how to get a reservation at Le Chantilly sooner than three weeks away; how to get a good table at Le Cygne; what great chefs of Europe have come to inspect their kitchens; who is the new pastry chef at The Four Seasons; what chef left which restaurant to start one of his own, etc., etc.

If we've been lucky enough to have eaten at one or more of the above once or twice, we may concede that the best meal we've ever had in the city was there. But still, these are never among New Yorkers' favorite restaurants, for a favorite restaurant is where we go constantly and know the menu intimately—neighborhood places usually. To have once eaten lunch at La Grenouille does not a favorite restaurant make.

If you should want to eat cheaply in this part of Midtown, you might want to know that aside from some coffee shops and sandwich shops scattered here and there (mostly in the Forties), some of the better inexpensive eating places are "hidden" inside other buildings. They include: **Zaro's** various counters (pasta, deli, bakery, yogurt, salads, baked potatoes) inside Grand Central Terminal; the **Oyster Bar**, also inside Grand Central, which is not really cheap, but compared to the Gloucester House, a seafood restaurant next to the Waldorf-Astoria, it is (also, the Oyster Bar is probably the only place you're ever likely to find ten varieties of oyster); the **Dining Commons** on the 18th floor of the City University of New York Graduate Center (33 West 42nd Street between Fifth and Sixth), which is a cafeteria that has the grace of serving wine in decanters; **Cafe Manhattan** inside the Manhattan Squash Club (41 West 42nd between Fifth and Sixth) for great hamburgers; the *soup, sandwich, and wine bars* in many of the Fifth Avenue department stores (Altman's, Lord & Taylor, Bergdorf's, Bonwit's); several cafés and the health-food restaurant inside the Citicorp Building's Market; and if an ice cream will tide you over, **Peppermint Park** inside the IND subway station on 53rd Street, just west of Fifth and across from the Museum of Modern Art, which sells delicious ice cream at about two-thirds the price of what ice cream anywhere else in Manhattan costs.

If you remember visiting New York as a child and delighting in getting food from behind the coin-operated windows of the various Horn & Hardart Automats, you might want to know that the only Automat left in the city—albeit on a much reduced scale—is the **Horn & Hardart** on 42nd Street just east of Grand Central. It's recommended not for food but for nostalgia.

# Turtle Bay: *Tudor City* / *Beekman Place* / *Sutton Place* / *United Nations*

Turtle Bay (the mid-to-upper Forties east of Third Avenue) and the East Fifties east of Third (including Sutton Place and Beekman Place) are essentially residential neighborhoods. They are also essentially wealthy, WASP residential neighborhoods—"middle-income" Tudor City, the United Nations, a huge collection of ethnic restaurants, and the Sutton Place Synagogue notwithstanding. Three or four children are rumored to be living in the East Forties and Fifties. You will not see much stoopball being played here.

If one doesn't live here, the most obvious reasons to come to this area are either to eat out or to count the number of Mercedeses and Rolls-Royces parked along Sutton Place and Beekman Place. These are two of the city's absolutely ritziest addresses—comparable to Fifth Avenue along Central Park, the difference being that here on Sutton or Beekman Place the rich have chosen a river view over a park view.

Though tourists will come to this neighborhood to visit the United Nations, we New Yorkers never do. If there is one attraction that interests us less than the Empire State Building, it is the U.N.

New Yorkers who live in the East Forties and Fifties east of Third—East Forties residents in particular—have always insisted that living here is different from living on the *Upper* East Side east of Third: quieter, less commercial, less trendy, more diverse, and more of a neighborhood, they say. (Which is why they insist upon being called East Siders, never Upper East Siders.) Here little old ladies plant flowers and trees in Tudor City. Here the iconoclastic, reclusive Katharine Hepburn and Greta Garbo reside (in Turtle Bay and on Beekman Place, respectively). Here—and because of these differences—three administrative assistants at the U.N. who share a two-bedroom apartment in Tudor City have always felt vastly superior to three stewardesses who share a two-bedroom apartment on East 77th just off First.

In the most general sense, these differences between the Forties and Fifties and the Upper East Side still do exist. However, the degree of difference is smaller than it was, and shrinking all the time. The feeling is that the quiet residential East Forties and Fifties have quietly become less quiet than they were.

Every other week—with the opening of a new restaurant with piano bar—First and Second Avenues below 59th come to look more and more like First and Second above 59th Street. Every other month—with the erection of another faceless, white-brick apartment building—First and Second below 59th Street appear more and more to be a clone of First and Second above 59th. The small service stores—cleaners, stationeries, newsstands, shoe-repair places—which once characterized First and Second Avenues have yielded to the likes of The Quilted Giraffe restaurant and Sedutto's Ice Cream. And knowing one's local maitre d' is just not the same as knowing one's local newspaperman.

Though the three administrative assistants who live in Tudor City still feel vastly superior to the three stewardesses who live on East 77th, it seems they now have a lot less cause to. Walk up Second Avenue through the Forties and Fifties into the Sixties and Seventies and judge for yourself.

## OF INTEREST

**1)** The view from **Tudor City**   (East 40th to 43rd between First and Second Avenues). Residents of Tudor City insist that if you stand here at 42nd Street and look west, you get one of the best views anywhere in the city—all the way to the New Jersey Palisades. Caveat to visitors: the Chrysler Building is *not* the Empire State.

**2)** Atrium of the **Ford Foundation**   (320 East 43rd Street between First and Second). Trees grow in Brooklyn *and* inside the Ford Foundation Building. Walking through the atrium is fun—sort of like walking through a greenhouse.

**3) Amster Yard**   (211 East 49th Street between Second and Third Avenues). This is a hidden private courtyard, which during the day is open to the public. Not open to the public at any time are the gardens that lie between the rows of town houses on 49th and 48th Streets (called **Turtle Bay Gardens**). Maybe Katharine Hepburn, who lives here, will let you into the gardens through her apartment.

**4) Greenacre Park**   (51st Street just east of Third Avenue). Not nearly as well known as Paley Park on 53rd just east of Fifth, Greenacre is actually a larger, much more neighborhood-type pocket park with a more interesting fountain-waterfall than Paley's. Come here in the morning and you see neighborhood residents eating breakfast.

The concession in Greenacre Park is one of the few places left in Manhattan where you can still get a 35¢ cup of coffee. This is particularly significant so close to Sutton Place and Beekman Place, a neighborhood where stores sell food, sandwiches, and drinks at about 40 percent more than anywhere else.

**5) Beekman Place** and **Sutton Place** (Beekman runs from 49th to 51st Street just before you get to the FDR Drive, while Sutton Place extends from 53rd to 59th, also along the Drive). Perhaps the most discerning of souls can distinguish between Beekman and Sutton Places. To the more humble among us, they exude an equal dose of affluence. On either place, one can practically hear a pin—no doubt, diamond pin—drop, which in Midtown Manhattan is saying something.

Usually some resident or other is good enough to leave a street-level window or two open so that you can get a glimpse of how the exceedingly rich live—or at least cook, for the street-level windows usually look into the kitchen.

Throughout Beekman and Sutton Places, the streets lead out onto a park or plaza overlooking the FDR Drive and the East River. **Riverview Terrace** (just above Sutton Square at the end of 57th Street, behind the gates) never has fewer than two Mercedeses and an Aston Martin, it seems, parked on it. A ridiculously rarefied setting for New York City.

**6) River House** (435 East 52nd Street, as far east as you can go). Considered one of the very most exclusive buildings in the city (Henry and Nancy Kissinger, for instance, live here), River House succeeded in proving just how exclusive it is when it recently refused to allow Gloria Vanderbilt (of Vanderbilt family and Vanderbilt jeans fame) to buy a million-dollar co-op apartment in the building.

**7) St. James Towers** (415 East 54th Street) and **River Tower** (420 East 54th Street). These two buildings, opposite each other on 54th Street between First Avenue and Sutton Place, are among two of the most superluxurious of the "superluxury" apartment buildings that have been built in the East Fifties in recent years. At the St. James, a co-op, the price of an apartment ranges from $360,000 (for a one-bedroom apartment) to $7 million (for a penthouse apartment that was made by joining what had originally been planned as three separate penthouses). At the River Tower, a rental building (premised on the belief that there are still people in New York who would rather rent than buy), apartments go for anywhere from about $4,000 a month (for a two-bedroom apartment) to almost $7,000 a month (for certain of the three-bedroom apartments).

**8) Recreation Center**    (348 East 54th Street between First and Second Avenues). There is no justice in the world. Here in the midst of one of Manhattan's most exclusive neighborhoods—and just one block down from the St. James Towers and River Tower described earlier—is a city recreation center with gym, running track, and pool, open to the public, and *all for free*. During the summer, with adults off to their summer places and kids off to camp, the facilities go virtually unused.

**9) Michael's Pub**    (211 East 55th Street between Second and Third Avenues). This is where Woody Allen plays Dixieland jazz on Monday nights. When he didn't show up at the Academy Awards to accept his Oscar for *Annie Hall*, his excuse was that it was Monday night, and he had to play at Michael's.

**10) Male Prostitutes**    (in the low and mid-Fifties between Second and Third Avenues). Young male prostitutes walk these streets, for the Fifties have a huge gay male population—older and richer than gay men who live in the Village, generally. The gay scene—beyond the prostitutes—is nowhere as overt as the Village, but it's pervasive nonetheless. There are many gay bars throughout the Fifties, and the Mayfair Restaurant on First Avenue between 52nd and 53rd Streets is well known in the area as a favorite dining place for gay men.

## EATING PLACES

This part of Manhattan has the unique distinction of having residents who consider Lutèce, Le Perigord, the Box Tree, and the Palm "great neighborhood restaurants." They may be great (Lutèce is considered by many New York City's finest restaurant), but most of us don't consider restaurants where dinner for two can cost $100 or more neighborhood places. (It must be the sawdust on the floor of the Palm that gives it a neighborhood-restaurant feeling.)

Eating places line both sides of First and Second Avenues, with additional—usually very expensive, usually French—restaurants on the cross streets. East 58th Street between Second and Third has thirteen or fourteen restaurants on one block alone. (Called "Restaurant

Row" by neighborhood people, somewhat derogatorily, one detects. It does remind one of La Cienega Boulevard in Los Angeles.)

New Yorkers who live here swear that the Chinese restaurants are better than those in Chinatown. Those who have tried them all say **Hunam** (845 Second Avenue) is the best of the restaurants run by "the Shun Lee people" (proprietors of Shun Lee Dynasty and Shun Lee Palace as well). And the absolute best of all the Chinese restaurants is said to be **Sichuan Pavilion** (322 East 44th Street), which is run by the Chinese government.

Everyone talks about the lines outside **Hobeau's** (963 First Avenue)—primarily a fish place—and for that reason everyone assumes it must be a good restaurant, though one gets the feeling that personal experiences didn't necessarily confirm that assumption. Nonetheless, it is an inexpensive restaurant in a neighborhood not known for inexpensive restaurants.

Other fairly inexpensive eating places include the Indian restaurants, such as **India Pavilion** (325 East 54th Street), **Nupur** (819 Second Avenue), and **Madras-Woodlands Restaurant** (310 East 44th Street), an Indian vegetarian restaurant. Nupur is probably the cheapest of the three, and Madras Woodlands probably the best.

Among the better-known eating places in the area is **Goldberg's Pizzeria** (996 Second Avenue). It wins *New York* magazine's pizza award for its deep-dish pizza. Not quite as well known is **Nyborg & Nelson** (937 Second Avenue), located on the second floor above a Scandinavian deli. A perfectly acceptable lunch (serves lunches only) can be had for about $4.00 or $5.00. And among the least-known eating places is the **Delegates' Dining Room** in the United Nations, which apparently everyone believes is off limits to all but U.N. personnel. It's not, though you do need a visitor's pass to get in. Lunch only is served here, and the only pervasive complaint seems to be that the food isn't always piping hot. Eating lunch next to the Secretary General of the United Nations may be compensation for that.

Two unusual bars in the neighborhood are **Costello's** (225 East 44th Street), where you get the opportunity to drink with *Daily News* reporters, since the Daily News Building is nearby; and the glass-enclosed bar on top of the **Beekman Towers Hotel** (3 Mitchell Place, at the foot of Beekman Place) for an outstanding view of the city, the East River, and the Pepsi-Cola sign in Queens.

# 20 Uptown

## Upper West Side: *Lincoln Center/ Morningside Heights*

Though certain East Siders consider the Upper West Side "the other side of the tracks" so to speak, most other New Yorkers have always thought of it as one of the city's most highly desirable residential neighborhoods. Historically, it has been in particular favor among middle- and upper-income New Yorkers of a Jewish, liberal, cultural, intellectual, or artistic bent, though admittedly that characterization is less true now than it once was.

The reasons for the great appeal of the Upper West Side are obvious. Lincoln Center is at one end, Columbia at the other, and Zabar's gourmet deli in between. It is near both Central and Riverside Parks.

Old, elegant, high-ceilinged apartment buildings line Central Park West, Riverside Drive, and West End Avenue—buildings in which apartments are large enough to accommodate one's family, one's grand piano, and one's live-in help if need be. There are magnificent brownstone and whitestone blocks throughout. Plus, the Upper West Side abounds with food stores, movie theaters, bookstores, boutiques, antique stores, and restaurants (to whose ranks another fifty or so restaurants-cum-sidewalk-café have been added along the recently gentrified stretches of Columbus and Amsterdam Avenues in the Seventies, and heading north).

What is not so obvious, however—and what distinguishes the Upper West Side from all other highly favored Manhattan neighborhoods—is that it is also filled with public housing, transient hotels, blighted blocks of tenements and abandoned buildings, West Side shopping-bag ladies, West Side crazies, addicts, and drunks. The consequences of this for middle- and upper-income West Siders are interesting.

On the negative side: The Upper West Side is a high-crime area (it is unique among the city's high-crime areas in that it is the only one in which you will find the defendant, his legal-aid lawyer, *and* the judge in the case all living within a block or two of each other); it is a checkerboard of "safe" and "unsafe" zones, which means the shortest distance between the 93rd Street exit of the IRT subway station on Broadway and one's apartment on 93rd and Riverside is not necessarily a straight line; and its block parties, once devoted to raising money for trees, are now devoted to raising money to pay for private security guards.

On the positive side: The Upper West Side is not a cloister—that is, no one escapes New York City by living on the West Side; it is nothing like the Upper East Side (it has always been the case that Upper West Siders derive their identity not so much from residing here as from not living on the Upper East Side); and one can live on the Upper West Side and still feel like a liberal. (As long as there is a methadone clinic nearby, one can live in a ten-room Central Park West co-op and still feel one is liberal. As long as poor Haitians and Dominicans live on Amsterdam Avenue, one can live in a duplex on any number of the beautiful brownstone blocks between Amsterdam and Columbus and still feel that one lives in a racially and economically integrated neighborhood. And as long as one's son gets his skateboard stolen every now and then, one can assuage one's guilt for sending him to a $5,000-a-year progressive West Side private school in lieu of the local public schools.)

Since the apartment-vacancy rate on the Upper West Side has in recent years been less than 1 percent, a rate that is lower than in many other areas of the city, it seems clear that the positives far outweigh the negatives.

As already mentioned, the *raison d'être* of the Upper West Side has always been that it not be like the Upper East Side. Therefore, the recent observations that West Side rents are becoming as high as those on the East Side, and that Columbus Avenue in the Seventies looks like the singles scene of First Avenue in the Sixties, have caused a certain amount of consternation to West Siders. The concern, despite the validity of the observations, still seems somewhat premature.

For the Upper West Side to become just like the Upper East Side, the following would have to occur: all the remaining transient hotels on and off Broadway would have to be converted to luxury co-op apartments; the public housing on Amsterdam Avenue would have to be demolished and the low- and middle-income subsidized housing on Columbus Avenue in the Nineties would have to be eliminated; and the restaurants and boutiques on Columbus and Amsterdam in the Seventies would have to extend through the Eighties, Nineties, and Hundreds as well.

Before the West Side becomes exactly like the East Side, all psychiatric practices would have to change to gynecology; luncheonettes to coffee shops; Red Apple supermarkets to Gristede's; the repertory film houses to first-run theaters; and the secondhand furniture stores to art galleries.

The Upper West Side won't be like the Upper East Side until blacks, Hispanics, old people, and poor people disappear; until the *Wall Street Journal* starts outselling *The New York Review of Books*; until its political representatives have names like Carter Burden. Or until one no longer hears Yiddish, Spanish, or Creole being spoken; until one no longer hears the sound of typewriters or musical instruments or voices singing scales; and until one no longer has to walk over and around bodies sprawled on the sidewalk in order to get into Zabar's.

This won't happen overnight—Columbus Avenue and Amsterdam Avenue in the Seventies notwithstanding. We hope never.

As a matter of orientation, you should know that the Upper West Side is wealthiest near the parks—Riverside and Central. Central Park West is the Upper West Side's most fashionable address, its Fifth Avenue, and Riverside Drive is the second most fashionable address, with West End Avenue close behind. Generally, the West Side becomes less rich as one goes toward Broadway from the direction of either Riverside or Central Park.

Broadway, on the other hand, is the heart and soul of the Upper West Side—its commercial, shopping, and entertainment center. Broadway is the West Side's magnetic north. Whenever anyone runs into someone one knows on the Upper West Side, it almost always occurs on Broadway. Broadway *is* the Upper West Side.

# OF INTEREST

*Along Riverside Drive*

**1) 79th Street Boat Basin**    (actually west of Riverside on the Hudson at 79th Street). This is proof that not only do people own boats in Manhattan and keep them moored here, but that they live on them too. The Boat Basin claims about a hundred residents. In past summers, the rotunda of the Boat Basin has served as an outdoor theater as well.

**2) New York Buddhist Church**    (332 Riverside Drive at 105th Street). The "Jewish Upper West Side's" only Buddhist church. Just around the corner from the church, on **105th between Riverside and West End**, you'll find one of the Upper West Side's loveliest blocks; called "the whitestone block."

**3) Children's Mansion**    (351 Riverside Drive at 107th Street). New York's only day-care center located inside a mansion.

**4)** Mosaic benches surrounding **Grant's Tomb**    (Riverside Drive at 122nd Street). The colorful and whimsical benches and arches around Grant's Tomb have been called folk art by their supporters and a disgrace upon the dignity of the tomb by their detractors. The controversy surrounding their installation is the only thing that prompts New Yorkers to visit Grant's Tomb. One purpose of the project was to involve community kids in its construction and thereby discourage the covering of the tomb itself with graffiti "art." In that respect the project has failed, since Grant's Tomb is covered by almost as much graffiti as some of the subway cars on the Broadway–7th Avenue line.

*Along West End Avenue*

**1) Penn Central Railroad Yards**    (actually west of West End Avenue from 57th to 72nd Street). This sixty-two-acre site—the largest undeveloped plot of land in Manhattan, and abandoned for the past twenty years—has been slated as the site of the proposed Lincoln West housing project. Lincoln West is to be a $1 billion, mostly luxury housing complex of more than four thousand apartments. Lincoln West won approval despite objections of many West Siders who feared what an additional ten thousand residents would do to an already crowded neighborhood, and who doubted that luxury housing is the answer to the city's housing shortage. Why, then, was it approved? Jobs and taxes, of course.

**2) Calhoun School**    (433 West End Avenue at 81st Street). What looks like a giant television set is actually a private school. Calhoun is among what must amount to thirty or forty private schools on the Upper West Side.

**3) No. 924 West End Avenue**    (at 105th Street). On top of this thirteen-story cooperative apartment building are about 120 solar collectors. Constructed in 1978, they represent an experiment to provide hot water for a huge New York City apartment house by means of solar energy. It is now several years, several breakdowns, several months of 60-degree "hot" water, and about $200,000 later. Whether the experiment has proved successful is not altogether clear.

**4) West Side Marxist Center**    (955 West End Avenue at 107th Street). That the West Side has a neighborhood Marxist Center and the East Side never would marks another major difference between East and West.

*Along Broadway*

**1) Needle Park**    (in the middle of Broadway at 72nd Street). Though it's officially named Verdi Square, the park is more widely known as Needle Park. Any doubts as to whether this referred to its shape or to a particular park activity were resolved when Hollywood produced the film *Panic in Needle Park*, featuring Al Pacino as a heroin addict.

Though Needle Park has been renovated, it's not clear whether sociologically anything else here has changed. Needle Park, incidentally, marks the point on Broadway where bench-sitting on the island that runs up the middle of Broadway begins. The image of old people and down-and-out West Siders—mostly from nearby transient hotels—sitting along the median strip and inhaling auto fumes from all sides is one of the more enduring ones we have of the Upper West Side.

**2) Ansonia Hotel**    (west side of Broadway between 73rd and 74th Streets). Though the Ansonia is mostly written about for its architectural grandeur (Beaux-Arts design inside and out), it is mostly known as the former site of the Continental Baths, where the singer Bette Midler would perform before audiences of gay men wrapped in towels; and as the former site of Plato's Retreat, one of the city's best-known sex clubs.

**3) Zabar's**   (west side of Broadway at 80th Street). Next to Macy's, Gimbels, and Bloomingdale's, this gourmet deli is probably the best-known store in New York. You find people in London walking around with Zabar's shopping bags. It's been featured in books and films, and they'll probably write a play about Zabar's someday.

If you decide to visit (about twenty thousand people each day do), unless you go five minutes after it opens or five minutes before it closes, be prepared to spend a lot of time on lines.

**4) Thalia Theater**   (West 95th Street just west of Broadway). The Thalia is known as the city's funkiest movie house, but also the theater where more New York City film buffs have been "educated" than anywhere else. One caveat about the Thalia: it slopes down and then up, so if you don't want someone's head blocking your view, avoid the "gully" in the middle at all costs.

**5)**   Instead of waiting inside the lobby of the Thalia for the next show to begin (where, by the way, you can't help but overhear the soundtrack of the film you're about to see), you might consider visiting **Pomander Walk**, just half a block down from the Thalia (Pomander Walk can be entered from either West 95th or 94th). It is the Upper West Side's only mews. Not as "perfect" as MacDougal Alley, Grove Court, Washington Mews, or any of the other mews in the Village, but then nothing on the Upper West Side is as perfect as anything in the Village.

**6) SRO (Single-Room-Occupancy) Hotels**   (on and off Broadway, mostly in the Seventies, Eighties, and Nineties). Any building on the Upper West Side called "hotel something or other" is not a tourist hotel. These are resident hotels occupied primarily by welfare recipients, the elderly poor, transients, and a hodgepodge of West Side down-and-out characters. They have been a major dumping ground for mental-hospital patients released—often prematurely—from the overcrowded state mental institutions. SROs are also rife with crime, prostitution, and drug addiction.

Single-room-occupancy hotels have been a fixture on the West Side for a long time. Part of the West Side "renaissance" has entailed forcing out SRO tenants and converting the hotels into luxury housing. Once about eighty SROs dotted the Upper West Side; now fewer than forty do, and the number is constantly declining (and the number of people sleeping on the streets of the city is simultaneously—and not just coincidentally—increasing).

The controversy involving SROs is a major one on the West Side. It is a particularly thorny issue for Upper West Side liberals, who might go out of their way to avoid walking on a block lined with transient hotels but nevertheless decry their conversion to co-op apartments.

**7) Morningside Heights**    (110th Street to 125th between Riverside Park and Morningside Park, but with Broadway at its spine). Morningside Heights *is* Columbia University (Barnard too). What Columbia doesn't actually use, it owns (it's said that Columbia owns something like one out of every five buildings in the area). Morningside Heights is the New York City version of a college town, which means it doesn't resemble a college town at all if Ann Arbor, Madison, or Berkeley are the standards.

Contrary to popular belief, 110th Street on the Upper West Side is not central Harlem. Ivy League schools are not to be found in Harlem. Columbia is near—not in—Harlem, which is a world of difference.

### Along Amsterdam Avenue and Columbus Avenue

**1) Akitas of Distinction**    (532 Columbus Avenue between 85th and 86th Streets). How drastically has this part of the Upper West Side changed? In what a few years ago was probably a bodega is now a store exclusively devoted to the sale of Akitas (dogs that look like huskies but are actually indigenous to Japan, not Alaska), the new "in" dog in New York City. Price? About $500 to $3,000.

**2) West Side Urban Renewal Project**    (87th Street to 97th Street between Amsterdam and Central Park West). Nestled between the clearly gentrified Seventies and the clearly ungentrified Hundreds are the Eighties and Nineties, which make up the West Side Urban Renewal Project. The project represents an attempt at urban renewal that would include community participation in the decision-making process; low-, middle-, and upper-income housing (and most of the new high-rises in the Nineties include this combination); and massive renovation rather than massive demolition. The project has had its problems—the fact that it was started about twenty-five years ago and remains unfinished being among them. But despite that, the area of the project is one of the most racially and economically mixed residential neighborhoods in Manhattan. No small accomplishment indeed.

While in the neighborhood, you might want to take a peek at the **People's Garden** (Columbus Avenue between 89th and 90th Streets), of which there are a scant few in New York.

**3) Manhattan Valley**    (100th to 110th Street between Amsterdam and Central Park West). When New Yorkers talk about the gentrified West Side, the new West Side, the West Side brownstone renaissance, and so on, this is *not* the area of which they speak. Predominantly poor and primarily Hispanic (mostly Dominican but with many Cubans, Haitians, and other West Indians), the area is easily recognizable as you walk up, say, Amsterdam. It's where the street life turns from sidewalk cafés to dice games, dominos, card games, and salsa music. Where hardware stores displaying tastefully placed pieces of driftwood in the window turn into undecorated tire repair shops, bodegas, numbers joints, and luncheonette-sized places serving Spanish food. Manhattan Valley presents the challenge that all poor neighborhoods in the city do—how to upgrade it without gentrifying it, how to save the neighborhood without destroying it at the same time.

*Along Central Park West*

**1) The Dakota**    (Central Park West at 72nd Street). This is the Upper West Side's most exclusive co-op apartment building—some say the city's most exclusive building. (As everyone seems to know by now, the name derives from the fact that when the Dakota was built in the latter part of the nineteenth century, it was so far from the center of Manhattan activity that it was as if it were as far away as the Dakotas.) This is the building where John Lennon lived and in front of which he was shot. (At the time of his death, he and Yoko were said to have owned something like five apartments—totaling more than 20 rooms—in the Dakota.) Other famous residents include Lauren Bacall, Leonard Bernstein, Rex Reed, and Roberta Flack.

Almost as famous as the Dakota is the **San Remo**, two blocks north at Central Park West and 74th. Among its celebrity residents are Diane Keaton, Dustin Hoffman, Tony Randall, and Barry Manilow.

## EATING PLACES

The Upper West Side is best known for its Chinese restaurants (probably more here than in any other neighborhood save Chinatown), its Cuban-Chinese restaurants, and its sidewalk-café restaurants (concentrated around Lincoln Center and on Amsterdam and Columbus in the Seventies, but moving north quickly). Sidewalk dining has become *de rigueur* on the West Side. Even ice cream shops and coffee shops now have sidewalk tables.

One doesn't need much advice regarding the slew of new eating places that have opened on Columbus and Amsterdam within the past few years. All one need do is start walking north in the high Sixties. Almost every other establishment is a restaurant, and what isn't is related to food in some other way—bakery, gourmet food market, caterer, cookwares, and so on. You'll find the new restaurants along Columbus and Amsterdam strikingly similar, if not by virtue of cuisine, then by virtue of the sameness of decor or ambience, which, of course, you'll pay for—$6.00 for a bowl of chili or $7.00 for tacos at a Columbus Avenue "chili parlor."

Upper West Side eating places that are somewhat more obscure than those just referred to and are excellent, relatively inexpensive, and for the most part, long-established institutions include:

Chinese: **Hunan Royal** (2519 Broadway at 94th Street); **Empire Szechuan Gourmet** (2574 Broadway at 97th Street); and **Empire Szechuan Columbus** (Columbus Avenue at 68th Street). Cuban-Chinese: **La Caridad** (Broadway at 78th Street); **Pez Dorado II** (2492 Broadway at 93rd Street); and **Dollar de Oro** (208 West 96th Street). Cuban only: **Ideal** (2825 Broadway at 109th Street).

In the category of interesting hybrids: **Lévana's Cafe/Bake Shop** (148 West 67th Street), which serves Kosher Moroccan delicacies; **Cherry Restaurant** (335 Columbus Avenue at 76th Street), a combination Japanese-Chinese-American coffee shop; **Souen** (2444 Broadway at 91st Street), a Japanese-macrobiotic restaurant; and **Mi Tierra** (668 Amsterdam Avenue at 93rd Street), which serves Mexican-Venezuelan dishes.

Miscellaneous eating places: **Symposium** (544 West 113th Street) for Greek food; **Green Tree** (1034 Amsterdam Avenue at 111th Street) for Hungarian food; and **Amir's** (2885 Broadway at 112th Street) for falafel and other Middle Eastern dishes. (Since these three places all have a large Columbia student clientele, their prices are *very* moderate.) Also, **Swiss Chalet Bar-B-Q** (27 West 72nd Street), which has nothing to do with Swiss food, but rather specializes in barbecued chicken and ribs (hamburgers too) at incredibly low prices; **Kamon Japanese Restaurant** (307 Columbus Avenue at 75th Street) for very interesting Japanese dishes; **The West End Café** (2911 Broadway at 115th Street)—once a favorite hangout for Allen Ginsberg, Jack Kerouac, and others during the Beat Generation—which serves inexpensive food and has live jazz (gets a Columbia crowd); **Mikell's** (760 Columbus Avenue at 97th Street), which serves more expensive food and also has excellent live jazz; **Mills Luncheonette** (2895 Broadway between 112th and 113th Streets), the prototypical New York City luncheonette; and the **Hungarian Pastry Shop** (1030 Amsterdam Avenue at 111th Street), simply the finest café in New York City (more relationships on the Upper West Side have been discussed, dissected, and resurrected at the HPS than anywhere else).

"Hidden" eating places: **Aki** (420 West 119th Street), a Japanese restaurant in the bottom of an apartment building; and **Terrace Restaurant Atop Butler Hall** (400 West 119th Street), a very expensive restaurant serving nouvelle cuisine located on the top of Butler Hall, a Columbia-owned apartment building.

In addition to these restaurants, food-related places include: **H & H Bagels** (Broadway at 80th Street), just down from Zabar's and reputed to have the best bagels in the city, where you can buy the same bagels Zabar's sells but get them warmer and cheaper; **Miss Grimble's** (305 Columbus Avenue at 75th Street) for a $20 cheesecake; and **Grossinger's** (337 Columbus Avenue at 76th Street) for somewhat less expensive cheesecake.

Finally, At Our Place, a Middle Eastern restaurant on Broadway between 94th and 95th Street, deserves mention if for no other reason than this: it changed its name from "Cleopatra" to "At Our Place" merely by rearranging the letters and adding one.

# Upper East Side: *Yorkville / Roosevelt Island*

The Upper East Side is to the rest of New York what Georgetown is to the rest of Washington, D.C.—domain of the smart set and the jet set, movers and shakers, doers and goers. The Upper East Side is the "dressed-for-success look." It is the staple of *New York Times* columns about style, fashion, society, art, and food. *Times* nuptial announcements too.

Jackie O. lives on the Upper East Side. Estée Lauder, Arthur Schlesinger, and Calvin Klein do too. Richard Nixon and Reggie Jackson did. The "Cosmo Girl" lives there. So do young recent graduates of Vassar and other proper private schools whose parents allowed them to come to New York to work in the curatorial department of Sotheby's only on the condition they live on the respectable and fashionable Upper East Side (which probably entails sharing an apartment with three other Vassar grads and still needing to get some help from home to cover the rent). It is Manhattan's wealthiest, whitest, safest neighborhood.

While other Manhattan neighborhoods reflect the urban life in general, the Upper East Side represents the urban good life in particular, however variously defined that may be. For some it means living in a ten-room Fifth Avenue or Park Avenue co-op and having a distinguished-looking, elderly doorman to hail your cabs, open your doors, carry your packages, and pick up your dry cleaning. For others, the urban good life entails owning a town house on East 68th Street between Fifth and Lex (without renting out the two top floors to help cover the mortgage payments as Brooklyn brownstone owners do) and giving "small" catered dinner parties for twelve in the middle of the week.

For two-income professionals, the good life may mean living in a red, white, or yellow brick luxury apartment building on Third Avenue, eating out at swank Second Avenue restaurants four nights a week, and ordering gourmet takeout from William Poll's on the other three. For young singles, the good life may consist of sharing a fifth-floor walk-up on York Avenue in the high Eighties with three friends and eating hamburgers at Jackson Hole coffee shops, but also jogging along the East River by morning and going to First Avenue singles bars by night.

For all Upper East Siders, the urban good life means that during the summer, one takes the "urban" out of one's life: one summers in the Hamptons where half the Upper East Side owns summer homes and half merely rents shares in summer homes—which, incidentally, is the distinction on the Upper East Side between the haves and have-nots.

Indeed, about the only negative aspect to living on the Upper East

Side is having to endure the verbal slings and arrows hurled by those of us who don't. Though admittedly part of the explanation for this verbal abuse may be sour grapes, there is, nevertheless, the undeniable truth that non–Upper East Siders think of the Upper East Side in more or less the same way New Yorkers think of Los Angeles. And that's not particularly kindly.

This is partially attributable to the fact that Madison Avenue in the Sixties—with its international boutiques—resembles Rodeo Drive in Beverly Hills; that being somewhat underdressed on the Upper East Side makes one feel as conspicuous as being somewhat overweight on an L.A. beach; that Upper East Siders don't walk anywhere (they take cabs); and, like Southern Californians, Upper East Siders have year-round tans.

As far as non–Upper East Siders are concerned, the Upper East Side, like Los Angeles, lacks a sense of neighborhood (being on a first-name basis with your doorman and the delivery boy from Gristede's is not the definition of neighborhood); it has no center (nothing, for example, like Broadway on the Upper West Side or Washington Square Park in the Village); and it lacks a *hamish* sense (which when translated from the Yiddish roughly means that it lacks warmth, character, a down-to-earth quality). The absence of *hamish-ness* is evidenced by the plethora of nail (as in pedicure) boutiques, by the existence of at least a dozen branches of Pasta & Cheese gourmet food stores, by the propensity of drugstores and pharmacies to call themselves "chemists," by the ability to name a store Pinch Penny Pick a Pocket without being the least bit self-conscious, and by the absence of residents who know what *hamish* means.

For their part, Upper East Siders deal with abuse from the others in one of two ways. The more prevalent response is to associate only with other East Siders, which is not all that difficult as one travels from one's Park Avenue apartment to one's Park Avenue law firm to one's weekend home in Amagansett.

The other response is simple: "Eat your hearts out" (he/she said, standing there tall, trim, tanned, well-coiffed in his/her jogging outfit and "top of the line" Nike running shoes on his/her way home to change before going out for the evening).

One way to approach the Upper East Side is to think of it as consisting of two Upper East Sides—one west of Third Avenue and the other east. The former is older, grander, wealthier, and not very singles-oriented at all. The latter is newer, brassier, and very much singles-oriented indeed.

## OF INTEREST

*From Fifth Avenue to Third Avenue*

**1) 90th Street Entrance to Central Park**   This leads to the Central Park Reservoir. Besides being a reservoir, it's one of the most popular jogging spots in the city. Between the hours of 5:00 and 7:00 P.M. it offers a view of a cross-section of Upper East Siders. Since the track around the Reservoir is elevated, it also offers one of the best views of Central Park and Central Park West for anyone not able to look at the Park from a Fifth Avenue apartment (which, by the way, sells for anywhere from about $300,000 for a one-bedroom to about $1,000,000 for a three-bedroom apartment).

**2) Nonprofit Organizations**   (from Fifth to Park Avenue, particularly on the cross streets). Citywide, out of a total of more than $70 billion worth of real estate, about $26 billion—or nearly 40 percent—is tax-exempt. The problem for the City of New York is the loss of about $2 billion a year in potential real-estate-tax revenues. Much of that loss comes from this part of the Upper East Side, for no other residential neighborhood has such valuable real estate or such a large number of tax-exempt organizations—schools, churches, synagogues, foundations, missions, consulates, and so on—occupying that valuable real estate.

**3) Madison Avenue Boutiques**   A great many stores along Madison keep their doors locked during business hours. To gain entrance, one rings a bell and if one looks appropriately respectable, one gets buzzed in. The only thing this security system fails to protect the boutiques against is the contingency of being robbed by an extremely well-dressed thief.

**4) Weintraub Gallery**   (992 Madison Avenue at 77th Street). One of Madison Avenue's best-known galleries, it made the news a few years back when *Ubatuba*, a $90,000 sculpture installed on the sidewalk in front of the Weintraub Gallery, was knocked over by vandals and damaged. Insisting they would never give in to vandals, Upper East Siders raised money and had *Ubatuba* repaired, reinstalled, and reinforced. A few weeks later, *Ubatuba* was knocked over and shattered once again. It has not been rereinstalled. Vandals have won on the Upper East Side, which gives Upper East Siders an idea of what the MTA (Metropolitan Transportation Authority) is up against.

Just up the block from the Weintraub Gallery is a **sidewalk designed by Alexander Calder**, which should serve as a valuable lesson for installing art in public places. Sidewalks cannot be knocked over.

**5) Lobel's Prime Meats**   (1096 Madison Avenue between 82nd and 83rd Streets). This may not be the typical Upper East Side market, but it's certainly not atypical either. Lobel's (which displays sides of beef in the window with the fat cut into decorative frills) boasts higher prices than almost any other butcher shop you're likely to find as well as a clientele characterized by the fact that 75 percent have charge accounts there and 90 percent order by phone.

Just a couple of blocks up is **The Gourmet Liquor Store** (1118 Madison Avenue), which advertises "temperature-controlled wine cellars." And over on Park Avenue, you'll find the **Bristol Market** (1110 Park Avenue between 89th and 90th Streets), which still closes on Thursday afternoons, historically the maid's day off.

**6) Gourmet takeout food stores and caterers**   (up and down Madison, Lexington, and Third). The growth industry for the 1980s on the Upper East Side is fancy food. These places line Madison (**E.A.T.** at both 72nd Street and 80th Street and **Ruslan** at 81st Street), Third (**Neuman & Bogdonoff** at 79th Street and **Lorenzo & Maria's** at 80th), and especially Lexington Avenue (**Demarchelier** at 69th Street, **Word of Mouth** at 72nd, **Betsy's Place** at 73rd, **William Poll** at 75th, **Self-Chef** at 82nd, **Country Host** at 93rd, and others). Indeed, at least one observer of the scene has been prompted to dub Lexington Avenue "the kitchen of the Upper East Side"—doing the cooking for people too busy to cook for themselves. These gourmet takeout food stores are to the Upper East Side what Kentucky Fried Chicken is to other neighborhoods. But instead of offering fried chicken, french fries, cole slaw, and ketchup, they offer dishes like smoked eel and sausage, baked eggplant with shallots and garlic, bass en croûte, cognac-glazed bay onions, fresh foie gras, brioche loaf, shrimp and lobster soup, chocolate-covered truffles, and chocolate-covered strawberries; or the more simple and basic beef and broccoli, canneloni, or veal tonnatto.

**7) Richard Nixon's Former Residence**   (142 East 65th Street between Lexington and Third). Is this town house really worth $2.6

million? That's what Dick and Pat sold it for just two years after purchasing it for a mere $750,000. (The Nixons took their tidy little profit and fled to the suburbs. They now reside in Saddle River, New Jersey.)

Down the block at **115 East 65th Street** is the town house owned by the Palestine Liberation Organization (the one with the steel mesh over the windows and the twenty-four-hour police guard out front). What with the PLO and the Nixons living on the same block, one can't help but fantasize about what East 65th Street Block Association meetings must have been like.

**8) 160 East 92nd Street**    (between Lexington and Third). Wood frame houses belong in the Village or in Brooklyn Heights, not on the Upper East Side. Yet here one is; and a really gorgeous wood frame house too.

Though 92nd Street is a beautiful Upper East Side block, by 95th Street you're in a poor, nearly all nonwhite East Harlem neighborhood. Over on Park Avenue the transition is even quicker and more dramatic. On Park just below 96th you find luxury apartment buildings with uniformed doormen. On Park just over 96th are public housing, tenements, and abandoned buildings. (Not coincidentally, the tracks leading from Grand Central Terminal and up the length of Park Avenue run underneath Park Avenue until 96th Street. At 97th Street the tracks surface.)

### From Third Avenue to East End Avenue

**1) Ruppert Green**    (East 93rd Street to East 94th between Second and Third Avenues). Upper East Siders are better known for eating out than for growing their own food. Yet here is the oldest community garden in Manhattan. It may be the largest one as well. (Two proposed high-rise apartment complexes threaten the future existence of the garden, at least in its current site.)

**2) Thrift Shops**    (along Second and Third Avenues in the Seventies and Eighties). For some unknown reason, one of the city's wealthiest neighborhoods seems to have more charity-sponsored thrift shops than any other part of the city. *Noblesse oblige?*

**3) Serendipity**    (225 East 60th Street between Second and Third Avenues). At least half the commercial establishments on the Upper East Side are either clothes boutiques or restaurants. Killing two birds with one store, Serendipity is a clothes boutique and restaurant.

**4) Vertical Fitness & Racquet Club** (330 East 61st Street between First and Second Avenues). How can one build a country club in the middle of Manhattan? Vertically, of course. This six-story "country club" includes swimming pool, saunas, running tracks, exercise gyms, tennis courts, racquetball courts, squash courts, restaurant, and sun deck.

**5) The Kennelworth** (519 East 72nd Street just east of York Avenue). Perhaps not as famous as the Plaza or the Sherry-Netherland, The Kennelworth nevertheless is a luxury hotel . . . for pets! Posted check-in and check-out times and all. The Kennelworth offers rooms of 28, 37, and 55 square feet as well as "cat rooms."

**6) Carl Schurz Park** (east of East End Avenue along the East River from 84th to 90th Street). This is probably the best-maintained public park in the city, largely because of the activism of neighborhood residents. It might also have something to do with the fact that Gracie Mansion—the official residence of the mayor of New York—is located in the middle of it. At any rate, the toilets here are clean and the water fountains work when that's not the case anywhere else but Central Park, a tourist attraction.

**7) Public Housing** (east of First Avenue from 92nd to 96th Street). Unknown to most New Yorkers—and to most Upper East Siders for that matter—there is low-income public housing on the Upper East Side, albeit tucked away in its most northeastern corner. To be sure, not everyone on the Upper East Side is rich, but low-income residents no more set the tone on the Upper East Side than do minority scholarship students set the tone at Harvard.

**8) Yorkville** (the heart of which is First and Second Avenues in the Seventies and Eighties). Historically Yorkville has been the ethnic enclave of the Upper East Side—German Yorkville (around 86th Street and Second Avenue); Hungarian Yorkville (on Second Avenue in the low Eighties); Czech Yorkville (around First Avenue in the low Seventies). Today, however, little remains of the ethnic communities save a few German, Hungarian, and Czech restaurants (if you can even find them interspersed as they are between all the Italian, Indian, Mexican, Chinese, Japanese, Thai, even Afghan restaurants that are now located on Second Avenue in the Seventies and Eighties), a few cafés, a couple of social clubs, and a couple of newsstands. In fact, to whatever extent gentrification is taking place on the Upper East Side, it is here in Yorkville, the only part of the Upper East Side where the gentry hasn't always been.

One of the most interesting Yorkville streets is **East 78th Street** from Third Avenue to Cherokee Place (Cherokee Place being the Upper East Side's least-known street; it's just east of York Avenue). East 78th is a quiet block of mixed residential and commercial use. Amid the small apartment buildings, walk-ups, and town houses are hand laundries, insurance and real-estate offices, flower and gift shops, woodworking shops, an electrical company, a reader-advisor, a local branch of the Metallic Lathers Union, an auto-parts store, cleaners, a copy center, antique shops, garages, a car service, a Hungarian bakery, a Hungarian pastry shop, and more. All in all, a very un-Upper-East-Side-like street. The mixed use would make Jane Jacobs, urban sociologist and mixed-use advocate, smile, and the neighborhood atmosphere serves as an exception to the rule that there is no sense of neighborhood on the Upper East Side.

**9) Roosevelt Island**   (the tram to which is at Second Avenue and 59th Street). This is New York City's version of a "New Town." In fact, Roosevelt Island, a self-contained community, was developed by the same people who built the New Town in Columbia, Maryland. Roosevelt Island offers the opportunity to be in the city but not of it, if that's what one wants. Housing on Roosevelt Island is primarily for middle-income and lower-middle-income residents. Housing for the former faces the East River and the Manhattan skyline. Housing for the latter faces a Con Ed plant and Queens.

The major criticism of Roosevelt Island is that it is antiseptic. But no matter what you think of Roosevelt Island itself, the tram ride there and back justifies the journey. The ride gives one the unique chance—especially during warm-weather months—to observe the rooftop life of Manhattan: penthouses, greenhouses, sunbathers, patios, gardens, hot tubs.

## EATING PLACES

At least half the restaurants on the Upper East Side are really singles bars posing as restaurants. Restaurant-bars dominate the Upper East

Side, especially on Third Avenue in the Seventies and Eighties and on First Avenue in the Sixties and Seventies.

You can easily spot singles-oriented restaurant-bars by the fact that they're almost always named after their owners. That some use just the first name (Rusty's, Gregory's, Mortimer's) and some the last (Harper, Hoexter's, Churchill's, Wilson's) seems to be the major distinction among them. You can also spot these places by how crowded they are. They are always packed (this despite the fact that all Upper East Siders deny frequenting them), which means you wait for a table while having drinks at the bar.

Though other neighborhoods have singles places—just not quite so many as here—what is unique to the Upper East Side are "face places." These are restaurants such as Jim McMullen's, Oren & Aretsky's, and Herlihy's, which cater to the beautiful people; beautiful both figuratively and literally. That is, no one has actually proved that you won't get a table if you're not good-looking, but no one has denied that it helps to be attractive either.

Somewhat more difficult to discover than singles places are the following restaurants, which are all of a decidedly un-singles, decidedly neighborhood, character:

**Gino** (780 Lexington Avenue), a very warm Italian restaurant with a high noise level but low prices; **Pandit India Restaurant** (303 East 80th Street), known to regulars as Ozzie's, an excellent, hole-in-the-wall-sized Indian restaurant; **Hsing Hua Chinese** (1108 Park Avenue), which is a smaller than a hole-in-the-wall-sized Chinese restaurant on a part of exclusive Park Avenue where one would not expect any commercial establishments, much less a neighborhood-type Chinese restaurant; **Chef Ho's Hunan Manor** (1464 Second Avenue), which certain Upper East Siders insist is the only decent Chinese restaurant in the neighborhood; **Tokubei** (1425 Second Avenue), which those same certain Upper East Siders swear is the only decent Japanese restaurant in the neighborhood; and **Chez Olga** (1350 Madison Avenue), perhaps the smallest, cheapest, and most northerly (between 94th and 95th Streets) French restaurant on the Upper East Side. It's certainly one of the very few bring-your-own-wine restaurants in that neighborhood.

Though there are now more Japanese and Mexican restaurants in Yorkville than German, Hungarian, or Czech restaurants, among the few old European ethnic places left in the Seventies and Eighties east of Third Avenue are: **Ideal** (238 East 86th Street) for German food, **Tip Top** (1489 Second Avenue) for Hungarian cooking, and **Vasata** (339 East 75th Street) for Czech food.

Don't expect Austrian dishes as you might know them at **Vienna '79** (320 East 79th Street). It offers nouvelle Viennese cuisine, which is to Viennese cooking what nouvelle French cuisine is to traditional French cooking—lighter, among other things. Vienna '79 was among the handful of restaurants in New York in the past few years to receive the highest rating of four stars from Mimi Sheraton of the *Times*. Expect to pay four-star prices.

Some final caveats: Elaine's reputation rests far more heavily on the reputation of its celebrity patrons than on the quality of its food; the Department of Consumer Affairs has accused Maxwell's Plum of using little or no vodka in its Bloody Marys; Rusty Staub—the Rusty of Rusty's—could better serve the eating public by devoting all his energy to playing professional baseball; and Jackson Hole's hamburgers are indeed 7 ounces as advertised, the only problem being their rolls are made to accommodate 4-ounce burgers.

# 21 Upper Manhattan

## Harlem: *East Harlem / Hamilton Heights*

Despite the belief in some quarters that most blacks in New York live in Harlem—or contrary to the claim by certain tourist guides that half do—Harlem is not even the city's largest black community. It is, however, the most famous black community—the historical and symbolic "black capital" of America—but not the largest, as it once was.

In truth, only 5 percent of the city's black population (80,000 of 1.7 million) resides in Harlem. (This figure applies to central Harlem only, the traditional black quarter, not to East Harlem—also known as Spanish Harlem or El Barrio—which is mostly Hispanic. Nor to West Harlem, a.k.a. Hamilton Heights, which is both black and Hispanic.) Which means only about a quarter of Manhattan's black population of 310,000 or so lives there, according to the 1980 census, at any rate.

Black flight from Harlem—middle-class black flight mostly—began in the 1940s and continued on through the 1970s. As a result, the size of its black population, in absolute terms, shrank to about half of what it was.

There seem to be two ways of interpreting the black flight from Harlem. One view maintains that blacks left because other neighborhoods in the city once closed to them opened up, proving, according to at least one major New York political figure, that integration is working. This is, to be sure, a minority view held by eleven or twelve conservative Republicans and by a handful of wishful thinkers.

The other view—held by just about everyone else—is that blacks left Harlem to escape its increasing blight. And if one were to look around Harlem and count the number of abandoned buildings, one would probably subscribe to this position as well. Half the buildings in Harlem are now owned by the City of New York, which assumed control after they were abandoned by their owners. *Over* half of Harlem's residential buildings are owned by the City of New York, putting it in the somewhat uneasy position of being the city's largest slumlord.

At this point, the argument over whether blight resulted from flight, or blight caused the flight seems moot, for in either case, it is generally conceded by all that Harlem has seen better days.

If there is some consensus about Harlem's glorious past—the Jazz Age, the Harlem Renaissance, the Cotton Club, the Savoy, Small's Paradise, the Polo Grounds, the Apollo, and more—and about its less glorious present, there is no consensus about its future. The talk now is that Harlem is ready to be gentrified; that it is Manhattan's last frontier of not-yet-gentrified neighborhoods. Essentially this means that brownstones can be bought cheap.

There is evidence that gentrification has already begun, evidence that after four decades of fleeing from Harlem, the middle class is ready to move back to reclaim its architecturally magnificent housing stock (albeit with a little prodding from the impossibly tight, expensive housing market below 96th Street). When the City of New York recently held a lottery to sell thirteen brownstones it owned around historic Mount Morris Park—now called Marcus Garvey Park—hundreds entered. And since *New York* magazine has already published articles about gentrification in Harlem, it *must* be happening.

The concern in Harlem is that gentrification will have the following negative results: First, the influx of upwardly mobile young professionals will, as it has everywhere else, raise property values and rents and push poor people out. (Though most assume that the majority of professionals moving to Harlem will be black, some actually fear that once gentrification begins in earnest, whites will move in. Harlem community boards and realtors report an increase in inquiries about properties from whites, though whether the intended purpose is to reside in Harlem or merely to speculate in Harlem real estate is unclear. The latter seems more plausible for the time being.) Thus, although Harlem will be upgraded, it won't do any good for the poor. They'll still be poor. The difference will be that they'll be poor in the Bronx, where they'll be forced to move.

Second, gentrification won't improve the lot of poor residents who remain (since there are a dozen public-housing projects in central Harlem alone, there will always be huge numbers of low-income people who will reside in Harlem). In other words, if gentrification in Harlem results only in the proliferation of "nouvelle soul food" restaurants as opposed to, say, a public high school (there is no public high school), it won't do Harlem's poor a bit of good.

The majority of visitors to New York either ignore Harlem altogether or take tour buses through it. (You can always, for instance, see busloads of Dutch and German tourists standing in front of the Schomburg Library, which houses the largest collection on black history in the world, taking pictures of nearby abandoned buildings.) Neither response seems particularly enlightening. A more rewarding approach would be to walk Harlem and visit its sights and attractions the way you would any other neighborhood in the city.

Without having to belabor the obvious about race, poverty, drugs, crime, and related matters, suffice it to say that there are parts of Harlem more receptive to visitors than others. Consider the following "easy-to-travel" sections. In central Harlem: 125th Street (particularly in the vicinity of the State Office Building), and Lenox Avenue in the area of Harlem Hospital and the Schomburg Library. In west Harlem: around City College, and Sugar Hill, the area just north of City College on and off Convent Avenue. In East Harlem: East 116th Street.

## OF INTEREST

*In central Harlem*

**1) Theresa Towers**    (125th Street and Adam Clayton Powell, Jr., Boulevard, formerly called Seventh Avenue). Until the 1960s, this was the Theresa Hotel, reputed to be the largest hotel in the world catering to blacks. Fidel Castro—shunning the Hilton, the Plaza, the Pierre, and all other Midtown hotels—stayed at the Theresa when he visited New York in 1960. Today, the Theresa is an office building as well as the site of Malcolm-King College.

**2) Apollo Theatre**    (253 West 125th Street between Frederick Douglass Boulevard, formerly called Eighth Avenue, and Adam Clayton Powell, Jr., Boulevard). The Apollo was at one time the most famous theater in the world for black entertainers—singers, musicians, comics, and dancers. For a number of years, it may also have been New York's most famous unused theater (it and the Vivian Beaumont at Lincoln Center, though for different reasons). In the past ten years, the Apollo has been closed, reopened, and closed again. Its opening and closing is probably as good a bellwether of Harlem's economic health as anything else. Just recently, plans to renovate the Apollo into a cable television studio broadcasting weekly live performances were announced.

**3) Lenox Terrace**    (West 135th Street between Lenox Avenue and Fifth Avenue). This is Harlem's best-known luxury apartment building. Apparently it is the only apartment building in Harlem that still has a *uniformed* doorman. Moms Mabley once lived here. So did Nipsey Russell and Melba Moore. Among its better-known residents today are Basil Patterson, former New York Secretary of State, and Percy Sutton, former Manhattan Borough President.

Just east of Lenox Terrace on the north side of 135th Street are the **Riverton Houses**, which are among Harlem's few co-op apartment buildings. Lenox Terrace and Riverton Houses together probably make up the largest concentration of middle- and upper-middle-class blacks in Harlem.

**4) Striver's Row**    (West 138th and 139th Streets between Frederick Douglass Boulevard and Adam Clayton Powell, Jr., Boulevard). Striver's Row stands for the proposition that Harlem may not be nearly so amenable to gentrification as some now presume. These two blocks of gorgeous row houses have for years been owned and occupied by some of Harlem's wealthiest residents. Yet they've never had any gentrifying effect in the area beyond the two blocks. Nor do any of the commercial establishments at either end reflect the relative economic wealth that exists here. Rather, Striver's Row—as well as other middle-class enclaves in Harlem—has always been a two-block oasis amidst rubble.

In any case, Striver's Row must be seen; 139th Street is one of the most beautiful town-house blocks in New York City (the north side of the street consists of houses designed by Stanford White). It surprises many New Yorkers who see it for the first time that such a block exists in Harlem.

**5) Signs that read "Urban Renewal Project, John Lindsay, Mayor."** Throughout Harlem are abandoned, boarded-up buildings with these signs on them, indicating they were once designated for rehabilitation, but the work never went past the posting of the signs. These are particularly poignant reminders of good intentions never realized, since as you may or may not remember, John Lindsay last served as mayor of New York in 1973—just as vast sums of federal housing money were drying up under the Nixon Administration.

**6) Rucker Pro Tournament**   (Holcomb Rucker Memorial Park at 155th Street and Frederick Douglass Boulevard). The Rucker Tournament used to be *the* premier summer basketball tournament. It was loaded with pro ballplayers, many of whom have since abandoned its hard asphalt surface for the softer wood floor of the gym at City College, also in Harlem, where another summer pro league now runs. Or else the pros go out to L.A. and play in a summer pro basketball league out there.

Still, some of the best New York City–style basketball is played at the Rucker Tournament, including superb women's basketball, which precede the men's games. New York City basketball was created on such playgrounds as here. Not seeing a basketball game on a Harlem playground is like going to Spain and not seeing a bullfight.

*In West Harlem (Hamilton Heights)*

**1) Sugar Hill**   (140th to 155th Street along and off Convent Avenue). Sugar Hill is the most solidly gentrified neighborhood in Harlem. It's the black equivalent of the poshest sections of Park Slope in Brooklyn. Physically—that is, architecturally—it looks a lot like Park Slope also, every bit as architecturally elegant and diverse. If you think of Harlem only in terms of what you see and hear on the six o'clock news, you'll be surprised to see the likes of Sugar Hill.

**2) Aunt Len's Doll and Toy Museum**   (6 Hamilton Terrace just east of Convent Avenue, above 141st Street). The museum is housed on two floors of a town house in the middle of Sugar Hill. Tours are made by appointment and are conducted by Aunt Len herself.

**3) Sylvan Terrace**   (between Amsterdam Avenue and Jumel Terrace at 161st Street, just across from the Jumel Mansion, which makes this officially Washington Heights). Sylvan Terrace may be

Upper Manhattan's only mews. The homes are all a hundred years old, recently renovated, and unbelievably quaint.

*In East Harlem*

**1) La Marqueta**   (Park Avenue between 111th and 116th Streets). If you're looking to purchase goat meat, rabbits, tropical fruits, or tropical vegetables, this is the place to do it. La Marqueta is a five-block-long complex of mainly Spanish food stalls.

If you do decide to shop here, you may want to know that not long ago the City Department of Consumer Affairs did a check of La Marqueta and found two-thirds of the meat stalls engaged in the practice of "short-weighing," or representing meat to weigh more than it does. Which is the old story of the poor having to pay more for less.

Around La Marqueta are dozens of street merchants selling clothing and other dry goods, which makes it seem like a Hispanic Orchard Street, the area of outdoor clothing and apparel stalls on the Jewish Lower East Side.

**2) Cosmo Theatre**   (176 East 116th Street between Lexington and Third Avenues). Harlem's *only* movie theater.

**3) Taino Towers**   (122nd to 123rd Street between Second and Third Avenues). This project's thirty-five-story white concrete towers can be seen from virtually any point in East Harlem. Though from the outside it may look like luxury housing, Taino Towers is, in fact, public housing—one of about thirteen or fourteen low-income public-housing projects in East Harlem (this is in addition to the dozen projects in central Harlem).

Taino Towers took over ten years to complete and cost something like $100 million. When it is fully occupied, it will house about 650 families. Which prompted someone to write a letter to the editor of the *Times* and point out that instead of building Taino Towers, the government could have simply given each of the 650 families an outright bequest of $150,000. Or, if the $100 million was invested at 15 percent interest a year, it would generate enough income to provide each family an annual income of over $20,000. All of which leads one to ask, "What if he's right?"

**4) Little Italy**   (primarily in the vicinity of 116th Street and First Avenue). It comes as a surprise to most to discover that Spanish Harlem has an Italian community. Actually, Italians were in East Harlem long before Hispanics.

Though East Harlem's Little Italy once numbered in the thousands, it has since dwindled to minuscule proportions. Starting after the Second World War, Italians moved out of East Harlem en masse as Puerto Ricans en masse moved in. Today just a small number of Italian residents and Italian restaurants, cafés, food stores, social clubs, and funeral parlors remain.

East Harlem's Little Italy may be the grittiest, most tenacious Italian community around. Its survival all these years gives one the sense that a bomb couldn't displace it now.

## EATING PLACES

Though, as a rule, New Yorkers don't go to Harlem just to eat, that doesn't mean there aren't very good restaurants in Harlem. Among the good eating places in or near "easy-to-travel-in" neighborhoods are the following:

For soul-food cooking there are **La Famille** (2071 Fifth Avenue just below 125th Street) and **Sylvia's** (328 Lenox Avenue just above 125th). (Though many insist **Adele's**, on Frederick Douglass Boulevard and 119th Street, is better than Sylvia's, Adele's may be too close for comfort to the 116th Street drug scene.)

**Twenty Two West** (22 West 135th Street near the Schomburg Library, Harlem Hospital, and Lenox Terrace Apartments) is a coffee shop, restaurant, cocktail lounge, supper club, and disco! Its menu is that of a coffee shop–restaurant (including its 30¢ cup of coffee). During the lunch hour, Twenty Two West is a gathering spot for Harlem politicos.

**Bombay India** (465 West 125th Street) is an excellent Indian restaurant that has been in business for twenty-five years or more. It is actually closer to the center of Columbia University than to the center of Harlem.

In East Harlem, **Ponce de Leon** (171 East 116th Street) and the **San Juan** (167 East 116th) are probably the two best-known Spanish-American restaurants. Consensus is that the San Juan is the better of the two, and that **Del Pueblo** (2118 Third Avenue just below 116th Street), which is not as well known as either, is better than both.

**Rao's** (455 East 114th Street at Pleasant Avenue) is probably the best-known restaurant in East Harlem's Little Italy; or it certainly was after *The New York Times* reviewed it a few years ago. (Perhaps the only restaurant the *Times* has ever reviewed that is located in the bottom of an otherwise boarded up, abandoned building.) **Patsy's** (2287 First Avenue between 117th and 118th Streets) is also extremely well known, though community opinion seems split between it and **Andy's** (corner of First Avenue and 116th).

Finally, one of the great, nearly hidden pleasures of Little Italy is the **Café Espresso** (2281 First Avenue between 117th and 118th Streets). One knows this tiny place is called Café Espresso only by asking its owner. There is no sign out front indicating its name; just a small, almost obstructed, sign in the lower corner of the window that says "Italian food." Locals merely say, "Go have Angelo cook something for you. He cooks good." And so he does. Since there is no printed menu, one chooses from what happens to have been prepared that day, which changes every day. One also has the distinct feeling that the size of the servings and the price vary from customer to customer, and that the more often you go, the larger the portions become and the lower the price goes. Open only till four in the afternoon, Café Espresso is one of the few places of its kind left in the city. Dining there is not unlike eating in the home—in the kitchen—of an old Italian family.

# Washington Heights: *Inwood*

If you care to know what the Bronx is like without actually having to trek to the Bronx, you could just visit Washington Heights and Inwood. Not that the Heights-Inwood area of Manhattan is exactly like the Bronx, but it certainly smacks of the Bronx; certainly has more things in common with it than with the rest of Manhattan. Which is not a value judgment, even though Heights-Inwood residents themselves wince at the identification with the Bronx.

For instance, Heights-Inwood, like the Bronx, was once largely Jewish and Irish but is now largely Hispanic. (There is still a substantial Jewish presence in Washington Heights and a large Irish presence in Inwood, but overall, Hispanics—mostly Puerto Ricans, Cubans, Dominicans, and Ecuadorians—make up over 50 percent of the population, Dominicans being the largest Hispanic immigrant group and Ecuadorians the newest.) And as in the Bronx—not considering the very wealthy Riverdale section of the Bronx nor the very poor South

Bronx—Heights-Inwood residents are mostly New Yorkers of moderate means.

Heights-Inwood further shares with the Bronx a deep sense of neighborhood as well as a sense of great distance—albeit not geographical—from Manhattan. And like the Bronx, it suffers the ignominy of being largely ignored by Manhattanites (visitors to the Cloisters or Columbia Presbyterian Hospital being the two notable exceptions); or, at least, Manhattanites who live below 96th Street and who not only believe Heights-Inwood is like the Bronx but think it *is* in the Bronx.

## OF INTEREST

Recognizing the reality that one is not likely to traipse up to Heights-Inwood except to see the Cloisters—actually the uptown branch of the Metropolitan Museum of Art, which houses the Met's medieval art-and-architecture collection—the following are all within walking distance of the Cloisters:

**1)** View from **Fort Tryon** (**The Cloisters** is located in the middle of the park). From the lookout in the center of Fort Tryon Park, you get a superb view of the Hudson and the New Jersey Palisades. If you turn around, you then get a view of the Bronx.

One major difference between Fort Tryon Park—as well as **Inwood Hill Park** just north of it—and Central Park is that in Central Park you always have a sense that you are in a park in the middle of a city, but not so here. In fact, these parks provide the best opportunity in New York of finding out what the island of Manhattan was like before it was colonized.

**2) 16 West 186th Street**    (on the westernmost edge of 186th). This could be one of the most spectacular private homes in Manhattan. Half of it actually overhangs a cliff and is supported by two massive concrete pillars. It's the sort of house one expects to find in the Hollywood Hills, not in Manhattan.

**3) Castle Village Apartments**    (on Cabrini Boulevard between 181st and 186th Streets). In the back of these apartments are a great expanse of lawn and a promenade from which you get a magnificent view of the Hudson, the George Washington Bridge, and the Palisades. The view makes one wonder why residents of Beekman Place and Sutton Place would pay so much just to look out onto the Pepsi-

Cola sign in Queens. (A sign leading to the lawn and promenade says TENANTS ONLY, but if you walk quietly and discreetly, there should be no problem.)

**4) Hudson View Gardens** (entered from the front on Pinehurst Avenue at 183rd Street or from the rear on Cabrini Boulevard at 185th Street). This is Midtown Manhattan's Tudor City come to Upper Manhattan. If you can't ever imagine yourself living in a New York City apartment building, visit Hudson View Gardens. It may change your mind. (As for the Tenants Only sign, ditto the comments made above for the Castle Village Apartments.)

**5) Bench-sitters** in front of Dyckman House (Broadway and 204th Street). Most people come to Inwood to see Dyckman House, a restored eighteenth-century farmhouse, now a museum, which is interesting in its own right. But once you're here, don't miss the long line of New York City bench-sitters in front of Dyckman House. The southern exposure attracts professional bench-sitters the way honey attracts bees.

**6) Playground** (at West 207th Street and Seaman Avenue). This is the prototypical New York City playground—shuffleboard, basketball, handball, paddleball, tennis, volleyball, and about twenty different additional "devised" games adapted to the limited space available and to the asphalt surface.

**7) 207th Street** (west of Broadway). This street relates the ethnic history of Inwood, past and present. Old, old synagogues, bodegas galore, Irish bars, Kosher butchers, signs in Greek in store windows, and at places where newspapers are sold, papers in Yiddish, Greek, and Polish. Plus *El Diario* and the *Irish Echo*, of course.

## EATING PLACES

To quote even the most chauvinistic of Heights-Inwood residents: "This is a fantastic place to live but *not* to eat."

# 22 **Outer Boroughs**

Note: Though there is no reason why newcomers or visitors to New York shouldn't trek out to neighborhoods in the far reaches of Brooklyn, Queens, the Bronx, and Staten Island just to look around, the reality is that most won't. Most newcomers to the city will spend their initial months here exploring Manhattan and "doing Manhattan things." And most visitors will also spend most of their time—especially if it's limited—in Manhattan, and will journey to the outer boroughs only if there is an obvious tourist attraction or event to take them there. Hence, whereas all Manhattan neighborhoods have been described, the discussion of outer borough neighborhoods is limited to those in the vicinity—walking distance really—of tourist attractions, such as the Brooklyn Bridge, Shea Stadium, the Bronx Zoo, or the Staten Island Ferry.

## BROOKLYN

## Brooklyn Heights: *Fulton Ferry District / DUMBO / Downtown Shopping District / Cobble Hill / Boerum Hill / Carroll Gardens* (*at the foot of the BROOKLYN BRIDGE*)

About the only thing that Brooklyn Heights shares with the rest of Brooklyn is low buildings. (Indeed, the greater expanse of sky one sees because of the low buildings is usually the first thing that strikes someone coming to Brooklyn from Manhattan.) Otherwise you can say there is Brooklyn, and then there is Brooklyn Heights. In other words, if you meet someone who has an Ivy League degree, wears penny loafers, topsiders, or Pappagallos, regularly receives the L. L. Bean catalog, has a nanny for the kids when they're young, and sends them to private school when they're older—traits all very uncharacteristic of Brooklynites—and still claims to be a Brooklyn resident, you can safely assume he or she lives in Brooklyn Heights.

More specifically, Brooklyn Heights bears a much greater resemblance to the Upper East Side of Manhattan than it does to the rest of Brooklyn. Montague Street, its major commercial strip, is *the* chichi street in Brooklyn and could pass for an extension of Madison Avenue in the Eighties. Well, almost. Heights residents are mostly WASP and upper-income—lawyers, bankers, brokers. In truth, many of these residents would be living on the Upper East Side if it weren't for the fact they can walk to work from Brooklyn Heights; the Heights being at one end of the Brooklyn Bridge and Wall Street— where they work—being at the other.

While other neighborhoods in "Brownstone Brooklyn" have only recently been discovered as respectable places for Manhattan types to live, the Heights has enjoyed that reputation for a long time. For years it has been one of the wealthiest, most exclusive, and most desirable neighborhoods in all the city. Norman Mailer lives in the Heights. Truman Capote used to. Brooklyn Heights is to Manhattan as Hampstead is to London.

And though there are a number of New Yorkers who consider the Heights to be a rather stiff and unfriendly neighborhood, few consider it less than breathtakingly beautiful. It has been designated in its entirety as a landmark historic district. More than seven hundred of its houses were built between the 1820s and the Civil War. And its views of the river and the Manhattan skyline are incomparable. In short, there is no other New York City neighborhood quite so esthetically satisfying, none quite so peaceful, and none quite so enjoyable to walk around.

## OF INTEREST

*In Brooklyn Heights Proper*

**1) The Promenade**   (overlooking the East River). There is simply no better vantage point in all of New York for viewing the harbor and the lower Manhattan skyline. This magnificent view may explain why Norman Mailer, whose house backs on the Promenade, chooses to live in Brooklyn.

**2) Pierrepont Street Playground**   (just off the Promenade at Pierrepont Street). This playground will tell you as much about who lives in the Heights as anything else. Typically there seem to be as many nannies as mothers accompanying the children.

**3) No. 222 Columbia Heights**   (right next to the playground). No. 222 is the newest house in Brooklyn Heights. Built in 1980, it is about 120 years younger than any of the other brownstones on the block—and the only one with a swimming pool inside. And though its design required the approval of the Landmarks Preservation Commission, the house, nevertheless, raises the obvious question, "Does it work architecturally?"

**4) College Place**   (hidden between Hicks and Henry Streets and entered from Love Lane, which intersects Hicks and Henry just north of Pierrepont). This is the one carriage-house mews that most Heights residents themselves don't even know about, as opposed to the better-known **Grace Court Alley** (off Hicks Street between Remsen and Joralemon) or **Hunts Lane** (off Henry Street also between Remsen and Joralemon).

**5) Pineapple, Orange,** and **Cranberry Streets**   Not much in New York City, and certainly not in Brooklyn, gets described as quaint. Yet the ambience in the neighborhood of these streets, which is the oldest part of the Heights, is all quaintness and coziness on the order of an old New England town. That these streets were so named was the result of an attempt in the early 1800s to democratize the process of naming streets by having them named after random fruits rather than particular prominent citizens as in most of the rest of Brooklyn Heights.

**6) No. 135 Joralemon Street**   (between Clinton and Henry Streets). With its paint peeling, pillars rotting, and its roof looking as if it could cave in any minute, this house represents Brooklyn Heights' one eyesore. Apparently the owner has ignored appeals from both neighbors and the Landmarks Preservation Commission to clean the place up as well as six-figure offers from people who have wanted to buy the house from him. And if the house from the outside looks like a set from the horror film *Halloween III*, the interior is exquisite and impeccably kept. Go figure it out.

**7) Spencer Memorial Church**   (corner of Clinton and Remsen Streets). Brooklyn Heights may have more co-op apartments per square foot than any other neighborhood in the city. First the rental apartment buildings went co-op; then the resident hotels were converted to co-ops. And now this former church is a co-op apartment building too!

## Just on the outskirts of Brooklyn Heights

**1) Court Street.**   You'll notice that the office buildings are gradually being converted to apartment buildings, which points up the fact that downtown Brooklyn is becoming a better place to live than to do business.

**2) Atlantic Avenue**   (from the Brooklyn-Queens Expressway to Flatbush Avenue). From the Expressway to Court Street, Atlantic Avenue is the dividing line between Brooklyn Heights and Cobble Hill, and it is this stretch that constitutes the center of the Middle Eastern community in Brooklyn—in New York City, for that matter. Dozens of Middle Eastern (Yemeni and Lebanese mostly) restaurants, bakeries, and food and spice shops line Atlantic. Even Middle Eastern immigrants now living in Scarsdale come to Atlantic Avenue to load up on food supplies. And whenever there is upheaval anywhere in the Middle East, you can count on someone from Atlantic Avenue being interviewed on TV news for the reaction of America's Middle Eastern community; no matter that the crisis is in Iraq and the shopowner interviewed is from Yemen, which he left more than twenty years ago.

From Court Street to Flatbush Avenue, Atlantic Avenue runs through Boerum Hill, and this part of Atlantic is best known as a center for antiques—antique furniture mostly. It is also known for two of its "residences": the **Brooklyn House of Detention** (Atlantic Avenue at Boerum Place), which you can easily not notice, since it doesn't look that much different from a lot of New York City high-rises except for bars on *all* the windows, not just the ground floor windows; and **No. 423 Atlantic Avenue**, which to its occupants is a luxury co-op and to everyone else is the old Ex-Lax factory building.

*Just north of Brooklyn Heights*

**1) Fulton Ferry District**    (between Brooklyn Heights and the East River). What had a few years ago been a rather desolate industrial area is now a burgeoning residential neighborhood which even has tourist attractions. Among the more impressive examples of convert-ing a commercial building into a residential one is **No. 28 Cadman Plaza West**. This magnificent building was the Eagle Warehouse & Storage Company, on the site of an early office of the *Brooklyn Ea-gle*, the borough's very own daily newspaper up until the mid-1950s. If you've never seen the inside of a residential building converted from a commercial structure, ask a tenant coming out of No. 28 to let you in to just look around the lobby. *Très* chic.

Moored at Fulton Ferry Landing are two "barges" worth visiting: **Bargemusic**, which is actually a houseboat for most of the week, but on weekends is given over to musical performances—mostly cham-ber music; and **River Café**, which is built out on the water in the shadows of the Brooklyn Bridge and is hands-down the classiest res-taurant in all of Brooklyn. There are never fewer than about seven Jaguars in its parking lot, and you can usually read about who ate there in the daily gossip columns of the *Post*. If someone like Robert Redford says he's been to Brooklyn, what he really means is that he's been to the River Café.

**2) DUMBO**    (*D*own *U*nder the *M*anhattan *B*ridge *O*verpass). Not only is this one of Brooklyn's major industrial areas, in the past sev-eral years it has become Brooklyn's major artists' quarter as well. Art-ists who live and work here discovered DUMBO as a financially feasible alternative to SoHo, or anywhere else in Manhattan. (Loft dwellers here and in other parts of the city in commercial zones near bridges such as the Manhattan, Williamsburg, or 59th Street bridges, refer to themselves as the "bridge-and-tunnel people.") If you walk on **Front Street**, it will take you through the heart of the area's factory and warehouse buildings—the residential lofts are where there are lights on in the evenings and on weekends—and into **Vinegar Hill**, Brooklyn's least-known neighborhood. At the end of Front Street is an extraordinary white-clapboard mansion which used to belong to the Brooklyn Navy Yard but is now privately owned.

There are plans to develop this area as a residential, office, retail, and tourist center, so its days as an industrial and artists' quarter may be numbered.

## Just south of Brooklyn Heights

**1) Cobble Hill, Boerum Hill,** and **Carroll Gardens**    (Cobble Hill is south of Atlantic Avenue and west of Court Street; Boerum Hill is mostly south of Atlantic but east of Court; and Carroll Gardens is just south of both Cobble Hill and Boerum Hill, De Graw Street being the dividing line). These are among the more newly discovered neighborhoods of "Brownstone Brooklyn." A few years ago, these neighborhoods were referred to in the real-estate sections of the *Times* and *Voice* as "Brooklyn Heights Vicinity," since most read-ers wouldn't have known where these neighborhoods were other-wise. Now that they have been put on the gentrification map, their respective names in their own right attract upwardly mobile young professionals. On a gentrification scale of one to ten—Brooklyn Heights being a ten—Cobble Hill is about a seven, Boreum Hill a five, and Carroll Gardens a three. (A few years ago most Brooklyn-ites hadn't heard of Carroll Gardens, an old, stable predominantly working-class Italian neighborhood. Now recent arrivals to New York City who still have their Minnesota plates on their cars are mov-ing in.)

In Boerum Hill and Carroll Gardens particularly, the tensions be-tween the new breed of "brownstoners" and the older less affluent residents (in Boerum Hill they are mostly black and Hispanic and in Carroll Gardens Italian) are palpable. In Boerum Hill you see signs all over the place that say, for example, STOP DISPLACEMENT NOW. In Carroll Gardens it is impossible to be in a store or luncheonette and not hear a conversation about the "new people." "How the hell can someone who's twenty-five years old afford to pay $700 a month for rent?" "Why in the world do they rip up perfectly good linoleum and throw away practically new venetian blinds?" "And do they know that the parking spots left by their little foreign cars aren't big enough for our cars to get into?" And so forth and so on.

The politics of gentrification notwithstanding, all three of these neighborhoods have landmark historic blocks, and unlike Brooklyn neighborhoods farther out in the borough which tend to sprawl, these are eminently walkable. Under no circumstances should you miss **Warren Place** in Cobble Hill (off Warren Street, *i.e.*, through the gates, just west of Henry Street), which is the loveliest mews in New

York and will make you forget all Greenwich Village mews. Warren Place consists of two rows of eleven-foot-wide "town houses" built in the late 1800s as workingmen's housing but now anything but that.

And in Carroll Gardens, aside from **President Street** and **Carroll Street** (between Smith and Hoyt), its two landmark blocks, don't fail to stop in at **D'Amico's** (309 Court Street), where coffee beans are roasted throughout the day in a seventy-year-old cast-iron roasting machine; or **Cammareri's Bakery** (502 Henry Street), where bread is baked in a tiled oven over coals. These two stores—among the scores of small Italian shops and markets in the neighborhood—will give you some idea as to why the "new people" from Minnesota, North Carolina, *and* Manhattan find Carroll Gardens so authentic and so utterly old-world.

## EATING PLACES

*In Brooklyn Heights*
**Woerner's** (151 Remsen Street) for the best fresh baked-on-the-premises rolls and breads and desserts you're likely to find in any coffee-shop-restaurant; **Queen Italian Restaurant** (98 Court Street) for its pizza or its veal dishes; and **Jimmy's Falafel** (11 Court Street) for falafel.

Among the couple of dozen Atlantic Avenue Middle Eastern restaurants, according to those who have tried them all, the outstanding ones are: **Adnan's** (129 Atlantic Avenue); **Dar Lebnan** (151 Atlantic); the **Near East** (138 Court Street, just below Atlantic); and **Almontaser** (218 Court Street, about five blocks below Atlantic). About half the Middle Eastern restaurants in the area are owned by or were launched by the Almontaser family, in which case the cuisine is that of Yemen.

Though **India House** restaurant (139 Court Street) is easily overlooked among the profusion of Arabic eating places, it happens to be an absolutely outstanding Indian-Pakistani neighborhood restaurant—some say one of the best in all the city.

*In the Downtown Shopping District*
**Junior's** (386 Dekalb Avenue) for cheesecake (if it's not the very best cheesecake in the city, as *New York* magazine claimed ten years ago and Junior's personnel boast of with their "We're #1" buttons, it's

certainly among the very best cheesecake in the city). Also, for Jewish deli.

*In Cobble Hill*
**Veranda** restaurant (268 Clinton Street) for northern European cuisine including such Norwegian specialties as fresh poached salmon with Norwegian pepper-root sauce.

*In Boerum Hill*
**Lisanne** (448 Atlantic Avenue), one of the elegant, perfectly delightful, and perfectly appointed French restaurants that have recently opened in this part of Brooklyn—which, incidentally, makes Brooklyn the only outer borough with French restaurants (there is a "French restaurant" on Queens Boulevard in the Sunnyside section of Queens that does indeed serve onion soup, escargot, and chateaubriand, but as it also serves steak pizzaiola, jumbo ravioli parmigiana, and baked ziti, it does not count).

*In Carroll Gardens*
**Nino's Luncheonette Pizzeria** (531 Henry Street) for fantastic spinach pizza (maybe the only spinach pizza in the city); the **House of Pizza and Calzone** (132 Union Street) for first-rate traditional pizza; and **Ferdinando's Focacceria** (151 Union Street), a Sicilian restaurant serving lunch primarily, for panelli (sandwiches of deep-fried chickpea patties, mozzarella, and ricotta cheese served hot) and for vasteddi (same as panelli except that cow's spleen takes the place of chickpea patties). And while there are some good Italian restaurants in Carroll Gardens—**Casa Rosa** (384 Court Street) being the best among them—one always will find a contingent of Carroll Gardens cognoscenti at **Crisci's** (593 Lorimar Street) in the Greenpoint section of Brooklyn.

# Park Slope *(along the western boundary of PROSPECT PARK and an easy walk from either the BROOKLYN BOTANIC GARDENS or the BROOKLYN MUSEUM)*

If Brooklyn Heights (Brooklyn's answer to the Upper East Side) is the borough's best-known, most elegant, and most exclusive neighborhood, then Park Slope (Brooklyn's version of the Upper West Side) runs a close second in all three respects. Or at least this applies to the gentrified core of Park Slope—the north Slope from Sixth Avenue to Prospect Park between Flatbush Avenue and Ninth Street. Beyond Ninth Street, Park Slope is mostly poor and working-class Irish, Italian, Hispanic. Below Sixth Avenue, the Slope is mostly poor Hispanic.

Still, there are substantial differences between the Slope and the Heights, even though Seventh Avenue gets to look more like Montague Street all the time, to say nothing of the rapidly climbing rents. One major difference is that the Slope is more informal and less uptight than the Heights. As related by a longtime Heights resident who recently moved to Park Slope: "If people in the Slope aren't in fact friendlier than Heights residents, they at least seem friendlier. When we lived in the Heights, it took about three years before anyone said hello to us."

The Slope has its literary types (there are a slew of writers and editors who live in the Slope) as well as a few celebrities. Governor Carey lived on President Street and Prospect Park West for years, and when the actress Shirley MacLaine and the writer Pete Hamill were an item, they shared a Park Slope brownstone. But the dominant character of the north Slope is created by the young professionals who flocked here during the 1960s and 1970s when houses—usually in need of repair—could be bought cheap, rents were low, and the Slope was a clear alternative to both Manhattan and Brooklyn Heights. And although now the price of a house is about five times what it was in the 1970s and renting is becoming passé in the wave of co-op conversions—which means many of the original "pioneers" are now moving south to become pioneers in Windsor Terrace—the Slope still manages to retain some of the best of its older traits.

It is still a neighborhood that by New York City standards feels small-townish. Notices on bulletin boards and in shop windows announce cooperative playgroups for toddlers, infant swim programs, community chorales, neighborhood "alternative schools," food coop meetings, block-association meetings, film programs, stoop sales, and community crime-prevention meetings.

The Slope also remains a neighborhood with at least some residents who profess a political and social concern. If there is one Brooklyn neighborhood where there will be leafletting for a demonstration to protest U.S. involvement in El Salvador, for instance, it is Park Slope. If there are any neighborhoods left in the city that could still mobilize residents to prevent, say, a McDonald's from opening up, Park Slope is certainly one of them. If the West Village teems with gay men, the Slope abounds with gay women. And if elsewhere couples give lip service to shared parenting, in Park Slope it is *de rigueur*, as evidenced by the large number of men pushing baby carriages—or more likely, carrying babies in back carriers—in the middle of the week in the middle of the day.

And then too, the Slope—that is, the north Slope—remains one of the loveliest neighborhoods with some of the most diverse residential housing in New York. Most of the Slope between Seventh Avenue and Prospect Park, in fact, has been designated a historic district. Though the physical beauty of the Slope—as well as all the outward appearances of community involvement and concern—tends to mask the very real tensions that exist between the gentry of the north Slope and the working-class and poor residents in and around it who haven't yet been pushed out, still, by New York City standards at least, most would concede that Park Slope remains one of the city's most "livable" neighborhoods.

## OF INTEREST

**1) Soldiers' and Sailors' Memorial Arch**    (Grand Army Plaza at northern entrance to Prospect Park). Unbeknownst to most people, there are stairs within the arch that lead to the top. The Arch is open to the public, though only on weekends and holidays.

**2) Montgomery Place** and **Carroll Street**    (the latter from Seventh Avenue to the park). If you only have time to see two streets in Park Slope, see these two. There are none more beautiful—Carroll Street between Seventh and Eighth Avenues and the park for uniformity and Montgomery Place for diversity.

**3) Montauk Club**    (Eighth Avenue at Lincoln Place). This is the must-see building in Park Slope. It's been used as a movie location. It also has what could be the only outdoor paddle-tennis court in all of New York City.

**4) Seventh Avenue** and **Fifth Avenue.**    There is no better reflection of the two Slopes—the white middle- and upper-middle-income north Slope and the Irish, Italian, Hispanic working-class and poor south and west Slopes—than Seventh Avenue and Fifth Avenue, respectively. There is nothing on Fifth Avenue like **Le Parc Gourmet** (Seventh Avenue and Carroll Street), a four-story building devoted to fine food and dining (a café on the first floor, a fancy-food restaurant on the second, lounges on the third, and private dining rooms on the fourth). And there is nothing on Seventh Avenue like the abandoned stores along the commercially moribund stretches of Fifth Avenue north of about Union Street (a center of the city's shopsteading programs, under which abandoned stores now owned by the City of New York are turned over to shopkeepers who agree to fix them up); nor anything so prosaic as a Thom McAn shoe store, which you'll find along Fifth Avenue's commercially robust stretches south of 5th Street.

**5) John Jay High School**   (Seventh Avenue between 4th and 5th Streets). John Jay is a typical New York City high school. It's huge (between 4,000 and 5,000 students); it's mostly nonwhite (70 to 80 percent); and its enrollment does not include any of the middle- and upper-middle-class kids who live in the brownstones around the corner.

## EATING PLACES
The **Thai Lagoon** (238 Flatbush Avenue) for excellent Thai cuisine; **Circle's Café** (514 Seventh Avenue) for vegetarian and nonvegetarian food; and **Our Daily Bread** (330 Seventh Avenue) and **La Papaya** (331 Flatbush Avenue) for vegetarian dining only. La Papaya, incidentally, is a feminist vegetarian gourmet restaurant, with a women's bookstore above—that welcomes men to dine only on Tuesday evenings and at Sunday brunch.

And then there is **La Villa Storica** (225 9th Street), located in a huge, old (circa 1840), quasi-Victorian, quasi-Gothic house. Though dinners are served in the second-floor dining room—or out back in the garden during the summer—you're welcome to roam throughout the house, which is filled with period pieces of the mid-1800s. La Villa Storica serves Corsican dishes primarily (basically northern Italian cooking with a French influence).

An added attraction at La Villa Storica is the wall built around it, which you have to go around to 8th Street to see. Built of bricks from neighboring structures that had been razed—with statuettes and other ornate touches added—the wall explains the "villa" in La Villa Storica. It is a rather unlikely sight for Brooklyn in general and this block in particular, which is why you should see the wall by all means.

## Crown Heights: *Bedford-Stuyvesant (within easy walking distance of the BROOKLYN BOTANIC GARDENS, the BROOKLYN MUSEUM—the seventh-largest art museum in the country—and the BROOKLYN CHILDREN'S MUSEUM—the world's first museum for children that is devoted to natural science and natural history)*

Middle-income residences have more or less been the hallmark of Crown Heights through much of its history. In the early 1900s, middle-income Jews poured into Crown Heights—a move that from, say, the Lower East Side, was considered a substantial step up in the world. More recently, Crown Heights has become a step up for middle-income blacks who moved here from poorer Brooklyn neighborhoods like Bedford-Stuyvesant, which borders on Crown Heights to the north.

Aside from its lower-middle-to-middle-income character and its diverse, often elegant housing stock, what is a distinguishing and perhaps the most interesting trait of Crown Heights today is the fact that West Indian blacks and Hasidic Jews now make up much of Crown Heights' population. If there are two more culturally disparate ethnic groups, it's hard to imagine who they are. (The West Indians are from Jamaica, Trinidad, and Haiti primarily; and these include a number of Rastafarians. The Hasidim—ultra-Orthodox Jews—in Crown Heights are of the Lubavitcher sect, as distinguished from the Satmar Hasidim in the Williamsburg section of Brooklyn and the Belz Hasidim in the Borough Park section. Among the distinctions between the various Hasidic sects are the degree of their orthodoxy and their positions *vis-à-vis* the state of Israel.) North of Eastern Parkway, Crown Heights is almost all black. South of Eastern Parkway, blacks and Hasidic Jews live side by side.

If the coexistence of West Indians and Hasidic Jews is somewhat unusual, it's also somewhat uneasy. In truth, blacks and Hasidim in Crown Heights don't have all that much to do with each other, nor do they very willingly share political power in the community. Indeed there's a lot of tension between them. Blacks are constantly claiming the Hasidim are buying and developing more and more property and are thus trying to push blacks out of Crown Heights. The Hasidim, of course, deny this. And a few years ago, it seemed almost daily that one read about Jews getting beat up by blacks or vice versa.

In any case, the situation here seems to be less volatile than it was. Now the news is more often about some new biracial committee that was just formed than about the separate black or Jewish security patrol groups that used to grab the headlines just a short time ago.

## OF INTEREST

*North of Eastern Parkway*
The immediate vicinity of the Children's Museum is a solidly black middle-class area. Six or seven blocks north of the museum marks the beginning of Bedford-Stuyvesant.

**1) St. Marks Avenue** (between Brooklyn Avenue and Kingston Avenue). In Manhattan, Fifth Avenue, above 60th Street is called Millionaire's Row because of the mansions built by Carnegies, Astors, Vanderbilts, and Whitneys. In Brooklyn, however, this is Millionaire's Row.

**2) No. 166–168 Brooklyn Avenue** (between St. Marks Avenue and Prospect Place, just across from the Children's Museum). This is an example of the city program to place window and door decals on abandoned, boarded-up buildings located on otherwise good blocks. The theory is that the decals (of shutters, hanging plants, half-opened shades, and the like) will prevent the buildings from being an eyesore, and by creating "the occupied look" vandalism will be discouraged also. In this case, at any rate, the theory seems to have worked.

**3) St. Marks Avenue** and **Prospect Place** (both between Kingston Avenue and Albany Avenue). These two blocks are known as the **Super Blocks** because the street and the public places on the street were designed by famed architect I. M. Pei. The Super Blocks are worth seeing, though it's doubtful they'll be included in any book representing a retrospective of Pei's work.

**4) Bedford-Stuyvesant** (Atlantic Avenue is the official dividing line between Crown Heights and Bed-Stuy). Bedford-Stuyvesant is among the largest black neighborhoods—if it isn't *the* largest—in New York City. It, together with Crown Heights, Bushwick, Brownsville, and East New York, is part of the vast center core of Brooklyn where most of the borough's 700,000-plus blacks reside, which, incidentally, gives Brooklyn the largest black population of the five boroughs.

(Brooklyn is basically white on the edges and black on the inside. From working-class Greenpoint to upper-class Brooklyn Heights to middle-income Bay Ridge, Bensonhurst, Sheepshead Bay, Marine Park, Mill Basin, and Canarsie, the neighborhoods around the perimeter of Brooklyn are overwhelmingly white. As you move toward the center of the borough, you find communities like Bed-Stuy, which are as pervasively black and Hispanic—though the number of blacks in Brooklyn is about double the number of Hispanics—as those around the edges of the borough are white. And though all of these central Brooklyn neighborhoods—which up until the 1950s were predominantly Jewish—have middle-class pockets, they nevertheless constitute Brooklyn's largest impoverished areas. It is said that in Brownsville, for instance, there is enough public housing to accommodate the entire populations of the Westchester communities of Scarsdale and Bronxville. Hence, they are both literally and figuratively Brooklyn's inner-city neighborhoods.)

In Bed-Stuy visit the **Bedford-Stuyvesant Restoration Plaza** (1368 Fulton Street at Marcy Avenue), which is part social-services agencies and part shopping center and is the major accomplishment of the Bed-Stuy Restoration Corporation. The Bed-Stuy Restoration Corporation, considered one of the most successful urban antipoverty projects in the country, was a pet project of Bobby Kennedy's when he was U.S. Senator from New York. (Its executive director, Franklin Thomas, has since gone on to become president of the Ford Foundation.)

Just east of Restoration Plaza is one of the black middle-class residential enclaves within Bed-Stuy: **Macon**, **Macdonough**, and **Decatur Streets** between Tompkins Avenue and Stuyvesant Avenue, which are filled with handsome representatives of the neoclassical styles of town house architecture popular in New York City in the early twentieth century. As such, these streets have been designated part of the Stuyvesant Heights Historic District.

Although you're not likely to see even a fraction of them, there are said to be over four hundred **storefront churches** in Bedford-Stuyvesant!

*South of Eastern Parkway*
**1) Kingston Avenue** and **Nostrand Avenue.** These are the major Hasidic and black commercial strips, respectively. Blacks do patron-

ize the Hasidic shops (including the Kosher pizza and falafel stands and Kosher meat markets) but not vice versa.

**2) Union Street, President Street,** and **Carroll Street** (just below Kingston Avenue). These streets are notable for at least three reasons: their beauty (especially President Street, whose huge houses with lawns would seem more appropriate on Main Street in some small town in Upstate New York around the Finger Lakes than in Brooklyn); the very high degree of housing integration between blacks and Jews; and the phenomenon of black children playing on one side of a stoop and Jewish children on the other without paying the least bit of attention to each other.

## EATING PLACES

**Allan's Bakery** (1111 Nostrand Avenue), just south of Crown Heights in Prospect Lefferts Gardens, for West Indian baked goods—hardo bread, beef patties, coconut bread, spice buns (which you can buy warm from the oven in the mornings), and the like. And in Bed-Stuy just east of the Stuyvesant Historic District is **McDonald's Dining Room** (327 Stuyvesant Avenue at Macon Street), which opened in about 1948 and is thus by now a neighborhood institution. McDonald's serves Southern-style food. Breakfasts, for example, include salmon and grits. Lunch and dinners include steaks, chops, fried chicken, barbecued ribs and beef, collard greens, sweet-potato pie, black-eyed peas—all home cooked.

Flatbush *(specifically the Prospect Park South section of Flatbush, which is just south of PROSPECT PARK and within easy walking distance of the BROOKLYN BOTANIC GARDENS)*

Flatbush *is* Brooklyn. It is the stuff of Brooklyn lore—the old Brooklyn Dodgers, Brooklyn College, Erasmus Hall High School, a nice Brooklyn boy, a nice Brooklyn girl, seltzer in siphon bottles, sitting in beach chairs in front of your apartment building, *A Tree Grows in Brooklyn*, *Sophie's Choice*, and on and on.

In 1950 the borough of Brooklyn was 90 percent white, had over a million Jews, and in the minds of many was synonymous with lower-middle- and middle-class Jews of upper-middle-class suburban aspirations. Flatbush more than any other Brooklyn neighborhood reflected those traits. (Actually, in 1950 Flatbush was about 98 percent white.) And in 1980, when Brooklyn had become almost 50 percent nonwhite, had lost half its Jewish population, but still remained the city's largest Jewish borough, Flatbush reflected those trends as well.

Although Prospect Park South is but a sliver of Flatbush—and not very deep into Flatbush at that—it still will give you a glimpse and a taste of the area. Prospect Park South reveals the essential family orientation of Flatbush, its unabashedly unchic nature, the utter lack of similarity between Flatbush and anything you're likely to find in Manhattan. (Flatbush is to the Upper East Side as any suburb of London is to Bloomsbury.)

One thing Prospect Park South might not reveal is the answer to the conundrum of why anytime in a room of mixed company—that is, Brooklynites and anyone else—the mere mention of the word *Flatbush* invariably elicits titters. That will probably remain a mystery to you as it always has to Brooklynites.

## OF INTEREST

**1) Church Avenue** and **Flatbush Avenue.**    These are the major commercial streets, and also the northern and eastern boundaries of Prospect Park South, respectively. Though there are still some Jewish delis, bakeries, and appetizing stores on Church and Flatbush, the number of West Indian food stores and bakeries far outnumber the Jewish ones. This mirrors, of course, the major demographic change in this part of Brooklyn. (Prospect Park South itself remains predominantly white—mostly upper-middle-income Jewish—but north and east of Prospect Park South is predominantly nonwhite, and this is obvious on Church and Flatbush Avenues.)

Flatbush Avenue, by the way, is to Brooklyn what Broadway is to Manhattan—its heart and soul.

**2) Buckingham Road**    (between Church Avenue and Albemarle Road) and **Albemarle Road** (west of Buckingham). Mansions in Flatbush? In salt-of-the-earth Flatbush? Yes, and ones that are among the grandest houses in all New York. There are mansions built in all styles: Victorian, Edwardian, Colonial, even Japanese-pagoda style

(131 Buckingham Road). These houses would not look out of place in Beverly Hills, where they'd be worth millions.

The mansions, to be sure, account for but a minority of the houses in the area south of Church Avenue, most of which fall into the category of tasteful, old suburban. Indeed this neighborhood of Prospect Park South just below Church Avenue could be the most suburban-looking neighborhood in New York City. It's as if a small piece of Palo Alto, California, had been dropped in the middle of Brooklyn. And the result is as incongruous as if a small section of Brooklyn had been dropped in the middle of Palo Alto. Nevertheless, the old houses here in Prospect Park South are considered among the great house bargains available in the city; which may explain why after generations of upwardly mobile young people moved out of Flatbush, some are starting to move back. That someone like the playwright Jack Gelber and his family would move from the Upper West Side of Manhattan to Prospect Park South in Flatbush was unheard of until just a few years ago.

## EATING PLACES

Located within walking distance of Prospect Park South—in the heart of Flatbush—is **Grillo's** (19 Newkirk Plaza just off Newkirk Avenue at East 16th Street), an excellent, inexpensive, austere, "very Brooklyn" fish restaurant.

## Coney Island: *Brighton Beach* (within a stone's throw of the BEACH, AMUSEMENT PARK, and the AQUARIUM)

Note: To take either the F or D train to and from Coney Island is to see a great deal of Brooklyn, since both these subways on the IND Sixth Avenue line run aboveground through much of the borough.

Don't expect Disneyland; don't even expect Atlantic City. Coney Island's best days are long behind it. Indeed, it is precisely because of its past as a premier amusement park (the Disneyland of the early 1900s), popular summer resort, and solid residential community that visiting Coney Island today is so poignant. Coney Island raises the question, "How could it have come to this?"

The beach does still manage to attract hundreds of thousands on any given summer weekend, whether or not the water is off-limits to swimming because of pollution. (Being the easiest beach to reach by public transportation, Coney Island is *the* beach of subway riders, the poor man's Fire Island.) And the one amusement-park area remaining still attracts crowds despite an undeniable tackiness, new coats of paint each season notwithstanding. But the neighborhood itself just barely survives.

Some 25 percent of Coney Island's residents are on welfare, much of its housing stock west of Stillwell Avenue is blighted or abandoned altogether, and of the approximately four hundred stores that once lined Mermaid Avenue, fifty or fewer remain in business. All of which may explain why Coney Island residents who live in the middle-income Trump Village or Warbasse Houses co-ops (mostly middle-income Jews, as opposed to the rest of Coney Island's population, which is largely poor or working-class Italian, black, and Hispanic) claim not to live in Coney Island at all, but rather in "West Brighton."

As for Coney Island's future? They've already built loads of public-housing and subsidized-housing projects. Casino gambling has been discussed but doesn't seem to be in the cards. So the talk now is to build one, two, and three-family houses in Coney Island—where the old Steeplechase Amusement Park once stood—in order to lure the middle class to the area.

## OF INTEREST

**1) Brighton Beach**   (just east of Coney Island, Ocean Parkway being the dividing line). Three notable facts about Brighton Beach are: It has the largest elderly Jewish population in New York City, which explains why the boardwalk is always more crowded than the beach and why anyone running for office in New York as a liberal Democrat goes out of his or her way to press flesh in Brighton more often than in any other neighborhood; Brighton Beach has the largest Russian Jewish immigrant community in New York (supposedly Brighton looks like Odessa), and if you're on the D or F train and overhear Russian or see people reading a Russian paper, you can usually assume they are on their way home to Brighton; and it is the handball capital of the world. National handball championships have been held here at the Brighton Beach Baths.

Brighton Beach is quite a fascinating little community. **Brighton Beach Avenue**, from Ocean Parkway to Coney Island Avenue, may just be the best food shopping and dining street in the city, lined with fruit and vegetable markets, fish markets (with the largest selection and lowest prices you're likely to find anywhere), Jewish dairy restaurants and delis, Jewish appetizing stores, Jewish bakeries, and Russian food markets and restaurants. And the **Boardwalk** may be the city's best people-watching and people-listening strip (to be sure, someone on the Boardwalk along Brighton Beach has the answer to the world's problems; just ask).

Brighton is also home to the **Brighton Beach Baths** (at Coney Island Avenue between Brighton Beach Avenue and the Boardwalk; best seen from the Boardwalk), perhaps the world's most *hamish* (down-to-earth; unfashionable) "country club." It is a country club that could only be found in New York City. What other place would have a country club that deemphasizes golf and tennis and instead offers paddle tennis, racquetball, basketball, volleyball, shuffleboard, *miniature golf*, Ping-Pong, mah jongg, chess, and cards?

Finally, whereas in Manhattan there are apartment buildings called the Dakota, San Remo, or River House, in Brighton Beach you'll discover an apartment building named after Mother Jones, the labor organizer and activist of the late nineteenth and early twentieth century (3102–16 Brighton 1 Place). Which tells you what kind of place Brighton Beach is—or was.

## EATING PLACES

*In Coney Island*

**Nathan's Famous** (at Surf and Stillwell Avenues just off the Boardwalk), whose frankfurters and french fries many still consider the best in the city; **Gargiulo's** (2911 West 15th Street) and **Carolina** (1409 Mermaid Avenue), for Italian food and for a cast of colorful characters; and the **Sea Garden** restaurant (518 Neptune Avenue in the Trump Village Shopping Center), a classic coffee-shop-restaurant of the sort that is found only in Jewish neighborhoods in Brooklyn, noted for its fish dishes and desserts. Incidentally, **Gerace's Bakery** (1408 Neptune Avenue) sells an extraordinarily delicious Italian bread.

*In Brighton Beach*

Among the several Russian restaurants that serve the Russian community of Brighton, one excellent place is **Kavka's Restaurant** (405

Brighton Beach Avenue), where among the appetizers is the obliga-
tory red or black caviar. Although they are not restaurants per se,
food places not to be missed include **M & I International Foods** (249
Brighton Beach Avenue), an appetizing store offering a potpourri of
"continental" foods and Brighton Beach's answer to Zabar's; and either **Israel's Take-Home Foods** (409 Brighton Beach Avenue) or
**Schechter's Take-Home Foods** (509 Brighton Beach Avenue), which
offer Jewish take-home foods—knishes, kreplach, pirogen, kugel,
stuffed derma, flanken, fricassee, gefilte fish, matzoh-ball soup, potato pancakes, stuffed cabbage, and more. Either place is an education
in Jewish cooking. (Israel's Take-Home Foods has a few tables, so it's
possible to eat there.)

And, of course, there is the inimitable **Mrs. Stahl's Knishes** (1001
Brighton Beach Avenue) for more kinds of knishes than you would
imagine ever existed. In addition to the standard potato and kasha
knishes, there are knishes stuffed with cabbage, spinach, cheese,
mushrooms and potato, sweet potato, cherries, strawberries, apples,
blueberries, pineapple—and who knows how many more.

# QUEENS

## Astoria: *Long Island City (just three or four subway stops from Manhattan and a short walk from the ASTORIA STUDIOS and the ASTORIA MOTION PICTURE AND TELEVISION FOUNDATION MUSEUM at 34–31 35th Street just below Broadway\*)*

Astoria is New York's "Little Athens." More Greeks are said to live in
Astoria than in any other city outside of Greece. And while other European ethnic communities in the city dwindle in size with the dis-

---

*The studios themselves—where they recently made *The Wiz, Hair, All That Jazz,
Ragtime, The World According to Garp, Author, Author,* and other films—have not
been open to the general public, though that policy could change. The museum, however, is open to the public, though at present only for group tours. (It should be open
to the public on a regular basis by mid-1984, when its new facility is completed.) The
museum's collection of photographs, posters, costumes, set designs, props, photographic and projection equipment, and various other movie memorabilia document-
ing the history of filmmaking on the East Coast makes it the only major museum in
the country devoted entirely to the history of motion pictures and television.

persal of second- and third-generation members to Long Island, Staten Island, New Jersey, and beyond, this seems not to be the case with Astoria's Greek population, which is actually growing.

Although it has been repeatedly profiled in the *Times* as an interesting ethnic neighborhood to visit, "Greek Astoria" has not become a tourist attraction at all. It remains an essentially residential neighborhood whose bustling street life is created by the bustle of indigenous people rather than visitors.

That Astoria has not become a tourist attraction despite the imprimatur of *The New York Times* proves just how difficult it is for any place in Queens to attract visitors. Astoria, like most of Queens, seems "tourist-proof." Indeed, Manhattanites for whom Astoria is as close to Midtown as is, say, Greenwich Village—would sooner travel to Greece itself than to Astoria in Queens.

Although New Yorkers associate Astoria solely with its Greek community, it also has a very substantial Italian population. The size of the Italian community could very well equal that of the 70,000-plus Greek population of Astoria. In fact, if you count the number of commercial establishments—restaurants, cafés, bakeries, fruit-and-vegetable markets, groceries—it's a toss-up as to whether the Greek or Italian enterprises prevail. In some cases they've merged and now go by the name "Mediterranean this or that," selling Greek *and* Italian imports.

Like much of Queens, Astoria is characterized by one- and two-family houses, a high school that fields a football team, a plethora of army-navy and work-clothes stores, and a residential population that is predominantly white. (Queens was 62 percent white in 1980—having been 90 percent white in 1960. Only Staten Island has a smaller percentage of blacks and Hispanics than Queens.) Like the rest of Queens, Astoria has hyphenated street addresses, which serve to absolutely befuddle the Manhattanites who deign to journey to Queens. (Actually, it's quite a simple matter. The number that precedes the hyphen indicates the cross street or avenue. Thus, 34-31 35th Street translates to No. 31 35th Street at 34th Avenue.) And like most of Queens, Astoria lacks anything that is trendy, shows no signs whatsoever of gentrification, and, *vis-à-vis* Manhattan, raises the question, "How can it be so close and yet so far away?"

On the other hand, Astoria is unlike a good deal of Queens in that it is old, its ambience is more working-class than middle-class, and its ethnic makeup is European rather than Hispanic, Asian, and Israeli—

the newer immigrant groups that have been settling in Queens. Astoria is also less amorphous and therefore has a greater sense of neighborhood than most of Queens—particularly the eastern half of the borough, where the closer you get to the Nassau County line, the more like Long Island Queens becomes. (Bayside, Little Neck, and Douglaston, for example, seem indistinguishable from Long Island towns. Half of Bellerose is actually in Nassau.) And finally, unlike most of Queens, Astoria is eminently walkable.

## OF INTEREST

**1) Ditmars Boulevard**   (from 31st Street—or the El—to Steinway), **30th Avenue** (from 31st Street across Steinway into the high Thirties and Forties), and **Broadway** (also from 31st Street into the Forties on the other side of Steinway). Though originally the center of Greek Astoria was Ditmars Boulevard, the Greek presence has grown sufficiently to become obvious on 30th Avenue and Broadway as well. These streets are lined with dozens upon dozens of Greek and Italian commercial establishments. Steinway Street above 28th Avenue is actually more Italian than Greek, the focal point of the Italian presence here being the **bocci courts** (consider it Italian lawn bowling) in the park on Steinway between 23rd Avenue and Ditmars Boulevard.

**2) Astoria Indoor Paddleball**   (34-38 38th Street). If you understand why an indoor paddleball center is typically Queens—in the same way that an indoor skateboarding center is—then you're well on your way to understanding what Queens is all about. Remember, this is paddleball played against a single wall and not paddle tennis, racquetball, or squash.

**3) Long Island City**   (just south of Astoria and actually reachable by foot from Roosevelt Island). Long Island City is the L.I.C. stamped on just about all products manufactured in New York. This is another way of saying Long Island City is largely industrial. This is another way of saying Long Island City looks a lot like Akron, Ohio, though its status as a place to live has apparently been elevated in recent years since artists started moving in. (Previously Long Island City residents would often claim to live in Astoria—Broadway is the official boundary—Astoria having the higher status of the two.) In fact, one of the more interesting things to see in Long Island City, aside from the extraordinary views of Manhattan, is **P.S. 1** (46-01 21st Street), which houses workspaces and exhibition space for artists as well as an art gallery open to the public. P.S. 1, which stands for Project Studios One, is in what had actually been Public School No. 1, built in the 1800s and renovated to its current use in the 1970s.

Around the corner from P.S. 1 is the one block in the entire borough of Queens to be designated a landmark historic district. **Forty-fifth Avenue** (between 21st and 23rd Streets) is lined with beautifully preserved late-nineteenth-century row houses. That Queens has but a single block designated a historic district, while nearly all of Greenwich Village or all of Brooklyn Heights, for example, is so designated, highlights the amazing dearth of buildings of architectural interest in Queens.

## EATING PLACES

*In Astoria*
Among the many Greek restaurants, outsiders recommend **Roumeli's** (33-04 Broadway) while neighborhood people swear by **Kalyva** (36-15 Ditmars Boulevard). And among the many Italian dining places, two neighborhood restaurants—both of which you could easily miss since they're off the major commercial streets—are: **La Penna** (31-86 31st Street just off Broadway) and **Piccola Venezia** (42-01 28th Avenue).

**HBH Bakery** (29-28 30th Avenue), a.k.a. HBH Greek Pastry Shop–European Tea Room, is typical of several Greek pastry-shop cafés in Astoria. It is cavernous, has plastic hanging plants, and serves delicious pastry you're not likely to recognize by name, such as amygdalou, sokolatina, ganioteko, galaktoboureka, dipla, karidopita, and kataïfi. Mercifully, there is baklava too.

*In Long Island City*
**Paul's Café** (24-16 Jackson Avenue) is undoubtedly the only place in Long Island City that serves quiche, something you can either thank or blame the newly arrived community of artists for.

## Flushing: *Forest Hills (within walking distance—or else one subway stop—from SHEA STADIUM, the NATIONAL TENNIS CENTER, the QUEENS MUSEUM, and FLUSHING MEADOWS–CORONA PARK)*

Note: To take the No. 7 Flushing train, which runs aboveground in Queens, is to get an excellent introduction to the borough. The No.

7 first goes through industrial Long Island City and then through the red-brick—with a little aluminum siding thrown in here and there—residential Queens communities of Sunnyside, Woodside, Jackson Heights, Elmhurst, Corona, and Flushing.

Consider Flushing as the kind of offspring that might emerge from a marriage between Manhattan and Long Island. Neither city nor suburb, it lacks some of the best, and the worst, traits of both.

To know Flushing is to know Queens, for it is prototypically Queens. When Manhattanites talk of Queens—which they do superciliously as though it were culturally, intellectually, politically, and sartorially middle America—it is Flushing, or a neighborhood very much like Flushing, that they have in mind. Like much of Queens, Flushing is demonstrably middle-income. Though predominantly white, it also displays the great ethnic variety that has come to characterize so much of Queens, particularly the influx of Asians (Chinese, Koreans, Japanese, Vietnamese, Indians) and Israelis.

Like other Queens communities, Flushing is very self-contained, has a plethora of cemeteries (wonderful for bird-watching), and has public schools the middle class has not abandoned (Queens public schools record the highest reading scores in the city year in and year out). As in other places in Queens, you typically must take a subway and then a bus to get where you want to go. And like all of Queens, Flushing is built almost entirely of red brick—red-brick one-, two-, and three-family houses; red-brick attached, detached, and semi-detached houses; red-brick garden apartments; and red-brick six- and seven-story apartment buildings. (In the beginning the world suffered from a surplus of red brick. Then they built Queens.)

## OF INTEREST

**1) Corona Subway Yards** (at the Shea Stadium subway stop). A new double-width chain-link fence topped with razor-edged metal coils (at a cost of $1.5 million) and two vicious German shepherds named Suzy and Red ($18,000 a year) are part of a security effort to make the Corona yards impenetrable by graffiti artists. In addition, the subway cars themselves have been repainted white both as a deterrent to graffitists and as a way of monitoring the effectiveness of the graffiti-proofing measures (at a cost of $2,200 per car). You can see for yourself whether it's worked.

**2) The Panorama**  (at the Queens Museum in Flushing Meadows–Corona Park). A permanent exhibit at the museum, the Panorama is a 200-foot-long, 100-foot-wide model of New York City with *every* single building in the city represented—850,000-plus of them. Created in 1964 for the World's Fair, the Panorama is constantly being updated as new buildings get constructed in the city. (Its scale is 1 inch to 100 feet, which makes the Empire State Building one foot high.)

If you don't know New York that well, particularly the physical relationship of things to each other, the Panorama is a terrific means of orientation. And if you're the sort of person who enjoys looking at maps, plan to spend hours here. A really marvelous thing.

**3) Main Street.**  The best way to see Flushing is to walk Main Street. Just below Northern Boulevard it runs through the "downtown shopping district"—Queens has about fifteen downtown shopping districts—which now has scores of Asian-owned and -operated stores: Chinese beauty parlors and real-estate offices, Japanese pizza parlors, Korean fruit-and-vegetable markets, or stores that simply go by the name of "Oriental" something or other and cater to all the Asian groups. (Queens and Nassau County residents now go to Flushing to buy their Chinese cooking supplies instead of going all the way into Chinatown.)

Farther south on Main Street, just above the **Queens Botanical Gardens**, is the center of Indian restaurants and stores. And south of the Botanical Gardens are neighborhoods where large numbers of Israelis have settled. "Haym Salomon Square" on Main Street is one hint that you're in such a neighborhood; Kosher-pizza and falafel stands are another.

Another way of gleaning the contemporary ethnic mix of Flushing is to visit the **Flushing Branch of the Public Library**. You will, for instance, discover a reading room filled with Asian schoolchildren doing homework, and you will find a magazine rack filled with current popular magazines from China, Korea, Japan, India, France, Greece, Italy, and Israel.

**4) Forest Hills**  (southeast of Flushing; south on Main Street and then east on Union Turnpike through Kew Gardens, the civic center—of sorts—of Queens, and into Forest Hills). Although it is a very, very long walk from Flushing to Forest Hills, to make that walk is to see Queens. Forest Hills itself is different from most of Flushing and most of the rest of Queens in that it (along with Jamaica Estates,

Douglaston, and a few other communities) is more upper-income. (In terms of status, Forest Hills is the Upper East Side of Queens.) Which may explain the extraordinary resistance in 1972 to a proposed low-income housing project to be built in the northern part of Forest Hills, near the Long Island Expressway. (This protracted, volatile controversy became very much a black-white—specifically Jewish—affair, which was finally settled by a compromise; instead of building three twenty-four-story towers as proposed, three eight-story towers were built.) Also, unlike most of Queens, which is distinguished by its undistinguished housing, Forest Hills is where you'll find **Forest Hills Gardens** (just south of Queens Boulevard at 71st Avenue), one of the more beautiful places in all the city to live. Built in the 1930s as a planned community of apartments and private houses with lawns and plenty of public spaces to encourage social interaction rather than privacy, it will make you realize where Roosevelt Island, another so-called planned community, went wrong.

Incidentally, **No. 110-11 Queens Boulevard** (near 110th Street and 72nd Road) is the tallest building in the entire borough—thirty-three stories.

## EATING PLACES

No one travels to Flushing just to eat, but as long as you're here, you should know that the downtown shopping area has a number of quite decent Chinese, Japanese, Korean, and Indian restaurants. For instance: **Kalpana Indian Restaurant** (42-87 Main Street near the Botanical Gardens), **Shere Punjab Restaurant** (136-27 Franklin Avenue just off Main Street), and **Sushikazu** (41-32 Main Street). And you should at least take notice of Marchels on the corner of Franklin and Main, since it is typical of the large diners that proliferate in Queens. Queens is the borough of diners. It must be the Nassau County influence.

# THE BRONX

## The Concourse (*just up from YANKEE STADIUM*)

The Concourse in and around 161st Street is neither the best nor worst Bronx neighborhood. It lies somewhere in between, though at one time it was considered among the borough's very best neighborhoods. In the early 1900s, the Grand Concourse (the familiar term for what is officially named the Grand Boulevard and Concourse) was the most exclusive address in the Bronx, the Bronx equivalent of Fifth Avenue. Well, almost. Babe Ruth himself lived on the Grand Concourse.

A solidly middle-income Jewish neighborhood through the 1950s and early 1960s, the Concourse is now predominantly nonwhite; some of its residents are middle-income (and live in the best buildings on the Grand Concourse), but most are not. The recent history of the Concourse, then, mirrors the history of much of the Bronx as a whole. And that is largely the history of white middle-class flight. (In the last ten years, the Bronx has been characterized not so much by an increase in the number of blacks and Hispanics—which, in fact, was relatively small between 1970 and 1980—as by a phenomenal decrease in the number of white residents. The Bronx was 60 percent white in 1970 but only 30 percent white by 1980, which makes it the least white of the five boroughs by far.)

One major difference, however, between the Concourse and other Bronx neighborhoods similarly afflicted by white flight—the South Bronx, Hunts Point, Morrisania, University Heights, or Tremont, to name a few—is that enough of the old still stands here so that you can see at least some evidence of that history. This as opposed to, say, the South Bronx, where large areas have simply been laid to rubble and where the past has thus been almost totally obliterated in the widespread waste and abandonment of the present.

Unlike these other neighborhoods, in the Concourse section most of the old housing stock still stands and is inhabited, and this includes the many fine old apartment buildings on the Grand Concourse itself. And if these buildings along the Grand Concourse— among the grandest in the Bronx—aren't all as well maintained as they once were, still their elegance sneaks through.

If you walk around the neighborhood, you'll see that many of the old synagogues still stand, though in most cases they no longer function as Jewish houses of worship. One large temple, for instance, now is a Girls Club. You'll notice also that some of the old businesses are still here (like the Kosher deli just below the Bronx County Courthouse on 161st Street) and that professional offices—doctors, lawyers, dentists—didn't leave en masse. They merely changed their signs to accommodate their changed clientele. Hence, Stone, Saltzman & Israel, Attorneys became Stone, Saltzman & Israel, Abogados.

And you'll even see a number of the old Jewish residents, all of whom appear to be in their eighties or, at a minimum, in their seventies. They are the stalwarts who didn't join the mass exodus to Co-op City, the middle-income housing complex in the northeast Bronx that opened in 1969 and drained the Concourse and other Bronx neighborhoods of their white middle-class base, as though a plug had been pulled in a bathtub.

And then, of course, another way the Concourse distinguishes itself from most other Bronx neighborhoods is that not only did the Concourse survive, it now seems to be on the upswing. Run-down buildings on the Grand Concourse are being refurbished. Well-maintained buildings are going co-op. Nary a storefront on 161st Street is empty. New businesses are opening. And who knows? Maybe one day soon they'll even mow the grass in Franz Siegel Park.

A word about the Grand Concourse itself. As Broadway is to Manhattan or as Flatbush Avenue is to Brooklyn, so the Grand Concourse is to the Bronx; it's the spine that runs almost the entire length of the borough, defines and gives it character, and serves as a focal point.

The Grand Concourse, first of all, is physically imposing, probably the widest street in all of New York City. (Its four lanes in each direction make one wish that either the East River Drive or West Side Highway were even half its width.) And too, the Grand Concourse is a sliver of relative stability in the turbulent west Bronx; in a real sense, the glue that has held certain neighborhoods together and prevented them from deteriorating past the point of no return. (In the neighborhood of the Concourse around 161st Street, there was a little help from Yankee Stadium and from the fact that the Bronx Civic Center—courts and municipal offices—is located in its midst.) If you were to travel the length of the Grand Concourse—from East 138th Street to Mosholu Parkway—you would see that it has remained viable throughout, both residentially and commercially. The same cannot be said of the neighborhoods of the west Bronx below or above the Grand Concourse.

## OF INTEREST

**1) Macombs Dam Park**    (161st Street and River Avenue just across the street from Yankee Stadium). In the mid-1970s, the New York Yankees announced that they would donate something like $35,000

to upgrade this city park. Lest this be judged as an act of great gener-
osity, one should know that this offer came only after the City of
New York had pumped about $75 million (some say $100 million)
into the refurbishing of Yankee Stadium.

(Unbeknownst to many, the city owns Yankee Stadium, which it
leases to the Yankees; the amount of the rent the Yankees pay is one
of the best-guarded secrets in New York. The city bought the stadium in the early 1970s and agreed to renovate it, a reaction to a threat
on the part of the then Yankee owners to move the team out of New
York. What had originally been announced as a $24 million renova-
tion project, which would also include a couple of million dollars for
the improvement of the immediate neighborhood, turned out to
cost no less than $75 million, with funds designated for neighbor-
hood improvement ultimately being eliminated. And though the city
has since tried to justify the extraordinary expense by saying a new
and improved Yankee Stadium would benefit the neighborhood—
make it more attractive and safer—that remains to be seen. Many argue that the old stadium was far more attractive than the new; it seated more people too. As for crime in the area, many residents claimed
that right after the stadium reopened in 1976, muggings and burglaries increased.)

In any event, regarding the $35,000 the Yankees pledged for up-
grading Macombs Dam Park *vis-à-vis* the $75 million or more the
city paid for upgrading Yankee Stadium . . . well, you be the judge as
to who came out on top.

**2) Real-estate offices**    (on 161st Street on either side of the Grand
Concourse). While prospective renters in other boroughs—particularly Manhattan—bemoan the fact that they must pay exorbitant fees
to real-estate agents in order to secure an apartment, here you find
realtors who advertise that landlords, not renters, pay their fee. And
this is one of the better neighborhoods in the Bronx, which tells you
something about the real-estate market in the borough.

**3) No. 800 Grand Concourse**    (at 158th Street). What may seem to
you to be just an ordinary-looking, well-maintained, seven-story red-
brick apartment building—of the sort one sees duplicated a thou-
sandfold throughout Queens—is quite extraordinary, at least to *The
New York Times*, which publishes articles about No. 800. The *Times*
thinks it is worth writing about because of its exquisite upkeep in an
area not known for well-kept buildings; because it is a middle-in-

come co-op in a neighborhood of scant few co-ops; and because it is a predominantly black co-op with an all-black co-op board in a borough in which the number of middle-income black co-ops can be counted on the fingers of one hand.

(The large number of air-conditioners in No. 800, and their conspicuous absence in the buildings on either side, tell you at a glance that it's a middle-income building, while the apartment buildings that flank it are not.)

## EATING PLACES

This is not a prime eating-out area. Because the Bronx Civic Center is here, the neighborhood primarily is one of deli-sandwich shops, coffee shops, and fast-food places (including a McDonald's). If you're famished, the advice is to tide yourself over with a hot dog from the Sabrett vendor in front of the Bronx County Courthouse and then go out to eat someplace else in the city.

# Belmont: *Fordham Road and the Grand Concourse* (just west of the *BRONX BOTANICAL GARDENS and the BRONX ZOO*)

Note: If you take the No. 2 or No. 5 IRT train, which travels aboveground through the Bronx, from 149th Street north you pass through the pervasive physical devastation and rubble of the South Bronx. Ever since Jimmy Carter visited the South Bronx in 1977—which he promised to save and of course didn't—it has supplanted Harlem, Watts, and Newark as the ultimate symbol of urban blight.

Compared to the Little Italy section of Manhattan, Belmont has many more Italian restaurants and Italian stores, and many fewer tourists—indeed, almost no tourists, which is why in the movie *The Godfather* the scenes of Manhattan's Little Italy were shot here.

While most of the Bronx seems to have been turned on its head and shaken loose in the past two decades—so great are the demographic and other changes throughout the borough—Belmont appears not to have changed at all in the past four decades, let alone the last two. It was, is, and perhaps always will be a large, vibrant, safe, stable working-class Italian neighborhood. About the only non-

Italians who reside in the Belmont section are some students from nearby Fordham University who decide to live off-campus. And where other predominantly Italian neighborhoods elsewhere in the city are threatened by non-Italian gentry moving in, no such threat exists in Belmont. Unlike Carroll Gardens in Brooklyn, for instance, whose beautiful brownstone blocks and nearness to Manhattan have attracted non-Italian, upwardly mobile professionals in recent years, Belmont, being totally devoid of brownstones and being miles from Manhattan, seems to be gentrification-proof.

(By the way, if you grew up in the 1950s, you might be interested to know that the Belmont section of the Bronx is whence the rock 'n' roll group Dion and the Belmonts hailed.)

## OF INTEREST

**1) Arthur Avenue**   (south of Fordham Road) and **187th Street** (between Southern Boulevard and about Hoffman Street). These are the two major commercial streets in the Belmont section. Together they have what must be the greatest density of Italian bakeries and pastry shops in New York.

Instead of going to twenty different little stores on Arthur Avenue or 187th, you could just go to the **Arthur Avenue Retail Market** (2344 Arthur Avenue), where under one roof is a collection of the various kinds of Italian food, housewares, and clothing stores you would find throughout the neighborhood. Arthur Avenue Retail Market is sort of an Italian version of the La Marqueta in Spanish Harlem.

**2) Fordham Road** and the **Grand Concourse**   (a fifteen- or twenty-minute walk from Belmont along Fordham Road). Past **Fordham University**—containing some historic landmark buildings that were built in the mid-1800s—you come to what is considered the downtown shopping district of the Bronx. What is interesting about the shopping area is that it reflects the actual racial composition of the Bronx more accurately than any of the residential neighborhoods, which tend to be either nearly all-white or nearly all nonwhite. Here on the streets around Fordham Road and the Concourse it is about one-third black, one-third Hispanic, and one-third white—roughly the racial breakdown for the borough.

Though new stores seem to come and go overnight, a few things in the area have not changed in ages: the **Loew's Paradise** (on the Grand Concourse just south of Fordham Road), one of the great

movie palaces of the 1920s, still stands, though it has been converted
to a quad cinema; **Alexander's** (at the intersection of Fordham Road
and the Concourse) remains the department store it's always been,
only with many more black mannequins in the display windows;
**Loehmann's** (on Fordham Road just west of Jerome Avenue) still attracts women from Manhattan and Westchester who come here just
to shop for designer dresses at bargain prices; and **Sutter's** (on the
Grand Concourse just north of Fordham Road) remains an oasis for
older ladies in the neighborhood who still wear white gloves and
meet here for lunch or tea.

## EATING PLACES

*In the Belmont Section*
Unlike Mario's Restaurant on Arthur Avenue, which advertises in *The
New York Times*, offers valet parking, and attracts patrons from outside the neighborhood, two Italian restaurants favored by locals are:
**Dominick's Restaurant & Bar** (2335 Arthur Avenue), where the plates
don't necessarily match but the food is excellent and the portions
enormous; and **Ann & Tony's** (2407 Arthur Avenue), which, in addition to serving dinners, has what some consider the best pizza in the
city.

*In the Fordham Road–Grand Concourse Section*
What is noteworthy about the Fordham Road–Grand Concourse area
is not so much the absence of good restaurants but the almost complete absence of restaurants of any kind. Doughnut shops yes; restaurants no. There are more restaurants on just one block of
Columbus Avenue in the Seventies than there are in this entire area
of the Bronx. If you're here and you're hungry, try one of the two
neighborhood delis: the **Palace Restaurant & Delicatessen** (122 East
188th Street at Creston Avenue) or **Mother's Delicatessen** (2458
Grand Concourse at East 188th Street).

## Pelham Parkway *(just east of the BRONX BOTANICAL GARDENS and the BRONX ZOO)*

When Jewish novelists reminisce about the old neighborhoods in
the Bronx where they grew up—where you never knew anyone who
wasn't Jewish and who didn't go to the Bronx High School of Sci-

ence, where eating out meant eating at the local deli or Chinese restaurant on Sunday afternoons, where on hot summer evenings kids hung out on corners and adults sat in beach chairs in front of their apartment buildings, and where the owners of the local candy or card-and-gift stores managed to send their children to Ivy League colleges—Pelham Parkway is among the neighborhoods of which they speak. What distinguishes Pelham Parkway from most of the other similarly described neighborhoods, however, is that while most of them no longer bear even the faintest resemblance to their former selves, Pelham Parkway seems not to have changed much at all.

It remains a predominantly Jewish, middle-class area (though now many of the Jewish residents are Israelis); it's considered one of the best residential neighborhoods in all the Bronx. ("Still a good neighborhood," in the words of Bronx residents or recent escapees of the Bronx.) In fact, among the outer-borough neighborhoods you hear about that are now beginning to attract young professional types from Manhattan, Pelham Parkway is mentioned. It could very well be the only Bronx neighborhood that has such an appeal. (Riverdale doesn't count. Riverdale is upper-income, wooded, and suburban and thus is *in* the Bronx but not *of* the Bronx. Riverdale residents don't even admit it is in the Bronx, despite its Bronx Zip code.)

## OF INTEREST

**1) White Plains Road**   (mostly between Lydig Avenue and Pelham Parkway) and **Lydig Avenue** (just south of Pelham Parkway and east of White Plains Road). These are the two major shopping streets of Pelham Parkway. Both are lined with every kind of mom-and-pop store imaginable, which restores one's faith that it's still possible to be a small businessman, that you don't have to be Waldenbooks to open a bookstore or Waldbaum's to open a food store. Lydig Avenue is food-oriented, with more Kosher meat and poultry markets than any other four blocks in the city. White Plains Road, on the other hand, has clothes. Many of the businesses on both White Plains Road and Lydig Avenue have been in business at the same location for at least thirty years, which is why the neighborhood generates a feeling of community and stability. And there is something very reassuring about that.

The streets that cross Lydig Avenue are filled with apartment houses (where you're sure to see the aforementioned persons sitting out front on beach chairs). But once you reach Matthews Avenue, the cross streets become streets of private homes primarily, which gives you the chance to see private homes, Bronx style—red-brick attached mostly.

**2) Children's playground**    (at the bottom of Lydig Avenue at Bronx Park East). If there is anything that gives meaning to the term "basic Bronx"—that which lacks embellishments, airs, or pretensions of any kind—this playground certainly does. No adventure playground here; just asphalt, swings, slides, seesaw, monkey bars, and sprinkler. That's it. The basics. Creative playthings? That's for sissies

## EATING PLACES

The common thread that binds the eating places in Pelham Parkway is that they're all classic outer-borough neighborhood restaurants—coffee shops, delis, and Chinese restaurants primarily. You might want to try the **Zion Delicatessen** (750 Lydig Avenue) for franks, hot corned-beef, pastrami, or tongue sandwiches, knishes, and Dr. Brown's Celray Tonic; or the **Twin Dragon** (2184 White Plains Road) for Chinese food. (While in the suburbs pizza parlors have home delivery, in New York City, neighborhood Chinese restaurants like the Twin Dragon deliver.)

Or, you might just want to walk up Lydig Avenue and buy some fresh fruit from one of the many outdoor fruit and vegetable markets; nuts, candies, or dried fruits from one of the Jewish appetizing stores; an egg cream at a candy-store–luncheonette; strudel or marble pound cake from one of the half-dozen or so Jewish bakeries; or some Jewish takeout (apple, potato, or sweet-potato kugel, kasha varniskas, knishes, and the like) at the **Meal Mart** (798 Lydig Avenue).

# STATEN ISLAND

## St. George: *Stapleton* (just up from the STATEN ISLAND FERRY)

The St. George section, which includes the downtown civic center, on the whole bears a greater resemblance to an old New England mill town (where the mills have long since stopped running) than it does to New York. Nevertheless it does have at least *some* things in common with the rest of the city. Most of the rest of Staten Island, on the other hand, has nothing in common with New York City. Which, of course, is the appeal of Staten Island to those who choose to live there and its lack of appeal to others.

While New York City is 50 percent white, Staten Island is 85 percent white. Whereas overall New York consistently votes Democratic, Staten Island consistently votes Republican. While New York City lost 10 percent of its population between 1970 and 1980, Staten Island actually grew by 20 percent. While in the rest of the city new housing, for lack of space, comes in the form of converting or renovating existing buildings, on Staten Island, because there is no dearth of undeveloped land, new suburban tract houses still get built. And while new ethnic restaurants of all types continue to open all over the city, Staten Island continues to get new Italian restaurants only.

St. George, unlike much of Staten Island but like much of the city, is old and has some high-rise apartment buildings, some public housing, some evidence of a black population, and no suburban tract houses. It also manifests some evidence of both urban blight and urban renaissance, and has something of a community of artists, writers, and other creative types, however small and recent that community is. Then too, unlike the rest of Staten Island and more like New York City as a whole, St. George is a politically liberal community. (Or at least it is part of the one Staten Island assembly district that Gerald Ford didn't carry in 1976 and Ronald Reagan didn't win in 1980.) And judging by the number of abandoned or just recently renovated houses, St. George, like the rest of the city but unlike the rest of Staten Island, probably experienced a population loss between 1970 and 1980 as well.

## OF INTEREST

**1) Westervelt Street**    (especially around Hamilton Avenue). Westervelt and the area around it capture the ambience of St. George as well as any area. You'll sense the feeling of neighborhood, and you'll see the spectrum of housing in St. George and other of Staten Island's old North Shore communities (as contrasted to the more recently developed, more suburban, more middle-income South Shore communities): big, old nondescript houses in various states of repair; big, old Victorian houses in various states of repair, including ones like Nos. 96, 88, 84, and 80 Westervelt Street, which are in beautiful condition (No. 88 in particular looks like a house that would be featured in *New York* magazine as an example of gentrification in St. George); high-rises and public housing too (Richmond Terrace Houses just east of Westervelt).

You're also likely to see some of those things you never see in the rest of New York City: Beware of Dog signs everywhere (Staten Island has guard dogs instead of doormen); people chopping wood in their backyards; old, dead automobiles sitting on people's front lawns; and the absence of any signs relating to alternate-side-of-the-street parking. There are no such regulations on Staten Island! Which proves it's really a suburb of New York in disguise.

**2) Scaglione's Bowling Center & Fishing Supplies**   (114 Victory Boulevard, three blocks up from Bay Street—technically Tompkinsville rather than St. George). New Yorkers neither bowl nor fish. Staten Islanders do both. Which is additional proof that Staten Island is a suburb of New York.

**3) *Staten Island Advance***   (at any newsstand. While the rest of New York reads the *Times*, *Post*, or *News*, Staten Islanders read the *Staten Island Advance*, a daily, conservative Newhouse-chain paper with a heavy emphasis on local Staten Island news. Staten Island is the only outer borough to have its own daily paper.

In a recent editorial, the *Advance* decried the evils of dirt bikers, whose motorized bikes were making a mess of public property and shattering the peace of quiet residential neighborhoods. More proof still that Staten Island is a suburb.

**4) Snug Harbor Cultural Center**   (a mile and a half from St. George in New Brighton). Staten Islanders claim that Snug Harbor will someday rival Lincoln Center. Though it seems highly doubtful, Snug Harbor is, nevertheless, a wonderful place to visit. What had been an eighty-acre, twenty-six-building home for retired sailors is now a center for the visual and performing arts. (Twenty-six acres of Snug Harbor make up the Staten Island Botanical Gardens.)

In addition to galleries, studios, and various activities of all kinds that go on there, the buildings themselves—mostly mid-nineteenth-century Greek Revival architecture—are now being renovated and are open to the public. They invite exploration.

During the summer, the Metropolitan Opera and the New York

Philharmonic give outdoor performances at Snug Harbor. Whereas in Central Park the boast is that 150,000 come to the outdoor concerts, at Snug Harbor the boast is that 150,000 *don't* come to the concerts. Which means you can sit close enough to actually see and hear the performances.

**5) Bay Street Landing** (along the waterfront just below Bay Street at Victory Boulevard). This recently constructed 500-apartment cooperative (in converted masonry warehouses and other assorted buildings) and 600-boat marina (the largest in New York City) defies all the clichés and characterizations of Staten Island offered heretofore. At least for the time being, consider this ultra-chic project—which smacks of Los Angeles—to be quite an aberration for Staten Island.

**6) Stapleton** (a mile from St. George). In many respects Stapleton is a lot like St. George. Like St. George, it is older, more urban, less middle-income, and more racially, ethnically, and economically mixed than most of Staten Island. It is also attracting gentry, as evidenced by the strip of antique shops along Bay Street beginning at around Canal Street and by the cozy, smart cafés and restaurants that are beginning to grace the area.

Also in Stapleton is the **Staten Island Children's Museum** (15 Beach Street), which will eventually be relocated to the Snug Harbor Cultural Center.

## EATING PLACES

There was a man who knew a man who knew a man who had an uncle who once went to Staten Island just to eat. Actually, **Montezuma's Revenge** (103 Stuyvesant Place), one of the very best Mexican (yes, Mexican on Staten Island) restaurants in the city, claims that a quarter of its clientele comes from off the island. That could mean from New Jersey, but in this case doesn't.

Montezuma's Revenge is open for dinner only. For lunch, try **Amos' Place** (at the Snug Harbor Cultural Center), which serves omelets, soups, sandwiches, chili, tacos, homemade desserts, and the like. Amos' serves dinners also.

# NYC Glossary

**Appetizing stores**—Jewish food stores (or counters within stores) specializing in cold cuts, lox, herring, whitefish, carp, pickles, bagels, bialies, pumpernickel, sweets (such as sesame candies, halvah, marzipan, brown licorice), nuts, dried fruits, and more. Readily identifiable by their wonderful and inimitable smell.

**Avenue of the Americas**—Sixth Avenue. Out-of-towners, not New Yorkers, refer to Sixth Avenue as the Avenue of the Americas.

**Bialy**—A Jewish onion roll. Well, sort of. The texture is somewhere between bagels and pizza dough, it has a depression in its center, and the more authentic ones are sold where the more authentic bagels are—in Jewish bakeries or in appetizing stores. The less authentic bialies can be found in the frozen-food section of any New York supermarket.

**Big Apple**—New York City. "Apple" is slang for city or town, and hence New York *is* the Big Apple. Jazz musicians in the 1930s talked of any big city they played as an apple, New York as the Big Apple, and Harlem as the main stem.

**Big MAC**—The Emergency Financial Control Board. Created by the State of New York in the midst of the 1975 fiscal crisis to oversee the city's financial situation. Since the state had already mandated the *M*unicipal *A*ssistance *C*orporation, referred to as MAC, ostensibly for that same purpose, the Emergency Financial Control Board was dubbed Big MAC.

**BMT**—*B*rooklyn *M*anhattan *T*ransit. One of the three divisions of the New York City subway system. The BMT is alternatively referred to by its specific lines—the J, LL, M, N, QB, RR, or the SS, the Franklin Avenue Shuttle.

**Bronx Science**—Bronx High School of Science. It is one of the city's competitive academic high schools, and although many consider it the city's most prestigious public high school, Stuyvesant High is actually the most difficult of the competitive academic high schools to gain entrance to.

**Brownout**—Reduced electrical power, a condition that typically occurs during the summer as a result of an unusually high use of electricity throughout the city, as on an especially hot day when everyone has air-conditioners going at the same time. Blackouts, by contrast, are when there is no electrical power, as occurred in the summer of 1977.

**Brownstone**—Originally, a nineteenth-century row house that actually had a 4-to-6-inch slab of brownstone (a kind of sandstone) over the brick, thus creating a brownstone façade. Now, however, the term is used to refer to almost any town house or row house, whether its façade is brownstone, whitestone, fieldstone, red brick, or wood, or aluminum siding.

**Brownstoner**—In the more general sense, anyone who lives in a brownstone. More specifically, brownstoners are New Yorkers who buy old brownstones in need of repair and then spend the next six years of their lives renovating them. Brownstoners are invariably in their mid-to-late thirties and, more often than not, live in Brooklyn.

**The bulldog**—The edition of the Sunday *New York Times* that is available on Saturday night.

**CCNY**—*C*ity *C*ollege of *N*ew *Y*ork. The oldest and best known of the senior, or four-year, colleges within the City University (CUNY) system. Once its enrollment exceeded 20,000. Now it's closer to 12,000, which is probably related to the fact that CCNY now charges tuition, something it didn't do for the first hundred years of its existence.

**The city**—Manhattan. This is despite the fact that the city really does include Brooklyn, Queens, the Bronx, and Staten Island as well. Outer-borough residents themselves, however, perpetuate the notion that New York City is Manhattan by saying, "We're going into the city," whenever they do travel into Manhattan. (See also "New York.")

**Con Ed**—Consolidated Edison Company. The electric power utility company "serving" New York City. Con Ed charges the highest electrical rates in the country.

**Co-op**—Cooperative apartment. The major form of apartment ownership in the city. It differs from a condominium in that with a co-op one buys shares in the building in which the apartment is located, while with a condominium one actually buys the apartment unit itself. Though co-ops are not unique to New York, what may be is the rate of converting existing rental units to cooperative apartments—about 100,000 such co-op conversions in 1981 alone.

**Co-op City**—A middle-income cooperative housing complex in the northeast Bronx in which some 65,000 New Yorkers reside. (Needless to say, its "rent" strike—since it's a co-op what was withheld was actually maintenance charges—in 1976 constituted the largest rent strike in the history of the world.) Built in the 1960s, Co-op City is where the first wave of white middle-class residents who fled their old Bronx neighborhoods escaped to.

**CUNY**—*C*ity *U*niversity of *N*ew *Y*ork. The City University system, within which there are eighteen two-year and four-year colleges. CUNY's total enrollment—undergraduate and graduate—is about 275,000, which makes it the largest public university system in the country.

**Dairy restaurants**—Jewish vegetarian restaurants. Aside from serving meatless "chopped liver," dairy restaurants specialize in "roasts" and "steaks" made of protose, egg dishes, sour cream and pot cheese dishes, fish dishes, soups, sandwiches, and so forth. They are where neophytes to Jewish cuisine can try their first blintzes, gefilte fish, herring in sour cream, knishes, lox and onion omelets, potato pancakes, noodle pudding, matzoh-ball soup, borsht, prunes with sweet cream, and cheesecake.

**DUMBO**—*D*own *U*nder the *M*anhattan *B*ridge *O*verpass. An area of industrial buildings in South Brooklyn that has become a popular place for artists to live and work ever since SoHo and other Manhattan neighborhoods became affordable only to artists who work for advertising agencies.

**Egg Cream**—A drink made with syrup (usually chocolate), milk, and seltzer. No eggs! (Folklore has it that there was a French druggist on the Lower East Side who would make a flavored soda, and for an additional penny or two would add cream: Voilà soda *et crème*. Mispronunciation and time did the rest.) The best egg creams are to be found in luncheonettes that use real seltzer. The worst ones come from places that use Perrier water instead of seltzer. The most expensive egg creams—which ordinarily are not expensive—are purchased from vendors who prowl around Midtown streetcorners and block parties.

**Face places**—Upper East Side restaurants owned by male models, or former models, that attract the beautiful people in a literal sense. No one has proved that you have to be good-looking to get a table, but, on the other hand, no one has proved that it hurts either.

**FDR**—*Franklin D. Roosevelt Drive.* More commonly referred to as either the East River Drive or East Side Highway.

**Flxible buses**—The six hundred or so buses delivered to the city in 1980, which quickly had to be pulled off the streets and sent back to the manufacturer because cracks developed in their under-carriages. Adding insult to injury, during the period of making repairs, the city borrowed twelve-year-old buses from Washington, D.C., which ran far better than the brand new Flxible buses ever had.

**Fort Apache**—The nickname that was given to the 41st Precinct Police Station in the South Bronx because of the high crime rate there. However, as buildings throughout the South Bronx have been abandoned and the population has declined, so has the rate of crime. Hence the 41st is no longer quite so commonly referred to as Fort Apache. (That didn't stop Hollywood from making a film called *Fort Apache, the Bronx* starring Paul Newman, about high crime and high drug use in the South Bronx, where, in fact, the film was shot amidst protests from community residents who decried the film's one-sided portrait of life in the South Bronx.)

**The Garden**—Madison Square Garden. Though now the home of the Knicks, Rangers, and Ice Capades, since the Knicks and Rangers threaten to move to New Jersey, the Garden could soon become home to the Ice Capades only.

**Gentrification**—the "upgrading" of previously run-down, marginal, or nonresidential neighborhoods as a result of an influx of middle-

and upper-income residents, gourmet takeout food shops, and pedicure boutiques. Gentrification can be analogized to supply-side economics; the notion is that neighborhoods will be improved by the trickle-down effect.

**Glatt Kosher**—Food prepared according to very strict adherence to Jewish dietary laws; as opposed to ordinary adherence, which makes the food simply Kosher. Glatt Kosher, then, is Kosher beyond any conceivable doubt.

**Great White Fleet**—Subway cars on the Flushing No. 7 line that have been repainted white to cover graffiti and to monitor the anti-graffiti security measures taken at the Corona subway yards in Queens, where the Great White Fleet is kept overnight.

**Gridlock**—The situation that occurs when traffic in all directions is frozen. Gridlock is the result of spillback, which is when cars get trapped in intersections when the light turns red, and cars on the cross streets are prevented from getting through. Laws making it a crime to cause gridlock are about as effective as laws against jaywalking.

**Guardian Angels**—A volunteer youth group that patrols New York City subways in an effort to help deter subway crime, though no one really knows whether in fact they do. Guardian Angels can be identified by their red berets. Subway riders appreciate them; cops hate them.

**Gypsy cabs**—Nonmedallion cabs which illegally cruise the streets for street hails, something only yellow medallions are allowed to do. Gypsy cabs operate mostly in the outer boroughs where licensed yellow cabs fear to tread.

**Hasidim**—Highly Orthodox, ultra-religious Jews. Hasidim literally means "pious ones." Hasidic men can be identified by their long, untrimmed beards; long locks of hair dangling down over their ears (called earlocks); dark—usually black—suits (often the coats are knee-length); white shirts (often buttoned at the neck with no tie); wide-brimmed black hats (often fur-trimmed); and always, the yarmulke or skullcap. The observation has been made that Hasidic men look like the Amish. Hasidic women, on the other hand, dress somewhat modishly, albeit modestly so. Most Hasidic women wear wigs—usually stylishly fashioned—since their hair is shaved after marriage as prescribed by Orthodox Jewish tradition.

**IND**—*Ind*ependent division of the New York City subway system. The IND is also referred to as the Eighth Avenue or Sixth Avenue lines, or as the A, AA, B, CC, D, E, F, and GG. Note that a double letter means it's a local.

**IRT**—*I*nterborough *R*apid *T*ransit division of the subway ·system. The IRT system runs on both the East and West sides of Manhattan, and is referred to as the Lexington Avenue Local or Express on the East Side, and the 7th Avenue Local or Express on the West Side. The IRT includes the nos. 4, 5, and 6 trains on the East Side and the nos. 1, 2, and 3 on the West. It also includes the Flushing Line no. 7 train and the Times Square–Grand Central shuttle.

The East Side and West Side IRT have the oldest cars in the entire system, and by almost every standard—on-time service, doors that work, lights that work, amount of litter, readability of subway maps, and so forth—are considered to be the worst of the city's subways. (This could change when the new cars ordered from Japan and Canada begin to be added to the IRT line, starting in 1984.)

**J-51**—A tax-incentive program under which real-estate developers receive tax exemptions and abatements for refurbishing old residential buildings or for converting nonresidential structures into residential housing. J-51 has been both praised and condemned as the major impetus behind the widescale conversion of the city's warehouses, churches, synagogues, firehouses, police stations, schools, factories, and single-room-occupancy hotels into luxury co-op apartments.

**JFK Express**—The special subway that goes to JFK International Airport—actually, only as far as Howard Beach, from where special buses take JFK Express passengers to the airport. Conventional wisdom maintains that a regular A train and then a regular city bus will get you to JFK faster and cheaper than the special JFK "Express."

**John Hour**—A program Mayor Koch started on the city-owned radio station, WNYC, during which the names of men convicted of patronizing prostitutes would be read over the air. Criticized by civil libertarians as an instance of the city taking the law into its own hands, and rejected by other radio stations and by newspapers as being simply a dumb idea, the John Hour was discontinued after one broadcast.

**Lex**—*Lex*ington Avenue. *The Lex*, however, is the Lexington Avenue Subway, also referred to as the East Side IRT, East Side Local or Express, or the nos. 4, 5, and 6 trains.

**Lofts**—Open floors of buildings where the plumbing and electrical fixtures are usually left to the tenant to install. There are now thousands of residential lofts throughout the city that have been converted from commercial lofts, albeit most are illegal. The Census Bureau considers lofts to be one-room apartments, even though their size may exceed 2,500 square feet.

**Maven**—Yiddish meaning expert, as in food maven, movie maven, music maven, clothes maven. Most New Yorkers consider themselves mavens about most things.

**Met**—Either the Metropolitan Museum of Art or the Metropolitan Opera.

**Mitchell-Lama**—Middle-income housing built under the provisions of a state law enacted in 1955. The law was written and sponsored by two state legislators, MacNeil Mitchell and Alfred Lama; hence their immortalization via Mitchell-Lama housing, which includes Co-op City in the Bronx.

**MoMA**—*M*useum *o*f *M*odern *A*rt (pronounced "móh-ma," not "M-O-M-A").

**MTA**—*M*etropolitan *T*ransportation *A*uthority. The agency that oversees the city's subways. Since it is a state agency, the MTA provides the city with the perfect scapegoat to blame for subway-fare hikes, subway strikes, terrible service, high crime, graffiti, and all other subway ills.

**Music and Art**—High School of Music and Art. One of the city's specialized high schools for which students must audition to be admitted. Among its graduates are Bess Myerson, Erica Jong, and Peter of Peter, Paul, and Mary.

**The New School**—The New School for Social Research. Located in Greenwich Village and famous for its adult evening division courses and for the *New School Bulletin*, which lists and describes those courses. The New School's area of specialization is dilettantism. Considered "a great place to meet someone"—better than a singles bar.

**New York**—What many outer-borough residents say to mean Manhattan, as when a Brooklyn resident, for example, says, "I'm going into New York." (See also "The city.")

**NoHo**—The section of Manhattan located *N*orth of *Ho*uston Street between Broadway and the Bowery. A once predominantly industrial and warehouse area, NoHo has in recent years seen many of its commercial lofts converted into residential lofts. Since it is somewhat cheaper and less chic than SoHo, more artists now probably live and work in NoHo than SoHo.

**Obie**—An award, sponsored by *The Village Voice*, honoring achievement in Off and Off-Off Broadway theater. (The name derives from the abbreviation of Off Broadway, OB.) The Obie is to Off and Off-Off Broadway what the Tony Awards are to Broadway.

**Off Broadway**—Plays performed in theaters, no matter where their location, that contain more than 100 seats but fewer than 500. Off Broadway theater must employ professional actors, members of Actors Equity.

**Off-Off Broadway**—Plays performed in theaters, no matter where their location, that contain fewer than 100 seats. Generally, compared to Off Broadway and especially Broadway, Off-Off Broadway theater is less professional, more experimental, and considerably cheaper. Off-Off Broadway "theaters" may be churches, storefronts, lofts, senior-citizen centers, garages, or the streets themselves.

**Op-Ed Page**—The page of opinion and public affairs columns of *The New York Times* located *op*posite the *ed*itorial page.

**OTB**—*O*ff-*T*rack *B*etting. These legalized horse-betting "parlors" are actually located throughout New York State, but since there are about five hunred more OTB outlets in New York City than anyplace else, they seem to be peculiarly New York City establishments The OTB parlors have actually been marginally profitable lately, and there is the possibility that they will soon be closed.

**Outer boroughs**—Brooklyn, Queens, the Bronx, and Staten Island.

**PA**—High School of *P*erforming *A*rts. Another of the city's specialized high schools, for which very rigorous auditions are required to be admitted (as portrayed in the film *Fame*). Anyone who aspires (or whose mother aspires for him or her) to be a Liza Minnelli, Al Pacino, Ben Vereen, or Pinchas Zukerman—all PA grads—tries to get into Performing Arts.

**Page Six**—The daily gossip page of the *New York Post* located on page six of that tabloid. Otherwise self-respecting *New York Times* readers have been known to get the *Post* every now and then and to turn to Page Six first thing.

**PATH**—*P*ort *A*uthority *T*rans *H*udson. The agency that operates the commuter train—the PATH—between New York and New Jersey. New Yorkers who have abandoned the city for Hoboken rationalize their move by saying "It only takes ten minutes to get into the city by PATH."

**Pegasus**—A clown-minstrel-storyteller who has been regaling children in Central Park for over a decade. Pegasus subsists on whatever he manages to collect from passing his hat.

**Pooper-scooper law**—Enacted in 1978, and officially known as the Canine Waste Law, a law that makes it an offense for any dog owner not to remove his or her dog's droppings from the sidewalks, streets, or other public areas. The pooper-scooper law, as everyone calls it, proved effective for approximately three weeks.

**Possibility line**—Neither a ticket-buyer's line nor a ticket-holder's line, but rather the unique invention of management of first-run movie theaters on the Upper East Side, a line for those who may or may not get into the theater at the last minute depending upon whether or not there are still seats available after one show clears and the audience for the next show is seated.

**R-46**—Not one of the robots in the movie *Star Wars* but rather the fleet of new subway cars that were discovered to have developed cracks in their undercarriages after they were delivered to the city in the late 1970s for use on the E and F IND lines. To cut down the risk of accidents, the R-46s are pulled out of service for about half of each day. Thus, the subway system's best—that is, newest—cars provide the worst service. (Little wonder, after the fiasco with the R-46, which was built by an American company, that the MTA chose a Japanese company and a Canadian company to build the new cars for the IRT line.)

**Rent control**—A system of rent regulation, applicable to about 400,000 apartments located in buildings constructed prior to 1947 and occupied continuously by the same tenant (or a member of his immediate family) since 1971, under which rents cannot be raised more than a certain amount each year, that is, 7½ percent. In divorce proceedings, the issue of who will retain custody of a rent-controlled apartment is often thornier than who will retain custody of the children.

**Rent stabilization**—A system of rent regulation, applicable to about 800,000 apartments in buildings constructed between 1947 and 1974 as well as to previously rent-controlled apartments that have been vacated, under which rents cannot be raised more than a certain amount each time a new lease is signed (increases are higher than those allowed for rent-controlled apartments).

**Seltzer**—A beverage consisting only of water and carbon dioxide. There's no salt in seltzer, as there is in club soda, which in New York is considered imitation seltzer. Seltzer is the key ingredient in egg creams. (It is common knowledge among matzoh-ball soup mavens that adding seltzer to the matzoh-ball batter instead of water results in especially light matzoh balls.) And though seltzer is not unique to New York, what might be is the home delivery of seltzer in siphon, or squirt, bottles.

**Shadow traffic**—Traffic reports given over the radio by the Shadow Network, a syndicated traffic-reporting service. Actually, the Shadow is believed to have originated in Philadelphia.

**Shopping-bag ladies**—Homeless women who live on the streets—more often on the West Side than the East Side—and who carry all their belongings in shopping bags. Though in almost every instance shopping-bag ladies have absolutely no money (they don't apply for or accept welfare), every once in a while one reads about a shopping-bag lady who dies with $100,000 in a savings account.

**Shopsteading**—A city program whereby city-owned properties, typically in run-down or marginal neighborhoods, are sold at very low prices in return for the promise from the purchasers to renovate the properties and start businesses in them. It is the commercial equivalent of the homesteading program (sweat-equity) employed in city-owned residential properties.

**Silk Stocking District**—A political district which includes the Upper East Side of Manhattan, notable for having an extremely wealthy constituency and for being the one district in politically liberal Manhattan that votes Republican.

**SIRTOA**—*S*taten *I*sland *R*apid *T*ransit *O*perating *A*uthority. Though Staten Island is known only for its ferry, it also has a passenger rail line operated by the SIRTOA.

**SoHo**—The section of Manhattan *S*outh of *Ho*uston Street. Originally SoHo was an industrial and commercial quarter, but then it became an industrial, commercial, and artists' quarter, then an artists' quarter, and now a tourists' quarter.

**Spaldeen**—A New Yorker's way of referring to the small pink rubber Spaulding ball used for playing stickball, stoopball, sidewalk handball, and many other city games.

**Spanglish**—A unique language among Hispanics that has evolved from mixing Spanish and English.

**SRO**—A *s*ingle-*r*oom *o*ccupancy hotel. These are resident hotels for the elderly, the poor, the down-and-out, and transients. In recent years, SROs all over the city have been converted into luxury housing. In 1975, there were about three hundred SROs in New York; by 1981, only slightly more than a hundred. As the number of SROs has decreased, the number of homeless men and women on the streets has increased.

**Suzy and Red**—The two German shepherd attack dogs who patrol the Corona subway yards in Queens as part of the antigraffiti security measures instituted there. Mayor Ed Koch used to refer to Suzy and Red as "the wolves."

**Taki 183**—The now famous, once-omnipresent signature that appeared all over New York City subways. Credited with beginning the great subway graffiti war. Taki was his name, and presumably he lived on 183rd Street.

**Taxi hustling**—The practice of charging the unwary exorbitant fares for cab rides—$50 to go crosstown instead of $3. Taxi hustling is rampant at the airports and near the East Side Terminal on First Avenue at 38th Street. Middle Eastern passengers are considered particularly vulnerable prey, since cabbies consider all Arabs to be oil sheiks.

**Three-card monte**—The card game one sees being played at 20-foot intervals along every block of Midtown. For a mere $20, one is given the "opportunity" to find the one odd card—say, the one red card, the one ace, the one face card. Three-card monte is both a hustle and a traffic obstruction. No one *ever* wins.

**Three-room apartment**—Indefinable. Can as likely be a studio apartment as a one-bedroom apartment, depending upon who is doing the counting and whether hallways, entryways, eating alcoves, sleeping alcoves, bathrooms, and closets are considered to be "rooms."

**TKTS**—The discount theater ticket booths located at Duffy Square (Broadway and 47th Street), at No. 2 World Trade Center, in downtown Brooklyn (Fulton Street and Dekalb Avenue), and at Bryant Park next to the New York Public Library. Here tickets for theater performances (at Bryant Park, for music and dance only) are sold for half-price on the day of performance. TKTS tickets are typically *not* for the best seats in the house.

**TriBeCa**—The area of Manhattan located within the *Tri*angle *Be*low *Ca*nal Street (the triangle formed by Canal Street, Hudson Street, and West Broadway). Once a predominantly commercial and warehouse area, TriBeCa is now a neighborhood of both commercial and residential lofts. As TriBeCa has become more residential, the once small triangle that defined its boundaries has gradually become a rather large trapezoid.

**Twofers**—Coupons one finds on counters of hotels, restaurants, supermarkets, and other places that allow one to buy theater tickets at a discount. The discount is usually not 50 percent, which was the original worth of twofers when they first appeared—that is, *two* tickets *for* the price of one, hence "twofer." It is the belief of some that twofers have saved Broadway theater, that they are responsible for generating as much as 40 percent of the weekly gross receipts of many Broadway shows.

**West Side crazy**—Any of a number of denizens of the Upper West Side whom you see carrying on a monologue as they walk. The subject of said monologue typically relates to World War III, poison in the city's water supply, race and ethnicity, life after death, or Henry Kissinger.

**Westway**—The proposed 4.2-mile-long highway that would replace the fallen West Side Highway from the Battery to 42nd Street. Westway has been debated for more than ten years and will take another ten years to complete once it is begun, if it ever is. Senator William Proxmire—citing Westway's estimated cost of $4 billion, or $1 billion per mile, which would make it the most expensive highway in the history of the world—has already given Westway one of his Golden Fleece awards for wasting taxpayers' money.

**WTC**—*W*orld *T*rade *C*enter.

# Index

293